SHAKESPEARE'S PERSONALITY

SHAKESPEARE'S PERSONALITY

Edited by Norman N. Holland,
Sidney Homan, and
Bernard J. Paris

University of California Press
Berkeley · Los Angeles · London

University of California Press
Berkeley and Los Angeles, California

University of California Press, Ltd.
London, England

© 1989 by
The Regents of the University of California

Printed in the United States of America
1   2   3   4   5   6   7   8   9

Library of Congress Cataloging-in-Publication Data

Shakespeare's personality / edited by Norman N. Holland, Sidney Homan,
and Bernard J. Paris.
p.   cm.
Bibliography: p.
Includes index.
ISBN 0-520-06317-1 (alk. paper)
1. Shakespeare, William, 1564–1616—Biography—Psychology—
Congresses. 2. Shakespeare, William, 1564–1616—Knowledge—
Psychology—Congresses. 3. Dramatists, English—Early
modern, 1500–1700—Psychology—Congresses. 4. Personality in
literature—Congresses. 5. Psychology and literature—Congresses.
6. Self in literature—Congresses. I. Holland, Norman Norwood,
1927–   . II. Homan, Sidney, 1938–   . III. Paris, Bernard J.
PR2909.S54   1989
822.3'3—dc19   88-31500
[B]   CIP

Contents

Acknowledgments

The essays in this collection emerged from a conference, Shakespeare's Personality, held on the University of Florida campus and at the university's Whitney Conference Hall, Marineland, March 7–10, 1985. Funds were generously provided by the Department of English, the Florida Endowment for the Humanities, and the Milbauer Endowment. In addition to the essays here presented, Maurice Charney, Robert Egan, Dennis Huston, Robert Kimbrough, Marvin Rosenberg, and Samuel Schoenbaum also gave papers, which because of limitations of space we could not include here. Murray Schwartz provided incisive commentary on the whole proceedings. We are grateful to all of these people, as well as to our colleagues Ira Clark, William Logan, Jack Perlette, James Sunwall, and Robert Thomson. Their participation proved, as always, special.

Introduction

Norman N. Holland

It is our fortune, good or bad, to complete this book on Shakespeare's personality at a moment in literary criticism when its "subject" (in several senses) has disappeared. Shakespeare is gone. So is his personality. Indeed, so is everybody's personality, yours and mine as well.

Some of today's most widely heeded literary critics proclaim that the very idea of self, personality, identity, character, or "the subject" has evaporated in the heat of recent theorizing. Ordinarily I would use this introduction to suggest the content and rationale of the essays that make up the book. In 1989, however, I shall probably do better to try to meet some of the fire currently directed at the idea of "Shakespeare's personality." On one flank an attack comes from the New Historicism, on the other from a radical postmodern skepticism. Both "problematize" (in current critical jargon) the very idea that we can intelligibly write about such a being as William Shakespeare. Merely to label some concept as problematic, however, does not quite seem to me to carry the day—any concept worth talking about must be problematic. We need to be more precise about these challenges.

When critics today speak of "the disappearance of the subject" or "the death of the author," what they are rejecting is the "humanist illusion" or "bourgeois fiction" of "an individual endowed with the freedom and capacity both to create himself and to shape his social and political environment." "In an age of mass communications, advertising, and state propaganda," writes David Quint, "it is difficult to speak of man shaping his own cultural identity or exercising an independent political will." Alas, yes. As a consequence, the literary text is no longer the author's, "the result of a personal selection among a series of constituent stylistic and ideological choices—but rather the product of choices that are largely made for him both by the literary system itself and by the ways of knowing, the 'epistemes' of the larger culture." From a deconstructionist point of view "the individual sub-jectivity that was supposed to speak through the text [is] a text itself, the product of other texts and discursive codes that both proliferate and coalesce under analysis" (Quint 1986, 5–7, 15). The Shakespeare we propose to analyze is just as much a text, determined by the sur-rounding discourse and the vagaries of language, as are the poems and plays we would use to analyze him.

If we believe that human beings are determined by their cultural surround (and surely they are), then the idea of an author whose unified personality shapes the style of what he or she writes becomes an illusion. To say that, however, forces an *either-or* that may not be necessary: either culture determines or the individual determines.

Wouldn't a *both-and* be truer to our experience, even in this day of the mass media? The idea that texts determine the individual does not exclude the idea that individuals determine texts. We are dealing with a dialectic or with the feedback processes described by modern cogni-tive psychology. This is not the place to try to develop a model that would adequately describe both cultural and personal determinism (see Holland 1985). We should not, however, embrace the fallacy of saying that *either* the culture *or* the individual controls. To insist that a certain play is either Shakespeare's or not Shakespeare's but his cul-ture's forces a dichotomy that a stronger model of our situation in culture would sidestep.

The deconstructionists' claim that Shakespeare is just as much a text as the texts we use to understand Shakespeare also avoids this dichotomy. Relying on the texts before us, we invent a text called Shakespeare just as Shakespeare himself invented plays from earlier narratives. That, however, is simply the human condition, not a reason for rejecting the analysis of "Shakespeare."

Often critics attacking the humanist illusion of an author have recourse to a widely quoted sentence by Michel Foucault: "These aspects of an individual, which we designate as an author . . . are projections, in terms always more or less psychological, of our way of handling texts: in the comparisons we make, the traits we extract as pertinent, the continuities we assign, or the exclusions we prac-tice" (1977, 127). Although some critics compress that idea into "the disappearance of the subject" or "the death of the author," Foucault himself is not so drastic, nor need we be. He simply replaces "au-thor" by "author-function," the latter being a construct by which we read the author's texts. Because it is a construct, we can acknowledge that an author-function has to do with our own wishes, feelings, and culture as well as with the poems and plays we are reading. The construct "author" (or author-function) is not a simple reality to be simply described—there is no such thing. It is a way to read a text, and psychology, Foucault points out, is the way to read our making of this author-function.

It is also worth noting that this critique of the idea of an organically unified personality has been a literary and philosophical move, not a psychological, psychoanalytic, or neuroscientific one. Freud himself wrote over and over again about the unifying function of the ego and of libido, or Eros, and—before he invented ego psychology—of the dream, the joke, the symptom, indeed the mind itself. Post-Freudian psychoanalysts like Karen Horney, D. W. Winnicott, Heinz Lichtenstein, Heinz Kohut, and Hans Loewald continue to find the idea of an organically unified psyche useful. To be sure, Lacan speaks of a disorganized, fragmented self, but his practice somewhat belies his theory. When he reanalyzes Freud's Rat Man, he does so in terms of "the neurotic's individual myth," which is not unlike Holland's or Lichtenstein's "identity theme" (albeit one formed before the Rat Man's birth). Similarly, cognitive psychologists find the idea of a personal "cognitive style" useful. Neuroscientists like J. Z. Young, Richard L. Gregory, Ragnar Granit, and Roger Sperry confirm the idea of a unified psyche from studies of the brain itself. Those who insist, for literary or philosophical reasons, on a fragmented psyche may be creating a new scholasticism, divorced like the old one from the science of its day.

Be that as it may, our authors base their readings of Shakespeare on contemporary psychoanalysis. This book therefore has a double point of view. What seems problematic, if looked at wholly from a literary or philosophical position, may seem less so if looked at simultaneously from the point of view of psychoanalysis and psychology. Because of their double perspective, most of our authors envision a real, historical William Shakespeare. Even those who accept Foucault's idea of an author-function see no inconsistency between that belief and a psychological study of "William Shakespeare." Psychology is one way to describe that author-function.

Moreover, most of our authors tend to use a psychology closer to that of the consulting room than to the increasingly abstract psychologies in contemporary literary theory. As a result, many (but not all) treat Shakespeare or "Shakespeare" as if he were unified along the traditional lines of ego psychology. We tend to assume that both Shakespeare and the "Shakespeare-function" have highly organized defenses and a coherent sexual nature or bias. Obviously one could "problematize" those assumptions. Most of us, however, have not felt the need to do so, even in the face of the questioning of modern literary theory, because they are close to what psychoanalysts actually experience.

In addition to the deconstruction of the author, literary theory mounts a second challenge to our enterprise, from the New Historicism (also known as cultural poetics or cultural materialism). From the perspective of Stephen Greenblatt (1986) a book like this, which tries to use psychoanalysis to study Shakespeare—be he man or construct—faces a double impossibility. First, our idea of the self differs from Shakespeare's (or more generally Renaissance thinkers') idea of the human subject. Second, psychoanalysis is a product of the Renaissance; hence psychoanalysis cannot step behind its own origins, as it were, to explain what gave rise to itself.

In the Renaissance mind, as Greenblatt and other New Historicists have convincingly shown, it took more than a mere psychic and bodily history to give a person identity or selfhood. The Renaissance individual gained identity by being granted and guaranteed a place in a complex community of kinship, ownership, duties, privileges, and rights (by custom and by contract). We can see this kind of identity in the (to us) mercenary way Shakespeare's lovers, even the most ardent, reckon up the beloved's estate. That estate is part of the essential Juliet, Portia, Hero, or Desdemona. Greenblatt is surely right when he claims that this Renaissance concept is very different from the psychoanalytic idea of self.

Or selves. Psychoanalysis does not have a single idea of the self. To be sure, Freud almost always wrote about a unified self bounded by that individual's skin. Since 1930, however, psychoanalysts have arrived increasingly at a self more like the Renaissance concept in being inextricably involved with its social surround. Lacan's alienated self rests on the idea that culture and language determine the "individual myth" of the self. Horney and subsequent object-relations theorists and those who today are working to integrate the insights of psychoanalysis with those of cognitive psychology have yet another idea of the self. They see it as a process, part of a system, inseparable from and "always already" interacting with its human and physical environment. Even the much-maligned ego psychologists regard the self as "always already" dealing, both actively and passively, with a reality outside itself. Here again we probably should not state the issue as a choice between either a cultural self or a personal, skin-bounded self. For the Renaissance, as for us when we think carefully about it, the issue is one of *both-and*, not *either-or*.

Nevertheless, Greenblatt is right when he says that the human subject that psychoanalysis seeks to understand is a relatively recent invention, even in these newer versions of psychoanalysis. Does that render a psychoanalytic account of Shakespeare impossible? I think not. When investigating fantasies of fatherhood in, say, the Trobriand Islands (as happened in the early Freud-Malinowski controversy), psychoanalysts are not bound to think only within the Trobrianders' fantasies. Rather, psychoanalysts draw on what they know as psychoanalysts about fantasies of fathering to explore what the Trobrianders think. Or what patients think, or what people in the Renaissance thought. The psychoanalyst studies an individual in the Renaissance as psychoanalysis defines the individual, not as the Renaissance defines it. Our authors are studying Shakespeare's personality as *we* understand personality, not as he would have understood it. That is as it should be and has to be.

Possibly the opposite view comes about from failing to acknowledge the claim that any psychology makes. A psychology, to be a psychology, must claim that its generalizations apply not only to the original evidence on which the generalization rests but also to all other evidence and even to imaginary or impossible cases—"contrafactuals." If there were a Santa Claus, he would have an Oedipus complex. It takes contrary examples to defeat that claim of lawfulness; that Hamlet, Santa Claus, or even Shakespeare or Montaigne could not themselves think in terms of an Oedipus complex is undeniable but not enough.

The psychoanalyst plays by different rules from the literary historian. A historian of Renaissance literature might feel it right, useful, or necessary to think always within the Renaissance concept of the self. Psychoanalysts feel just the opposite—that is the whole point of their enterprise. The psychoanalyst tries to interpret individuals—and, by extension, cultures—more fully than they can interpret themselves and (if dealing with patients) to pass that ability on to the patients themselves.

This is not to say that these scientific or interpretive claims ever cease to be part of a particular history and culture. A discipline's claims of universality do not gainsay its participation in the values of a given moment in history. In the current jargon, the "historicization" of a discipline goes side by side with its "scientization." Any adept player in the game of psychology, psychoanalysis, or literary criticism will claim a validity beyond the moment for what he or she asserts. Any honest player will recognize that that claim is also framed by a particular moment in time.

Greenblatt's second argument concerns the chronology of psychoanalysis. He says that psychoanalysis is the historical outcome of certain characteristic Renaissance strategies. Psychoanalysis stands, therefore, in a paradoxical position. It is a result of the Renaissance rather than a psychology that can explain the people or events of the Renaissance. Greenblatt writes of "the curious effect of a discourse that functions *as if* the psychological categories it invokes were not only simultaneous with but even prior to and themselves causes of the very phenomena of which in actual fact they were the results." Psychoanalysis, Greenblatt says, can "redeem its belatedness only when it historicizes its own procedures" (1986, 221).

Has Greenblatt pointed to a true dichotomy or a real paradox? Does the fact that psychoanalysis is a result of the Renaissance rule out its being an explainer of the Renaissance? Would we apply the same argument to other *sciences de l'homme*? Modern economics, sociology, and anthropology are, of course, all products of the Renaissance, yet we use modern economics to understand the enclosure movement, modern sociology to understand the results of primogeniture, and modern anthropology to understand the function of the drama (as Greenblatt himself expertly does). The same applicability may not extend to history, literary criticism, and philosophy, however. When sociologists, economists, and psychoanalysts assert laws, they claim them even for contrafactuals. Historians, literary critics, and philosophers rarely assert laws at all. If we demand that psychologists "historicize" themselves, we may simply be asking them to stop being psychologists.

We could ramify indefinitely these arguments and counterarguments about the self, understanding the self, and using psychologies to understand the self. The issues they raise are fascinating and complex but not, it seems to us, essential to our enterprise. Rather, they are something each of you who reads these essays should and will apply as you see fit. That is what our fourteen authors have done. Most have directed their inquiry to the historical Shakespeare; they include Barber, Wheeler, Paris, Hawkins, and Neely. Some, like myself, think in terms of an author-function. Others—Kerrigan, for example—hover between these two possibilities. Still others, like Freedman and Willbern, adopt the radical skepticism of the postmodern.

It is a bit surprising, therefore, given such a diversity of theoretical approaches, that we agree so markedly about William Shakespeare. Overall we see a Shakespeare who deals with a lot of aggression, which arises at least in part from his family situation—the birth of a younger brother, perhaps, or his father's financial and social failure. He justifies and defends his aggression by idealizing the established social order, although not without ambivalence. In the theater he was able to pursue his destiny more freely by being what he was not (as an actor) or by making himself invisible (as the author or the director). He could both act out and defend against his aggressive and sexual impulses by idealizing father-son relations and taming the feminine. At the same time, he tried to internalize feelings of trust, generosity, and nurturing, qualities he identified as feminine, and in his later career he succeeded in doing this to a marked degree.

C. L. Barber and Richard P. Wheeler find that the most striking feature of Shakespeare's early history was his father's loss of patriarchal authority as a result of his financial decline. This loss might have intensified the son's normal disillusionment with the idealized figure of early childhood and led to "an intense form of object hunger" as he sought "a substitute for the missing segment of [his] psychic structure." Shakespeare sought to satisfy this hunger in a creative way by imagining fictional characters, many of whom carry on the search for the ideal Shakespeare himself had lost.

His father's weakness, according to Barber and Wheeler, not only made it difficult for Shakespeare to experience power in himself, but, combined with his father's amiability, also made it hard for him to express aggressively his own independent identity. Instead, he put his aggression into his dramatic art, expressing it through the creation of aggressive characters, through the mockery of comedy or "the ruthless ironic knowledge" of tragedy. His mastery of the play as a whole, moreover, provided a self-assertion that balanced his "giving himself to the realization of other identities."

Like Barber and Wheeler, Sherman Hawkins sees the genres in which Shakespeare worked, especially that of the history plays, as at once exposing and displacing his own aggression. Hawkins suspects that the major effect of his father's decline was to fill Shakespeare with dreams of restoring the family fortunes. For him, as for Prince Hal, his task became the validating of his father's claims through his own victories. Whether his father's failure was its cause or not, Shakespeare clearly had a lot of aggressive ambition that is at odds both with "our image of the 'sweet' and 'gentle' Will" and with the traditional notions of social degree to which Shakespeare was committed. Hawkins feels that his commitment to order and hierarchy was, in part at least, a defense against "the turbulent aggressive energies that threaten[ed] to overthrow them." Barber and Wheeler ask what Shakespeare did with his aggression. Hawkins thinks one answer might be that he wrote history plays. These plays allowed him to experience aggression vicariously while preserving his sense of order by exposing its destructive and amoral consequences. In *Henry V,* however, his project was to redeem ambition by showing that the same drive that produces wrath and violence also makes for courage and that the craving for power can be directed to nobler ends. Henry's aggression is legitimized—indeed, idealized—by being put to the service of ethics and community. Shakespeare's ambivalence toward aggression is not fully resolved, however, as the skeptical responses of directors, audiences, and critics to Henry indicate, and it deepens as he approaches his tragic period.

In my own essay I also find Shakespeare's works to be based on an idealized relation of father to son. The son does for the father what the father does not or cannot do for himself, much as hawk, hound, and horse (all favorite Shakespearean images) act for their gentleman masters in aggressive contexts. This pattern applies to king and subject, master and servant, officer and soldier, and many other such pairs of figures. It thus provides the basis for Tillyard's and Spencer's well-known "Elizabethan world-picture."

Shakespeare, however, also imagines the son figure becoming the sexual delegate of the father figure—his phallus, as it were—and the anxiety and the potential for betrayal associated with this agency fuel the Sonnets and the problem comedies. Hence this father-son relationship can fail in two ways, through aggressive rebellion or sexual betrayal. Rebellion outrages Shakespeare, but he does not seem to find it nearly as galling as sexual betrayal.

In my view, Shakespeare began his career by treating the feminine as a threat to this right relation of father to son, one best dealt with by taming the shrew. Ideally woman should be to man as son is to father. The tamed shrew in the finale of that early farce acts as her husband's dog or hawk to hunt and fetch, to be bet on, and to endorse enthusiastically her own subordination. Other heroines in the early plays dress up as boys to serve their men. As Shakespeare matures, although he continues to fear and distrust women in military or aggressive roles, he comes to an accommodation, even a trust, of the feminine, allowing woman a sexual and generative power that comes to surpass and provide a foundation for male-male agency.

Like Hawkins, Kirby Farrell speculates about the impact on Shakespeare of his father's declining fortunes, and like me, he sees patriarchy as the background against which Shakespeare reacts. According to Farrell, what made patriarchy so valuable to the Elizabethans was its function as a defense against death. It invested the patriarch with godlike powers that could be shared by dependents through a worshipful self-effacement that gave them a feeling of vitality and invulnerability. Against the reductive, unimaginative patriarchal society in *Romeo and Juliet* Farrell opposes the act of individuating imagination. By it the lovers attempt to escape their fathers' control, even as they use, invariably, the metaphors and the theological assumptions of their world both within and outside the play. That is, they construe love as worship. The lovers substitute the beloved for father and God and "seek apotheosis in each other."

To Farrell, as to many of us, it appears that another defense for Shakespeare may have been his vocation as a playwright. Onstage he could give his experience new and authoritative forms yet nevertheless earn fame and the rank of a gentleman. In order to escape retaliation or guilt for turning his world's verities into fantasy, he adopted a style of equivocation that enabled him to honor venerable cultural forms even as he demythified them.

The Dutch psychoanalyst Conrad van Emde Boas (1951) has proposed that Shakespeare compensated for his "dethronement" at the birth of his younger brother Gilbert by renouncing his claims, denying his hostility, and identifying instead with his mother's desire to satisfy his rival. Van Emde Boas applies this model to the Sonnets. Barber and Wheeler and Marianne Novy suggest that it also accounts for Shakespeare's negative capability, his astonishing power to understand the "other" and imagine stage characters at once like and unlike his real self.

In her essay Novy elaborates the van Emde Boas hypothesis. Shakespeare, she points out, often alludes to the stories of Cain and Abel and of the prodigal son, in both of which an older brother is envious of a favored younger son. She suggests that such stories reflect the resentment that older brothers feel at the care and attention given to the younger, forgetting how they themselves were treated as infants. Although Shakespeare never wrote explicitly about brothers competing for a mother's affection, Novy points out that he did write frequently about a husband or lover who worries about a woman's fidelity, which she develops (following Dorothy Dinnerstein) as a parallel relationship. Themes of brotherhood and cuckoldry, she notes, converge in a number of plays, often with imagery that explicitly suggests conflict over a mother. The intensity of masculine anxiety about cuckoldry comes from the infant's anxiety about losing the mother who is his whole world. Since the women turn out to be faithful, Novy finds that Shakespeare is not only expressing his anxiety but also defending himself against it by blaming the male and identifying with the feminine perspective.

Carol Neely ingeniously discovers how Shakespeare imagined women by comparing his fictional women with the situations of real women in Stratford. In Shakespeare's real environment much formality attached to ecclesiastical licenses and the lengthy negotiation of marriage settlements, because marriages transferred money and lands. The women in the plays, however, are not associated with property in any realistic, negotiated way. The real world of Stratford tolerated sexual lapses, and women's sexual roles included not only marriage but also courtship, pregnancy, childbearing, and remarriage. The plays, though, narrowly define woman by two themes: Petrarchan love and cuckoldry. She is idealized or mistrusted, and when Shakespeare does show a "masterless" woman he represents her not in familial sexual roles but as a witch, shrew, lunatic, whore, or wayward wife. At its finale the play contains the power of such a woman by marriage, madness, or death.

Neely's essay shows that again and again Shakespeare imagined women as weaker in realistic ways and more powerful and dangerous in fantastic, unreal ways than the women he actually knew. Hence Neely can pose a disturbing question: granted that Elizabethan society was pervasively masculinist, was not Shakespeare even more so? Subsequent essays dealing with Shakespeare's attitudes toward women would seem to answer yes. Masculinist ideology, particularly the idea that women are dangerous, runs all through the plays.

Shirley Nelson Garner examines the five Shakespearean plays that deal with the actual or imagined infidelity of women. In all but one the woman in question is unusually virtuous, but the man becomes jealous quickly, at the merest suggestion of unfaithfulness. He rages at her and humiliates her, finally deciding she must die. She, in contrast, forgives him. As Shakespeare replays this drama from 1599 to 1611, suspicion comes more and more out of the lover's own diseased imagination without any evidence to support it. The men's haste shows how frail their bonds with women are. By the end of the canon it is as though Shakespeare's men need some woman to betray them.

These extreme reactions, Garner says, come from the men's idealizing of women (and Neely's essay confirms her theory). As Shakespeare proceeds in his career, he reacts against this idealization, notably in Hermione's stepping down from a pedestal to be a real woman instead of a statue. He comes to accept a more realistic view of women's sexuality (as Kerrigan's and my essays also suggest), but he never gives up the image of woman as divinely forgiving.

Janet Adelman also focuses on the theme of sexual betrayal, closely exploring the bed tricks in *All's Well That Ends Well* and *Measure for Measure*, which substitute a legal wife for the woman a man illegitimately desires. In these theatrical stratagems she finds a male desire to separate procreation from the sin of the flesh. In *All's Well* the bed trick separates the soiling of sexual intercourse from the sexual woman (because the man does not sleep with that woman) and motherhood from the man's desire (because the man does not desire that woman). By not fully imagining sex as sex, Shakespeare can relocate sexuality in a sacred family. Helena almost becomes a virgin mother.

Helena's unborn child in *All's Well* reappears as Juliet's pregnancy at the opening of *Measure for Measure*, where sexuality now leads to a sentence of death. Government can banish sexuality to brothels in the suburbs, but it returns to violate and pollute the inner space of both city and woman. In the Duke's paternal role as actor-director the play brings sexuality back under the control of a father figure, almost supplying a purely male creation. The Duke, however, surprises the audience when he proposes to Isabel. We cannot escape sexuality, and in subsequent plays Shakespeare charts the vicissitudes of sexuality in a world in which the father has departed, not to return until Prospero dominates the forces of sex and aggression in *The Tempest*.

The Duke in *Measure for Measure* is one of several characters who are like theatrical actors or directors. William Kerrigan singles out three aspects of these figures, all related to Shakespeare's sexual fantasies. First, from *Richard III* on, Shakespeare makes his most fascinating characters actors or directors. For Shakespeare the self becomes a self precisely by fashioning a self. Second, Shakespeare seems taken with the idea of mismatched love. Again and again he portrays heterosexual couples drawn inescapably to one another although they are from the start antagonists, foreigners, or unequals, people who face each other across a barrier. Third, Shakespeare frequently expresses nausea and disgust at the genitals of women (as in Adelman's reading of the bed tricks), treating the vagina as a damnation that cannot be avoided. Kerrigan thus adds both a physiological and a theological dimension to the theme of the danger of woman.

In *Antony and Cleopatra* these three themes converge to undo man's damnation through woman's unclean genitals. Cleopatra is an actress who dramatizes herself supremely. Instead of Christian eschatology, in this tragedy Roman stoicism and an imperial, masculine mentality (like that of Shakespeare's own time) confront her flamboyant sexuality. At her death Cleopatra's magnificent self-staging produces a "counter-epic" that overcomes disgust at sex by transforming femininity into motherhood.

Madelon Sprengnether also focuses on the death scene in *Antony and Cleopatra*. Just before her suicide Cleopatra imagines herself played in some future theater by a squeaking boy. Shakespeare's use of boy actors to impersonate females allowed him to consider issues of gender in a form not threatening to his male-dominated society and its theater. The antitheatrical tracts of Shakespeare's day show that the acting of the women's parts by boy actors made woman both "other" and "not other."

For Shakespeare woman represented a sexual difference that was alien, threatening, and untrustworthy. Antony submits to Cleopatra, who robs him of his Roman valor so that others regard him as dangerously effeminate. Yet, Sprengnether notes, the male hero portrays his own feeling self as feminine. Like the boy actor, he is a man who can turn into a woman or a woman who is really a man, and Cleopatra does indeed playfully dress Antony as a woman.

As the tragedy nears its end, Cleopatra more and more evokes feminine otherness, which is thus linked to Shakespeare's own arts of fancy and illusion as well as to deceit and deception. At exactly this moment Shakespeare reminds us that Cleopatra is being played by a boy, diminishing her threat at the very moment he maximizes it, as Cleopatra carries herself and Antony to their deaths. He thus refuses to fix the issue of gender, staging femininity contradictorily both as sexual difference and as an undeveloped potential within men. By equivocating on the issue of gender he can suspend the conventional gender hierarchy without finally overturning it.

For Bernard J. Paris, Prospero, Shakespeare's magician and play-wright, acts out his author's own need to punish others without corrupting himself, to release his aggression without violating his need to be virtuous. Like many protagonists in the history plays and tragedies, Prospero is enraged at those who have injured him. He craves a revenge that will assuage his anger and restore his self-esteem. He needs to see himself as a powerful, masterful, dangerous man who cannot be taken advantage of with impunity and who will strike back when he has been injured. Yet he also needs to see himself as humane, benevolent, and forgiving.

Through his magic Prospero is able to satisfy both these contradictory needs, for it enables him to inflict terrible suffering on his enemies without doing them physical harm and thereby losing his own nobility. *The Tempest* is above all a fantasy of innocent revenge. The revenge is Prospero's, but the fantasy is Shakespeare's, whose inner conflicts are similar to those of his protagonist. Paris concludes that Shakespeare had strong vindictive impulses but even stronger taboos against those impulses and a fear of the guilt and punishment to which he would be exposed if he acted them out. He imagined solutions to this problem by creating situations, like those in *Henry V* and *The Tempest*, that permit justified aggression and innocent revenge.

In the spirit of reader-response criticism David Willbern suggests that our interpretation of the playwright Shakespeare is itself relative. We read into him our own perfect artist and thus discover not the historical figure but rather ourselves. Even as Shakespeare, blessed with a "dramatic ego," rewrote himself in his characters and thus obscured his real self, so we, by duplicating his original act of self-projection, imitate him in the very act of interpreting the plays. Therefore, the man Shakespeare, let alone the playwright Shakespeare, does not exist, is nowhere to be found. Willbern, a professor of English, appropriately maintains that *his* Shakespeare is the English language itself, for language, that definitive quality of the human species, was taken to its final perfection by Shakespeare. The protean nature inside and outside the playhouse that our other authors describe becomes, in Willbern's analysis, the world of the pun, the metaphor, and the trope. We know Shakespeare—this man, this wordsmith, this symbol of our language—only through our selves, through our own reflections in his dramatic mirrors.

Barbara Freedman's essay goes even further than Willbern's into the theoretical issues involved in the concept of Shakespeare's personality. She combines the poet that so many critics (including the critics in this book) have described as having no identity with the Foucaultian vanishing of the subject to make, like a conjurer, the whole criticism of Shakespeare's personality disappear. Then, with a postmodern turn, she goes on to describe that very personality. Shakespeare's mode of self-presentation, she suggests, is not simply to be absent or elusive. Rather, his theme is to be what he is not, absence becoming a form of presence. In this sense, Freedman recuperates earlier psychological critics who found in Shakespeare a need to locate selfhood in another, in an "out there." Through these not-Shakespeares, Shakespeare encourages *us* to misread, to transfer, to dislocate ourselves. Like the anamorphic mirrors popular in the Renaissance, the characters' acting (commented on so often in this book) makes them people who cannot be seen, so that acting itself subverts the supposedly stable place of the critic. So too does the changing sense of self in the Renaissance—the sense pointed to by the New Historicists that self is something to be *made*.

All this recapitulates the *méconnaissance* of Jacques Lacan's version of psychoanalysis. The plays express the fictionalities by which the ego is constructed and maintained. "Shakespeare's personality" in this sense is just one more of the phantoms erected by our own desire, which itself is necessarily displaced and dislocated from our deepest selves.

...

Our essays move from early plays to late, from analysis of Shakespeare's historical surroundings to abstract theory, from a Shakespeare "out there" to a Shakespeare "in here." Yet despite the diversity, our story grows to something of great constancy.

The Shakespeare we agree on shared the aggressive male-male values of his society, possibly as a compensation for his father's deficiencies, possibly as a defense against his resentment of father or brother. He found sexuality between man and woman a far more troubling subject—dark, soiling, frightening—a feeling he overcame only at the end of his career. He construed his world as split between male and female, parent and child, private and public, love and war, word and deed, theater and polity, play and reality. These differences, deeply felt, harbored deep dangers.

Throughout, however, his verbal wit provided him a way of equivocating, even disappearing, amid the profound dualities of his mind. He could deal with the dangers and the differences by flowing easily from one side of the chasm to the other, by being, as the occasion admitted, male or female, parent or child, private man or public figure, lover or soldier, talker or doer, skeptic or idealist, rebel or conservative, presence or absence.

Having read and thought about these essays, I conjecture the following center for Shakespeare's personality: a division crossed by imaginatively being on both sides. Out of some such germ, Shakespeare flourished as actor, director, playwright, and the elusive subject of such enterprises as this. He became the "gentle Shakespeare" we take pleasure in admiring, studying, and imagining. "Having read and thought about these essays, I conjecture"—that is their purpose, and may it please you to do the same.

Shakespeare in the Rising Middle Class

C. L. Barber and Richard P. Wheeler

Shakespeare was so perfect an artist, so completely engaged and ful-filled by his creation, that it is notoriously difficult to talk about the man apart from his work. His separate humanity seems invisible, a transparent medium we see through but cannot see. His art is tactful: it makes troubling things acceptable, indeed enjoyable (with a few exceptions); it provides many kinds and levels of interest to hold atten-tion. There is no *necessity* to look at what points to the author in the individual play or in the succession of plays. Some feel that to do so involves disrespect or a violation of privacy and buttress their objec-tion with an "impersonal theory of poetry," as T. S. Eliot does in "Tradition and the Individual Talent" (1950). But we can see in the plays, and in patterns that emerge from them, something of the contri-bution of the individual sensibility that gave them their distinctive shape, hazardous as this attempt has often proved. Eliot himself effec-tually abandoned the impersonal theory in his later criticism, when in his own poetry he had become able to speak more directly in his own voice, and when he became concerned with understanding the whole oeuvre of various writers, notably Dante and Shakespeare.

Moreover, Shakespeare's supremely resonant adult works permit inferences—some tentative, some highly speculative—about the way the known circumstances of his early life shaped his sensibility. Here the relative scarcity of information is less an impediment than it might at first appear to be. We cannot know just how Shakespeare's working

This essay is adapted from chapter 2 of C. L. Barber and Richard P. Wheeler, *The Whole Journey: Shakespeare's Power of Development* (Berkeley and Los Angeles: University of California Press, 1986). In completing this project, left unfinished when Barber died in April 1980, I tried to produce a book that represents as closely as possible Barber's working design for it. "Shakespeare in the Rising Middle Class," based primarily on a draft chapter of that title by Barber, has been augmented with passages from other fragmentary drafts and with additions I have provided.—R. P. W.

life and the works he produced were conditioned by the experience of infancy, childhood, and youth, but we could not derive such inward matters simply from external data even if we had far more of them than we have. As with the psychoanalysis of adults, in which the kéy early situations and the events occasioning them emerge gradually as recollections and as reenactments, in the analytic situation biographical information must be read inferentially, in terms of Shakespeare's use of the theatrical institution.

The purpose of setting Shakespeare's works against what we know about his life is not, of course, to derive his creative achievement from, or reduce it to, such facts as we have. The bare facts suggest a pattern that could be consistent with many other outcomes, and the odds against any circumstances having led to the development of Shakespeare's genius are incalculable. But that Shakespeare came from a family where the father rose from humble origins to become bailiff (mayor) of a prosperous market town, having married the heiress of an affluent yeoman, and then when his eldest son was twelve withdrew from civic life and fell into debt; that Shakespeare worked and prospered in the social and financial situation of a booming joint stock company, the most successful company of players, who possessed their own theater, of which Shakespeare owned a share—these are circumstances that clearly helped to shape the attitudes and values expressed in his plays. The circumstances of his working life provided support for the poet's role as a man among men. The particular constellation of the burgher family he grew up in is consistent with the thematic preoccupations visible in his works. We shall look first at the circumstances of Shakespeare's early life in relation to some aspects of his development as an artist, then consider his adult working situation and its implications about his temperament and its equilibrium.

"This Most Balmy Time"

Shakespeare's father was a considerable person in a considerable world, a world all too frequently patronized by critics who adopt, half-consciously, the aristocratic perspective for which Shakespeare himself gave the cue in presenting such figures as Justice Shallow or the merry wives. John Shakespeare was a leading citizen, faithfully attending the council as alderman, holding several civic offices, serving a term as bailiff, buying two houses, dealing in wool and probably other commodities in his trade as a maker of soft leather goods. His fortunes had been enhanced considerably when, at about the age of thirty, he married the daughter of his father's landlord, a well-to-do farmer with connections to the long-established minor gentry.

The youngest child among ten daughters (eight by an earlier marriage) and two sons, Mary Arden was clearly her father's favorite. In his will, made as he lay dying in 1556, he left her all his principal property, after making modest provisions for a widow whom he had married late in life. In Schoenbaum we get the inventory of the property, of which Mary Arden was one of the executors, from eleven painted cloths through ample furnishings in the house to "a barn filled with wheat and barley, store of livestock, . . . wood in the yard and bacon in the roof" (Schoenbaum 1975, 19). Shortly after her elderly father's death Mary Arden married his tenant's son, who was considerably older than she was. John Shakespeare was already prospering, living in the house that became Shakespeare's birthplace and buying in 1556 the adjacent house, which became known as the Woolshop. In September 1558 the couple had a girl, christened Joan; in 1562 another girl, Margaret, who records show was buried five months later. Then William Shakespeare was christened on April 26, 1564. He was the eldest male child, and the eldest child to survive, for the next girl to be born, in 1569, was christened Joan like the first-born girl. Thus the first Joan was dead, but her death is unrecorded, and may have happened any time before 1569; she may or may not have been alive at the time of Shakespeare's birth.

Shakespeare grows up in a home that is also a prospering business. His hardworking, enterprising father is a man to whom his fellow citizens looked with admiration and confidence, which is obvious from the trusts he was given by the community—and with compassion, as is later made clear by their forbearance when he ceased to participate and got heavily into debt. In legal matters of which we have records, the role of women was so subordinate to that of men that all the surviving evidence about the mother concerns her inheritance, the christenings of her children, the dissipation of her inheritance by borrowing, and her death in 1608. But as we have seen, she was the youngest daughter of a father who gave her not "a third more opulent than your sisters' " but virtually all. She marries an exceptionally able older man of lower social origins, and after the disappointment of one girl-child's death (perhaps two), she gives birth to her first son. For two years and five months, until the birth of Gilbert in October 1566, William Shakespeare is her only child, or at least her only male child, at a time when her very successful, older husband is extremely busy.

Shakespeare's enormous resonance to life, his great capacity for play, and his set toward generous cherishing must have roots in this very early experience. The sort of timeless, blissful moment some of the Sonnets to the friend seek to recover would find an active, enduring prototype in "this most balmy time":

> Not mine own fears, nor the prophetic soul
> Of the wide world, dreaming on things to come,
> Can yet the lease of my true love control,
> Suppos'd as forfeit to a confin'd doom.
> The mortal moon hath her eclipse endur'd,
> And the sad augurs mock their own presage,
> Incertainties now crown themselves assur'd,
> And peace proclaims olives of endless age.
> Now with the drops of this most balmy time
> My love looks fresh, and Death to me subscribes,
> Since spite of him I'll live in this poor rhyme,
> While he insults o'er dull and speechless tribes;
>   And thou in this shalt find thy monument,
>   When tyrants' crests and tombs of brass are spent.

One can certainly read Sonnet 107 without reference to infancy, as the recovery of a private feeling of omnipotence through confident love in an auspicious moment of renewed public confidence. The poem swings around the experience of a threat overcome, which can be understood as the threat of a sibling expected and feared, but not ultimately decisive, because through the love of the young man the original situation has been restored almost beyond belief, and whole tribes of rivals can do nothing about it. To see this in the poem depends on its exquisite generalization by concrete suggestion, its openness to a multiplicity of readings. Through the cryptic reference to a "time" in which it is being written, it is open to, or conveys feelings from, an earlier time, like those adumbrated in the absences lamented in Sonnets 97 ("How like a winter hath my absence been") and 98 ("From you I have been absent in the spring"), when a child's fears are animated "by the prophetic soul" of his whole "world," "dreaming" not of him but of "things to come." Sonnet 107 evokes these "incertainties" as overcome: the maternal moon, whose loss was presaged by the sad auguries, has only been eclipsed. Now, in this new time, moist and "balmy," without conflict, the "death" of separation is overcome.

As elsewhere in the Sonnets, it is impossible in Sonnet 107 to separate the poet's love as his act of loving from his love as his object: "My love looks fresh, and Death to me subscribes." The whole thing is made possible by the poem, which holds, out of ordinary time, the loving and the beloved. The gesture abjuring conflict, the modesty in "this poor rhyme," in keeping with the peace proclaimed by "olives of endless age," is belied by the aggression that "insults o'er dull and speechless tribes," while the poet will "live in this poor rhyme." The couplet returns simply to the friend and the "rhyme"; the idea of death returns with "monument," but there is a final balancing aggression, which asserts victory for the poetry of private love over the pride of the mighty of this world.

The public event is made part of the private, but to assume that it is the sufficient cause of the exultant affirmation is utterly implausible. Quite probably the "mortal moon" refers to Queen Elizabeth, who survived the "eclipse" of a political or, more likely, an astrological danger. Shakespeare shared, of course, in the cult of "the imperial vot'ress" (*A Midsummer Night's Dream*, 2.1.103; see Yates 1975, 29–87). Courtly worship of her obviously drew on roots of feeling going back, often explicitly, to childhood; it included many adaptations of ceremonial adoration of the Virgin Mary, whose place Elizabeth in some ways took over. Sir Walter Raleigh, expressing in "The Ocean to Cynthia" his anguish, insecurity and frustration after his marriage temporarily lost him the queen's favor and love, at one point compares his loss to the loss of a mother's breast. But Raleigh's relationship was personal as well as the whole basis of his career. His love was indeed "the child of state"; Shakespeare describes such courtly loves in Sonnet 124, by contrast with his disinterested love, "which suffers not in smiling pomp, nor falls / Under the blow of thralled discontent." In Sonnet 107, clearly, the public situation is merely the occasion for the private renewal and becomes a trope for it as the poem turns from vehicle to tenor with the new surge of the third quatrain, "Now . . . / My love looks fresh."

In the earlier work identification with the maternal predominates, partly in compensation for fear of abandonment or of being overwhelmed (Barber and Wheeler 1986, chap. 1). The whole structure of Shakespeare's sensibility is deeply responsive to the "lines of life" that extend vertically across generations through the node of infancy and childhood; horizontal relationships in the same generation are decisively shaped by residues of the family constellation. The triumph of Sonnet 107 over fears of isolation within a "confined doom" recapitulates the recovery of the initial union with the mother as it opens out onto riches of sensuous and verbal experience. This recovery can be realized, in the period of the Sonnets, in poetry about adult human relationships and about the power of his art. But the need to enact such recovery conditions all phases of Shakespeare's work.

From first to last, Shakespeare in his art responds to life most deeply according to patterns of relating grounded in the bond to a mother—fulfillment through cherishing another, loss of self by abandonment or betrayal. The cherishing sympathy is rooted in a rich narcissism that extends outward by empathy, putting the self in others' places. But on practical levels Shakespeare clearly has a firm sense of "mine" and "thine," and the cherishing can move toward possessing others as confirmation of an egoism. His temperament is richly sociable, centered in kinship extended outward by a high valuation of kindness; evil is most intensely felt as a violation of kinship, as unkindness in the sense of unnatural, where "natural" means kinship. This temperament has its own type of selfishness and detachment: other people are extensions of self, and all relationships are provisional or contingent because they replace other relationships. At the core is the original loss of the parental objects and the possibility of its recurrence. When, in Shakespeare's later work, this threat is fully explored, the "everything" reached by a cherishing possession may suddenly become the "nothing" that echoes in *King Lear*.

Keats, in exploring his own nature, illuminated the receptive side of Shakespeare by speaking of him as the supreme example of "negative capability." This power to be "in for" other beings accounts for Shakespeare's being able, next after God or nature, to create most—to fill even the wings of the theater with human spirits bursting with life, to be the boy in act 1 and the old man in act 5, to be both Othello and Iago, as Stephen Dedalus says in Joyce's *Ulysses*. Keats also observed in himself, and guessed in Shakespeare, that this poetic capacity for "humility before life" went with a lack of self, with being almost without a determinate identity—as we can see in those sonnets where the poet's selfless cherishing of the friend leaves him in the lurch. Genius, working with the resources of poetry and theater, was crucial in enabling Shakespeare to live so fully in this mode. But his root sense of self and of self-enjoyment ("No, I am that I am"), together with his "deepest sense, how hard true sorrow hits," must reach back to the buoyant time when he was the only male child of a young mother, and to the inevitable discovery that such a time, despite its infinite promise, is "but a little moment" (Sonnets 121, 120, 15).

"His Virtues Else"

The birth of a new brother, with its inevitable dethronement of his majesty the baby, is the initial shock suggested by Shakespeare's biographical record; the second, much more striking shock is his father's failure, obvious to all by the time the boy is twelve. The familiar eldest child's experiences of dethronement and fear of abandonment in infancy seem to have fused in Shakespeare's imagination with sympathetic preoccupation with his amiable father's failure, thereby shaping the tendency to incorporate maternal qualities and powers toward an ideal of cherishing fatherhood. In the plays, especially those from the early phases of Shakespeare's development as an artist, we discover fear for, and sympathy with, generous, vulnerable men dramatized with full understanding of their weakness and its capacity to provoke their women.

John Shakespeare's rise was obviously helped materially by his marriage; how his decline was related to it we can never know with certainty. But his younger, better-born wife can scarcely have failed to feel deep resentment as she saw her inheritance dissipated, whatever likable qualities her husband possessed for the community. Soon after the death of her affluent father she had married another older, substantial man, the John Shakespeare of 1556 or 1557, who, after years of prosperity and civic responsibility, turned into something else. From the later 1570s he is repeatedly in financial trouble. He borrows £40 in 1578 on the security of his wife's inheritance, allegedly fails to repay it on time in 1580, and never recovers the disputed house and land, despite repeated legal efforts. Other property that came to him from Mary Arden is rented or sold in the late 1570s. In 1580 failure to appear in court results in a £20 fine. Another £20 fine was imposed on John Shakespeare when a hatmaker for whom he had stood surety failed to appear in court. Two other forfeits of £10 each for those for whom he had stood surety (a tinker and his brother Henry) suggest

bad judgment and generosity—or need for ready cash, since by standing surety one could collect a small fee (Schoenbaum 1975, 36–38).

After 1576 John Shakespeare abruptly stopped attending council
meetings and going to church. He was, however, kept on the council
for ten years, despite attendance at only one recorded session in that
period; fines for nonattendance were forgiven him, as well as contributions toward relief of the poor. He was never ruined, quite possibly
thanks to help from his successful son, who joined in the long, heart-
breaking legal struggle to recover his mother's inheritance, and who in
the late 1590s was still involved in legal action in Chancery. Near the
end of his life John Shakespeare was still living in the house where his
children were born. In the last year of his life, when "he must have
been in his early seventies" (Schoenbaum 1975, 40), he was listed in a
petition to London as one of those who could testify to the economic
difficulties Stratford was experiencing.

It is almost certain that John Shakespeare had Catholic sympathies,
at least briefly. There is strong evidence that he executed, presumably
under the influence of a secret Jesuit missionary, a Catholic "spiritual
testament" (a translation of a formulary by Cardinal Borromeo),
which such missionaries carried to England in 1580–81. The docu-
ment was found in the roof of his house in the middle of the eighteenth
century; maddeningly, only a transcript, lacking the first page, has
survived, but Schoenbaum and other archival scholars now regard it as
genuine. John Shakespeare may have executed the testament in a moment of enthusiasm and then hidden the little manuscript booklet
when persecution intensified (Schoenbaum 1975, 41–46). But his fellow townsmen, among whom on the council there were Catholics, did
not regard him as one; in 1592, when commissioners ordered to ferret
out recusants filed two reports, John Shakespeare is listed among nine
nonattenders who "coom not to Churche for feare of processe of
Debtte" (Schoenbaum 1975, 38).

Some inferences, speculative but consistent with the record, can be
made about the poet's relation to his father's failure and about consequences for Shakespeare of the episode of the Catholic testament.
The British psychoanalyst John Padel (1975) has suggested that the
self-disabling of the sonnets could have been shaped by identification
with the father when "in disgrace with fortune and men's eyes"
(Sonnet 29). Such "transference feeling" in the relationship to the
young man would be natural in those moments when a different

identity, maternally derived and based on the experience of being cherished, does not sustain the poet—when "all alone" he beweeps his "outcast state" (Sonnet 29). The degree to which parents' identities subsist at deep levels is more familiar to analysts than to most of us; their experience of the fluid, protected analytical process dramatizes such internalized presences in the transference to them. Parents are also omens for us all, often ill omens from which we struggle, consciously or unconsciously, to disassociate ourselves. There is no inconsistency in John Shakespeare's having been also a cherishing father. The "decrepit father" of Sonnet 37 "takes delight" in "his active child." If John Shakespeare came to combine weakness and generous love, he must have been both a poor model for manhood and a parent difficult to reject wholly.

One of Shakespeare's first great portraits is Henry VI, who cherishes his realm even as his weakness lets his nobles and his queen tear it to pieces. Henry's credulity is heavily stressed, along with his religious devotion, as in the scene, not required at all by the plot, where he superstitiously believes the "miracle" of a poor man's sight restored—a fraud that his uncle Gloucester handily exposes. Conceivably the connection between Henry's weakness and his gullible piety is partly shaped by recollections of John Shakespeare's Catholic profession of faith—though the "miracle" episode in 2 *Henry VI* (which comes from the chronicles) was calculated as drama to appeal to Protestant sentiment, and the religious preoccupation that goes with Henry's weakness is also historically derived.

The son's response to John Shakespeare's spiritual last will may be writ large, however, in the almost complete absence, from all his works, of religious resolutions of central dynamic stresses. Pious gestures at the moment of death or in oaths and appeals to ultimate authority are dramatic renderings of behavior in a Christian culture. Arguments have been mounted on the basis of Shakespeare's *sensibility* that he was either a Catholic or a devoted high Anglican. But the point of view his drama adopts never, in our judgment, involves religious eschatology. Such a this-worldly perspective fitted, of course, with the prohibition of religious themes in the theater, including the ban (which he frequently violates) on using the Lord's name. But it is in human beings and society that Shakespeare invests himself. To have watched at sixteen or seventeen a precarious father make and then take back an extreme religious gesture might well have contributed to

Shakespeare's resolute secularism, despite the religious need in his temperament.

Lawrence Stone has described the extreme patriarchal authority exercised by parents, especially fathers, in the sixteenth and earlier seventeenth centuries, which accompanied the rise of the nuclear family—a domination over children and a ritual subservience yielded by them that are often astonishing to our modern sensibilities. It seems highly unlikely that Shakespeare's father can have maintained such authority within his own house from the time he abdicated public authority, if he had not already lost it some time before. So we encounter extreme discrepancy between the father of Shakespeare's infancy and early childhood and the precarious figure implied by the public record after Shakespeare was twelve, an objective contrast much more drastic, involving more for a son to deal with, than the usual dismantling of infantile overestimation, which is part of growing up.

Heinz Kohut (1971) stresses the importance of the child's gradual disillusionment in dealing with idealized figures on whom parts of the self are patterned. "Under optimal circumstances," Kohut writes, the "child's evaluation of the idealized object becomes increasingly realistic"; a process of "gradual disappointment" permits the secure internalization of parental objects as structures of the self (45). A sudden intensification of the process of disillusionment forced by the abrupt failure of the idealized figure can lead to "what seems to be an intense form of object hunger. The intensity of the search for and of the dependency on these objects is due to the fact that they are striven for as a substitute for the missing segment of the psychic structure" (45). Of course, John Shakespeare's decline, which seems to have coincided with his son's early adolescent years, would not have presented the kind of "very early traumatic disturbances" with which Kohut is most concerned, disturbances that can lead to severely incapacitating disorders, as with "personalities who become addicts" (46). But the father's failure would have corresponded to years in which, in "optimal circumstances," the son's gradually dismantled idealization of the father leads into and becomes the basis for a boy's preoccupation with manhood—as ideal and identity.

There are, of course, difficulties with applying Kohut's account to Shakespeare. Common sense (and common prejudice) rejects the idea of making Shakespeare a "case." The process of taking new objects for old needs is, after all, universal, or nearly so. An expression such as "missing segment of the psychic structure" assumes as a psychological norm what in fact must be an achievement of culture. Yet there is surely evidence in the creative achievement for an exceptional need, along with exceptional mastery of it by means of heroic and romantic imagination balanced by a sense of reality that controls ironic awareness about the heroic and romantic. That need is itself consistent with the dominant concerns of the culture Shakespeare knew. In that culture the tension between received ideas of static, hierarchical society and the increasing social mobility, along with the loosening of earlier communal structures and their traditional religious reinforcements, place a new emphasis on reverential attitudes toward patriarchal authority and on the nuclear family and its survival through generations.

Shakespeare puts to creative use potentially disruptive trends such as Kohut describes: an "intense form of object hunger" is fulfilled in the dramatist's power to create others. Many of these created persons carry on the search for ideal embodiment in art. The poet of the Sonnets conducts such a search in his effort to live through the aristocratic manhood of his friend. Hamlet's effort to identify himself with the heroic manhood of his dead father launches a series of plays in which the protagonist's search for self-fulfillment in or through another ends in tragedy.

The action in *Hamlet* is determined by the violent dethronement and death of a father. But this father is the first to be apprehended as "a goodly king" (1.2.186), strong, majestic. As Shakespeare moves up, in social terms, beyond caste difference, to invest his creative powers in the son (Hamlet) who might inherit from such a father, he moves back, in terms of individual development, to derivatives of the world of childhood, where such a figure would have been known and then lost. Not lost, however, as is Hamlet's father, in the full vigor of his active manhood, but lost behind the abruptly and unaccountably diminished figure of a father whose failure makes him an object of pity rather than open confrontation. That Hamlet is not an adolescent but a grown man (thirty, if we accept the gravedigger's calendar) fits with the long delay and incomplete accomplishment in Shakespeare's own development of a process that in simpler or different natures, and different family situations, takes place earlier, if perhaps never completely. The situation in *Hamlet,* centered on the son's all-or-nothing struggle with a beloved father who commands his loyalty and with a hated stepfather who must be destroyed, seems to offer the son a second chance for confrontation and internalization.

When we consider Shakespeare's long delay in turning to the tragic exploration of such confrontation, it seems significant that his own father was likely a man not easy for a son to hate. On this point, at least with regard to John Shakespeare's social and civic relations, the external evidence is very strong: his being kept on the town council despite nonattendance, the forgiving of his fines and assessments for relief of the poor, his standing surety for others even after extensive losses had cut deeply into his wife's inheritance. It is hard to hit a man who is down, to release into the filial bond the aggression by which a son can assert his own independent identity, especially if the father is a kind man and the son is understanding. It is harder still if the father's failure has made him an object of disappointment—whether expressed as hostility or as pity—for a mother whose fortune he has brought down with him.

In the situation in *Hamlet,* however, there is the stepfather Claudius, who is very much up, a thoroughly hateable figure and a mighty opposite. The splitting of the father figure would seem to give license for the passage through hatred that can lead to atonement. Shakespeare brings Claudius, to the sound of cannon and of trumpets that "bray out / The triumph of his pledge" (1.4.11–12), into the beginning of the great scene on the battlements in which Hamlet will finally encounter the Ghost. Hamlet's clearheaded description, in the "nipping and . . . eager air" (1.4.2), of what is going on below is icy with scorn:

> The King doth wake to-night and takes his rouse,
> Keeps wassail, and the swagg'ring up-spring reels.
> (1.4.8–9)

But as Claudius "drains his draughts of Rhenish down" (1.4.10), Hamlet feels himself involved in, even shamed by, the wassailing custom he regrets, though he is "to the manner born" (1.4.15):

> This heavy-headed revel east and west
> Makes us traduc'd, and tax'd of other nations
> They clip us drunkards, and with swinish phrase
> Soil our addition, and indeed it takes
> From our achievements, though perform'd at height,
> The pith and marrow of our attribute,
> So oft it chances in particular men,
> That for some vicious mole of nature in them

As in their birth wherein they are not guilty,
(Since nature cannot choose his origin)
By their o'ergrowth of some complexion
Oft breaking down the pales and forts of reason,
Or by some habit, that too much o'er-leavens
The form of plausive manners, that these men
Carrying I say the stamp of one defect
Being nature's livery, or fortune's star,
His virtues else . . .

(1.4.17–33)*

As Hamlet shifts from scorn for those who perpetuate a national disgrace to compassion for those afflicted with an inescapable "defect," Claudius is left behind as the object of his meditation. The passage is often taken as a description of Hamlet himself and more generally of Shakespeare's tragic heroes, with support from "Oft breaking down the pales and forts of reason."

But the passage describes private persons—what often "chances in particular men"—and the first instance of a disabling "mole of nature" is "in their birth wherein they are not guilty, / (Since nature cannot choose his origin)." None of Shakespeare's heroes, least of all Hamlet, is lowborn. "By their o'ergrowth of some complexion" describes a developing character defect, not a rapid crisis such as we get in the tragedies; it is a long-term process that is spoken of as breaking down rational control. "Or by some habit, that too much o'er-leavens / The form of plausive manners" specifies a character defect that is social; the description would fit a social drinker who becomes an alcoholic: "plausive" suggests manners that are pleasing but lose their pith and become merely plausible. A suggestion of too much yeast, too much ferment, in the word "o'er-leavens" is picked up in the final summary drink image: "the dram of eale / Doth all the noble substance of a doubt / To his own scandal" (1.4.36–38). "Yeast" is probably the first meaning of "eale" (here retained from Q2), with only a punning suggestion of "evil." The small "dram" contrasts with the "draughts of Rhenish" Claudius "drains," even as it develops the theme. The result for such "particular men" is not final, tragic destruction but "scandal": they "in the general censure take corruption / From that particular fault" (1.4.35–36).

---

*The punctuation of the second quarto is here preserved to keep the huddled, sliding quality of the movement of the thought, which is broken up by modern punctuation; the comma after "attribute" (line 22) may not be a printer's error.

The oblique language, hovering between technical terminology and exquisitely suggestive metaphor, along with the poised enumeration of alternatives, suggests an impulse to keep a distance. But despite the emphatically objective tone, a gathering intensity of regret takes over as the reflections accelerate (by means of a doubling syntax that modern punctuation spoils):

> that these men
> Carrying I say the stamp of one defect
> Being nature's livery, or fortune's star,
> His virtues else be they as pure as grace,
> As infinite as man may undergo,
> Shall in the general censure take corruption
> From the particular fault: the dram of eale
> Doth all the noble substance of a doubt
> To his own scandal.
>   *Enter* Ghost.
> HORATIO: Look my lord it comes.
> HAMLET: Angels and ministers of grace defend us: . . .
>   (1.4.30–39; punctuation as in Q2)

The abruptness of the final lines of the long passage emphasizes the finality of the result of the process. Even as he recognizes sadly how the virtues are vitiated, Hamlet's regret pays tribute to them in the strongest terms. The subject shifts significantly from plural ("these men") to singular as a new start is made; "His virtues else be they as pure as grace" is high praise indeed, topped by "as infinite as man may undergo." The emphasis on "one" defect stresses what might have been, what was promised and lost.

These lines serve the dramatic purpose of diverting the audience— and Hamlet—so that the sudden apparition of the Ghost takes them by surprise (see Burke 1953, 29–30). The omission of these lines from the Folio version (and from the quite full version of the first act in the first quarto) shows that they are not a necessary business of the play. But in Shakespeare's own development, if this way of reading them is correct, they are a characteristically generous business of the author. E. Nicholas Knight, in an exhaustive and moving account of John Shakespeare's legal difficulties in his decline, takes the famous generalizing lines beginning "So oft it chances in particular men" to be a description of the dramatist's own father (1973, 28). The idea that the text moves into an account of men manqué is very compelling. Between Claudius, made present by ordnance and braying trumpets, and the appearance of the awesome Ghost—two potent fathers rooted in early childhood—Shakespeare puts Hamlet into relationship with a third father, neither villainous nor majestic. As he moves his hero toward an encounter with a most powerful, indeed overpowering, paternal presence, and thereby into high tragedy, Shakespeare writes a poignant valediction to the kind of flawed figure his own father had become. In the process, with marvelous associative freedom and resonance, the Prince moves from despising in his drink the heroically evil stepfather, Claudius, through reflections on the shame of a disabling weakness in quotidian life associated by imagery with drink, to regret for the noble substance so vitiated. Only then comes the ghostly return of a father whose noble substance is intact, though he is robbed of life.

That Claudius's drunkenness provides the link between Hamlet's scorn for the usurper and his compassion for particular men may further reflect conditions in the Stratford home. Though there is no evidence beyond congruence with other circumstances and one belated anecdote about a merry-cheeked, Falstaffian old man to make it certain that John Shakespeare's problem was drink, his economic decline and his withdrawal from civic affairs are remarkably consistent with a common alcoholic pattern. But one's sense of the whole situation does not depend on that specification. It is worth remarking that the lines about private men refer to a decline ending not in death but in "general censure." Such an assessment is consistent with the likelihood that Shakespeare's father was still alive when *Hamlet* was written (or at least first written). John Shakespeare was buried in September 1601; if, as most scholars judge, Gabriel Harvey's marginalia note that Shakespeare's "*Lucrece,* and his tragedy of Hamlet, Prince of Denmark, have it in them to please the wiser sort" (Harvey 1974, 1840) was penned not later than early 1601, then a version of the tragedy that could command such respect must have been written at the latest in 1600. It is not the actual father who is dramatized as returning from the grave; but the apparition of past greatness may have something to do with half-buried recollections of the dramatist's father in the red, furred gown of Stratford's bailiff, escorted to church by constables, as awesome a sight for a four-year-old son as, in heroic iconography, "the fair and warlike form / In which the majesty of buried Denmark / Did sometimes march. . . . We do it wrong, being so majestical, / To offer it the show of violence" (1.1.47–49, 143–44).

"An Absolute *Iohannes Fac Totum*"

That Shakespeare at eighteen should have married a woman eight years his senior accords with the dominance of the vertical axis of family relationships in his sensibility. That it was something that happened rather than something planned seems evident, precontract or no precontract, from the fact that the marriage was performed less than six months before the birth of their first child. An ecclesiastical license was sought and paid for to allow only one asking of the banns instead of three on successive Sundays so that the ceremony could take place before the Christmas season, when marriages were prohibited (Schoenbaum 1975, 62–65). The responses of commentators have varied, from explanations making it all respectable for the nineteenth century, to beating pots and pans in charivari, versions of that old ritual gesture against the confusion of sexuality by verticality—citing such passages from the plays as the following:

> LYSANDER: Or else misgraffed in respect of years—
> HERMIA: O spite! too old to be engag'd to young.
> (*A Midsummer Night's Dream* 1.1.137–38)

Stephen Dedalus's comment in *Ulysses* is exceptional in that Joyce, controlling the whole, makes Stephen's own involvement part of his interpretation:

> He chose badly? He was chosen, it seems to me. If others have their will Ann hath a way. By cock, she was to blame. She put the comether on him, sweet and twenty-six. The greyeyed goddess who bends over the boy Adonis, stooping to conquer, as prologue to the swelling act, is a boldfaced Stratford wench who tumbles in a cornfield a lover younger than herself.
>   And my turn? When?
>
> (Joyce 1934, 189)

That Shakespeare left Stratford for London but did not leave the marriage, begetting in its early years the first daughter and then twins, a daughter and the son who was to die at eleven and a half years of age—these are crucial facts, however bare. We do not know whether he joined a company traveling through Stratford, was for a period a schoolmaster in the country, or became a noverint, a legal secretary, as E. Nicholas Knight (1973) has argued plausibly but not compellingly. What is clear is that in making this move, as so many were doing, he brought to London a rich local heritage shaped both by civic experience and by the agricultural life surrounding his market town. What he encountered in the professional theater of London was an institution in the process of establishing its economic independence, a vocation that made it possible for a gifted writer to exist apart from aristocratic patronage.

With his usual multiple ironies, Shakespeare addresses the prospect of permanent financial patronage in *A Midsummer Night's Dream*, where the artisans lament Bottom's absence just before their play is scheduled to be put on:

> O sweet bully Bottom! Thus hath he lost sixpence a day during his life; he could not have scap'd sixpence a day. And the Duke had not given him sixpence a day for playing Pyramus, I'll be hang'd. He would have deserv'd it. Sixpence a day in Pyramus, or nothing.
>
> (4.2.19–24)

The noble persons for whom Shakespeare's marriage play may have first been written could scarcely miss this iteration. Though it can pass off as a joke about the palpable-gross play that follows, Shakespeare at this early stage of his career seems to be glancing at least at the possibility of steady financial patronage—though he may already be enjoying a glance back at a situation from which his successes in the commercial theater have released him, or promise to release him. A little earlier, in 1593 and 1594, there are the dedications of the poems to Southampton; though they are in the mode of devoted compliment customary in the period, they seem to point hopefully toward acquiring patronage, especially the second dedication: "What I have done is yours, what I have to do is yours, being part in all I have, devoted yours." But by about 1600, when *Hamlet* is written, the Prince, elated by the success of the play within the play, exclaims:

> Would not this, sir, and a forest of feathers—if the rest
> of my fortunes turn Turk with me—with two Provincial roses
> on my raz'd shoes, get me a fellowship in a cry of players?
> HORATIO: Half a share.
> HAMLET: A whole one, I.
>
> (3.2.275–80)

For all his enthusiasm about the traveling company, Hamlet thinks of them as self-supporting actors who share ownership won by their talents.

This financial independence, along with aristocratic sponsorship and intermittent performances with rewards at court, provided a relatively secure working situation and a measure of independence crucial for Shakespeare's productivity and the critical perspectives of his productions. Robert Greene's deathbed attack on Shakespeare in 1592 and its publisher Henry Chettle's subsequent apology speak volumes here and are worth dwelling on despite their familiarity. Greene, one of the University Wits who first gave educated voice to the burgeoning acting profession, warns Marlowe, Nashe, and Peele, "*those Gentlemen his Quondom acquaintance, that spend their wits in making plaies*," to take a lesson from his own miserable state, brought on by "those Puppets ... that spake from our mouths, those Anticks garnisht in our colours." If Greene, to whom such "burres" have sought "to cleave," has been forsaken by actors turned base imitators, shall not these three, "to whome they all have beene beholding," be forsaken as well?

> Yes trust them not: for there is an vpstart Crow, beautified with our feathers, that with his *Tygers hart wrapt in a Players hyde*, supposes he is as well able to bombast out a blank verse as the best of you: and beeing an absolute *Iohannes fac totum*, is in his owne conceit the only Shake-scene in a countrey. O that I might intreat your rare wits to be imploied in more profitable courses: & let those Apes imitate your past excellence, and neuer more acquaint them with your admired inuentions. I knowe the best husband of you all will neuer proue an Vsurer, and the kindest of them all will neuer proue a kind nurse: yet whilest you may, seeke you better Maisters; for it is pittie men of such rare wits, should be subiect to the pleasure of such rude groomes.
>
> (Greene [1592] 1974, 1835)

When one thinks of the stress to which the need for patronage subjected even such a well-derived poet as John Donne, despite the early recognition of his genius, once his marriage had alienated his patron, one is grateful that Shakespeare could provide for his life by "public means." He could feel, in relation to the world of his highborn friend, uncomfortable about his profession: "almost thence my nature is subdued / To what it works in, like the dyer's hand" (Sonnet 111). But if Shakespeare is associated with "rude groomes," the rude grooms have money—that is the root of the animus of poor Pierce Penniless Greene. In a time before theatrical copyright, to be the players' in-house playmaker was a secure way to make a solid living. Greene, at the end of the road of hand-to-mouth insecurity to which the University Wits were subject, speaks with a dilapidated gentleman's scorn of anyone who could "proue an Vsurer." To lend out some of his money at interest was just what Shakespeare in fact did, as did many members of the rising mercantile class, as well as alert members of the aristocracy.

Before the year 1592 was out, Henry Chettle responded to the stir caused by his posthumous publication of Greene's letter "to diuers play-makers," which had been "offensively by one or two of them taken." After defending his own reputation as a printer who had long "hindred the bitter inueying against schollers," Chettle went on to apologize for not deleting the remarks about Shakespeare:

> With neither of them that take offence was I acquainted, and with one of them [Marlowe] I care not if I neuer be: The other [Shakespeare], whome at that time I did not so much spare, as since I wish I had, for that as I haue moderated the heate of liuing writers, and might haue vsde my owne discretion (especially in such a case) the Author beeing dead, that I did not, I am as sory, as if the originall fault had beene my fault, because my selfe haue seene his demeanor no lesse ciuill than he excelent in the qualitie he professes: Besides, diuers of worship haue reported, his vprightnes of dealing, which argues his honesty, and his facetious grace in writting, that approoues his Art.
>
> (Chettle 1974, 1835–36)

It is striking that in many of the Sonnets, even as Shakespeare expresses his adulation of aristocratic heritage, he does so in prudential monetary and legal terms of middle-class provenance, terms used in upright dealing—or sharp practice (compare Sonnet 134). He feels his heritage as a stain in the situation of writing them, perhaps referring to his father's trade as a glover in "the dyer's hand." But from within the nascent middle class, in the dipolar society of the time, Chettle's praise defines Shakespeare's professional situation in complimentary, positive terms. His "facetious grace" in writing Shakespeare would have learned and polished in London, but the status Chettle describes with middle-class admiration extended what the dramatist brought with him from Stratford. If on one side Shakespeare's tough business success reflects determination not to be like the father who failed to carry through, the young playwright's model for "vprightnes of dealing," which "diuers of worship haue reported," must also have been that father and the firm-textured society in which he had earlier succeeded.

Greene's belittling turns inside out as one thinks of what it implies about Shakespeare's roles, besides what it says of his financial independence. The "*fac totum*," as he makes and "shakes" scenes and writes parts for everybody, is in the position, if he has the sense of form that Shakespeare had, to dominate the whole, to be *dominus factotum*—not a mere jack-of-all-trades, but master. It is ironic that Greene's attack on Shakespeare ("his *Tygers hart wrapt in a Players hyde*") suggests this dominance by likening the enterprising playwright to one of the domineering women prominent in his early work—Queen Margaret, as she violently usurps the power of British royalty. Having captured York, her great dynastic rival, Margaret taunts him fiendishly by wiping his face with a napkin soaked in the blood of his youngest son. York, about to die on her and Clifford's dagger, cries out:

> O tiger's heart wrapped in a woman's hide!
> How couldst thou drain the life-blood of the child,
> To bid his father wipe his eyes withal. . . .
> (*3 Henry VI* 1.4.137–39)

But Shakespeare's actual role in the theater—to be constantly giving, working within a team, creating parts to realize and nurture the talents of his fellows—is directly counter to Greene's jibe. It is a cherishing role, the very opposite of the dread maternal destructiveness portrayed, and thereby distanced, in Margaret.

Apart from Greene, Shakespeare's contemporaries speak of him as "gentle"; he has a supremely generous imagination. Identification with the cherishing role of the parents is built into Shakespeare's genius as player and playwright. In the Sonnets such cherishing goes with an inhibition on the middle-class poet's characterizing, and thereby limiting, the aristocratic young man. If we considered only the self-disabling adulation in the Sonnets, we might well ask: what did Shakespeare, in contrast with quarrelsome Marlowe and Jonson, do with his aggression? How was he spared the destructive effects when aggression not directed outward turns inward, back against the self?

It seems clear that Shakespeare puts aggression fully in the service of his dramatic art. He uses it in creating aggressive characters: Richard III, in Shakespeare's first great public hit, is utterly captivating as he plays ruthlessly and humorously for the crown. The dramatist also crucially uses aggression to shape and limit the characters he creates, subordinating each to the mastery of the whole production:

And let those that play your clowns speak no more than is set down for
them, for there be some that will themselves laugh to set on some
quantity of barren spectators to laugh too, though in the mean time
some necessary question of the play be then to be consider'd.

(*Hamlet*, 3.2.38–45)

The royal amateur of the theater who makes this speech is about to use
a play from the repertory of the visiting common players for extremely
aggressive purposes, to show royal crime its own image. Hamlet
speaks patronizingly of "a fellowship in a cry of players," but the
whole situation suggests the remarkable role the players had in their
relationship to the world of court and kings.

Leo Salingar (1974) has made the point that as a way of expressing
their special, new, undefined status, the poets of the common players
"found the equivalent of a professional emblem in the novel device of
inserting a play within the play," often with royal or noble spectators
(267). We can see Kyd doing this, with aggressive protest, in *The
Spanish Tragedy*, where a court official, unable to obtain justice for
the murder of his son, turns the play he is staging into a brutal attack
on his royal audience, destroying a whole dynastic line. Salingar sees
Shakespeare, in his comedies, balancing prerogatives, political ("the
real influence of the monarch") and artistic ("the idea of play-acting").
These polarized preoccupations reflect Shakespeare's "historically
novel situation, as a professional playwright in a mainly commercial
theatre, writing for, and even in a sense creating, a national public, but
depending first and last on aristocratic favour. At one pole of his
comic world is the actor-poet, at the other, his ultimate patron, the
prince" (256).

The two poles, with their class or caste difference, are implicit in
the interplay between admiration and irony in history and tragedy as
well as in comedy. Shakespeare in his art shares the assumption of
most Englishmen of the age that the fullness of life could be realized
only by the nobility and the gentry, with the royal family at what
should be the pinnacle. On occasion he could give the merry wives of
Windsor and other neighbors their due, but as Salingar observes,
"His stage world gravitates to the great house or the court. He depicts the gentry from outside, but they stand at the centre" (255).
The stage itself, however, was a middle-class property and vantage
point. In the commercial theater Shakespeare could use the power of

dramatic form to develop an aggressive, ironic understanding of the world of the court—its ideals and iconography, with the magical expectations they could foster.

The Elizabethan theater was very much open to life shaped by aristocratic expectations and values—generous in the sympathies it extended toward that life, but also ruthless. The lesser dramatists reveled in ruthlessness or sympathy as opportunity and convention offered. Marlowe's plays are often, in effect, acts of aggression in which the audience is invited to participate. But in Shakespeare the range of sympathy and the range of ruthlessness are perfectly matched and balanced, transforming aggression into dramatic irony. Irony is a form of aggression wherein the ironist does nothing to his object except as his audience joins with him. An ironic attack depends on somebody else seeing the point. When dramatic irony is present, the audience gives the aggression social validation, taking the burden off the dramatist's shoulders. So the ironist's aggression is also the audience's and is validated by the audience. This is as true of the large, tragic ironies implicit in *King Lear* as it is of a thrust of ironic wit or a satiric sally. The art puts aggression in the service of a common recognition of the ludicrous and tragic potentials of aristocratic values accepted, but only prima facie, by Shakespeare's art.

Shakespeare's remarkable unassertiveness in his own person as an author fits, we think, with his ability to transform aggression into the mirth of comedy or into the ruthless ironic knowledge that accompanies the ruth of tragedy. Wyndham Lewis (1927) and, more extensively, John Holloway (1961) have observed that in his tragedies Shakespeare conducts something like a public execution; something like a saturnalian public holiday is fundamental to his comedies (see Barber 1959, chap. 1). With the rhythms of comedy and tragedy he is able to realize aristocratic and royal identities but at the same time to limit them by dramatizing an understanding of them. In his role as unseen judge and executioner—or as lord of misrule—Shakespeare follows, in his most fully achieved works, the ironic logic of the very motives he is liberating and cherishing; the audience, in recognizing the irony, shares in the ruthlessness of his art. The whole play, not only as a composition of utterances but also as an event in the theater, provides a mode of self-assertion to balance Shakespeare's giving himself to the realization of other identities. Perhaps it was only possible for Shakespeare's personality, with its intense responsiveness, its negative capability, and its lack of ordinary self, to achieve domination in this social way through his art.

We have argued in chapter 1 of *The Whole Journey* (Barber and Wheeler 1986) that Shakespeare does not use his art to dramatize tragic male-to-male confrontation across generations until more than half of his plays have been written. In relation to the concerns of this essay, we can add that by the time Shakespeare comes to write *Hamlet* he has succeeded wonderfully, in middle-class terms, by his own role in a joint-stock company; has followed through with his father's earlier application for a coat of arms to make his father and himself gentry; and has invested a large part of his earnings in his native Stratford, including the purchase of New Place. In short, he does not make tragedy, with its dominant concerns of heritage and authority organized by the stresses of Oedipal conflict, his central form of expression until he has outdone his father in the rising middle class. From his own fully established place in the independent, commercial theater, Shakespeare could use his drama to risk testing the possibility of becoming the ideal, omnipotent father of infancy: he could begin to express in the major tragedies his longing for that figure of authority, with the parricidal rage, the immense anxiety, and the feared destruction that accompany it.

The shift into the preoccupations of the major tragedies can be summarized by the change from a special investment of self in Falstaff to such an investment in Hamlet. Falstaff, as William Empson long ago suggested, relates to Prince Hal somewhat as the speaker of the Sonnets relates to the highborn young man, but with "a savage and joyous externalization of self-contempt" (Empson 1935, 100). When one asks what happened in *Hamlet* to the gulf of caste or class difference that in part animates the Sonnets and the role of Falstaff, one can perhaps see a further contribution made to Shakespeare's art by his origins and his way of handling them. Hamlet can be gracious with the players or his old school fellows, but when the chips are down, the Prince puts them in their place: "Besides, to be demanded of a sponge, what replication should be made by the son of a king?" (4.2.12–13). Why is there not an element of wish fulfillment, a vicarious enjoyment making for sentimental or snobbish distortion in the player-dramatist's realizing the sense of self of a higher caste? Is not the answer, in part at least, that the whole spectacle is presented in the commercial theater, an independent place from which Shakespeare can stand and look with his awesome ironic understanding at the great world and its secular magic? There is no such control in the Jacobean court masques, which dramatize "expressions of royal power," as Stephen Orgel observes, not ironic explorations of it (1975, 45). The caste difference separating middle-class author, players, and much of the audience from the play's royal subject matter in Shakespearean tragedy contributes to the awe with which figures of authority and the struggle for it are invested, in agreement with the worshipful patterns of the secular hierarchy that shape expression in the Sonnets. But Shakespeare's middle-class difference and sense of tough realities simultaneously contribute to the increasing ironic clarity with which he makes us see that the social order, whose structure as such he does not question, fails to work. Moreover, the whole dramatization of aristocratic heroic struggles is made within the matrix of the early-based, cherishing sensibility, with its deep commitment to kinship and kindness that was also shaped in the family in middle-class Stratford.

The London in which Shakespeare practiced his dramatic art was the nerve and power center of England and was open to foreign influence by commerce, travel, and foreign residents, including the Huguenots, among whom he lived for a time. The four great dramatists of Athens all came from rural demes; in their work traditional attitudes, beliefs, and values are articulated (and put to tragic or comic test) by the cosmopolitan consciousness of a city that had become the crossroads of Greece and an imperial power. A great nascent moment seems regularly to involve such interplay. The English Renaissance, especially in Shakespeare's supreme example, is not primarily the recovery of classical resources so reborn—though it includes that. More fundamentally, it is the articulation of tradition-directed ways of living and thinking as these are brought into the field of developing metropolitan consciousness. The interplay of Stratford and London was crucial, even though the Stratford kind of experience is not a major subject, as such, in Shakespeare's works. The fact that he used his London earnings to establish himself in Stratford by the purchase of New Place in 1598 and returned to live there when his London career came to an end is in line with the characteristically English country-city polarity, crossed by the polarity, fundamental in his achievement, between his own middle-class heritage and his court-centered art.

Aggression and the Project
of the Histories

Sherman Hawkins

There are two very natural propensities which we may distinguish in the most virtuous and liberal dispositions, the love of pleasure and the love of action. If the former be refined . . . , improved . . . , and corrected . . . , it is productive of the greatest part of the happiness of private life. The love of action is a principle of a much stronger and more doubtful nature. It often leads to anger, to ambition, and to revenge; but, when it is guided by the sense of propriety and benevolence, it becomes the parent of every virtue; and if those virtues are accompanied with equal abilities, a family, a state, or an empire may be indebted for their safety and prosperity to the undaunted courage of a single man.

Gibbon

I

This essay is an experiment in generic psychology. I wish to explore Shakespeare's imagination—and the personality that is its source—not in any individual play but in an entire dramatic genre, the chronicle history. In contrast to one prevailing critical tendency, which stresses the autonomy and independence of each history play, I see both tetralogies as concerned with a single underlying psychological motive and working out a common psychological project. Such an approach must necessarily be general and schematic, both psychologically and critically, but it is not without particular critical relevance and usefulness. The culmination of all these histories, *Henry V,* deserves at present to be called a problem play as much as those that are usually termed so, and its hero remains one of Shakespeare's most controversial characters. Yet in the larger psychological context of the histories, I would argue, only one interpretation of *Henry V* makes sense. The main thrust of the play is toward the heroic, the ideal and exemplary. But the same psychological context explains why this impulse encounters resistance, counterstrains and countercurrents, in Shakespeare's imagination, so that we sense a tension, a discrepancy between purpose and result, between what Shakespeare sets out to do and what he does.

Though the histories deal with the public world of politics and the objective world of history, here we may be particularly close to Shakespeare's personal and private imagination. For unlike comedy and tragedy, the other major Shakespearean "kinds," the history play is a new genre unprecedented in classical drama. If it is not Shakespeare's invention, it is his individual achievement, his distinctive contribution to Elizabethan drama. Without him—despite *Edward II* and *Perkin Warbeck*—the genre would be negligible. But Shakespeare's plays, apparently concerned with the history and politics of a bygone era, still come alive in the theater—and sometimes even in the classroom. What, then, is the deeper subject of these plays, and why does it interest us? What prompted Shakespeare to write histories, and what impels audiences to go to see them, in his day and our own? A historical critic like E.M.W. Tillyard would probably cite the apparently boundless Elizabethan appetite for reading about the English past. But such an answer does not explain the hold such plays have on modern readers, who do not share this Elizabethan taste. Our answer must, I think, be psychological. And the psychology involved, if not for all time, cannot be for a particular age, whether Shakespeare's or our own. For the appeal of these plays is, I suspect, primary and even primitive. I am irresistibly reminded of a recent cartoon showing two sober Elizabethan matrons shaking their heads over advertisements for *Romeo and Juliet, King Lear,* and *Macbeth:* "I'm sick of it . . . another fall line-up of sex and violence, sex and violence." We laugh—but are not sex and violence what most of Shakespeare's plays at some primary level are all about?

II

It may seem odd to begin a discussion of Shakespeare's histories with *The Tempest.* But that final generic synthesis blends not only comedy and tragedy; in its action of usurpation and conspiracy and its themes of true authority and the just commonwealth *The Tempest* echoes the history plays as well. Prospero, Shakespeare's last and greatest image of the poet-dramatist, is also an image of the governor. At the end of the play Prospero surrenders his art but not his sovereignty. Even though every third thought is now his grave, Prospero returns to Milan to rule. His sense of consummation and release in the epilogue results as much from power regained as from pardon conferred:

> Let me not,
> Since I have my dukedom got,
> And pardon'd the deceiver, dwell
> In this bare island by your spell.
> (*The Tempest*, Epi. 5–7)

This concluding stress on power and rule, the "dukedom got," answers to a strain we may find puzzling in Shakespeare's plays and in their author. Even though Shakespeare virtually abandons the history play after 1600, all his great tragedies are profoundly political—*Othello* being the deliberate variant that proves the generic rule. Why is a poet so absorbed in politics? Though at least one critic of the histories maintains that Shakespeare wrote political plays only because the Elizabethans expected to find princes and generals on the stage (Palmer 1948, 1), I think we must conclude that Shakespeare shared his audience's relish for these charismatic figures, that he found something dramatic about politics. But much that we understand by "politics" never appears at all in Shakespeare's histories. Rather, as their very titles imply, these are plays about kings. Kings fascinate Shakespeare—and still, I think, fascinate us—as embodiments of power. And this supremacy, this power, symbolized by the crown, is an object of profound desire.

Generic contrast helps us grasp the nature of this desire. There is a striking and suggestive symmetry to the first half of Shakespeare's career as a playwright. In the dozen or so years before *Hamlet* Shakespeare produces exactly the same number of comedies and histories—nine of each—plus one experiment that thrusts the least historical personage of the histories, Falstaff, into the most realistic of the comedies, *The Merry Wives of Windsor*. It would be symbolically—though of course not literally and chronologically—true to think of Shakespeare as producing comedies and histories in regular alternation through the 1590s until he subsumes and synthesizes the concerns of both in tragedy. *Titus Andronicus* is an early attempt at such a synthesis, but the other tragedies Shakespeare writes in this period conform to the two dominant genres: *Romeo and Juliet* is a romantic comedy with an unhappy ending, and *Julius Caesar* offers us a tragic perspective on politics and history.

Comedy and history are thus antithetical but complementary in the evolving dialectic of Shakespeare's dramatic imagination. Appropriately, each genre has its archetypal gender. The histories deal with the masculine world of politics and war, dominated by the hero and his male antagonists. Even in the first tetralogy, women are felt as intruders in this world: they are mostly pathetic victims, seductive temptresses, or mannish viragoes like the warrior Joan, the ambitious Eleanor, or Margaret herself, a queen who was in "stomack and corage," Edward Hall declares, "more like to a man, then a woman" (Bullough 1960, 3:102). But in the second tetralogy, especially in the three plays that are our main concern, women have almost disappeared. The comedies, on the other hand, deal with the feminine world of romantic love, dominated increasingly by the heroine. Here too we see an evolution. In his early comedies Shakespeare shifts the sexual focus back and forth, even experimenting with a dominant male in *The Taming of the Shrew*. But in the later and greater plays charismatic and enchanting women are wooed by such comparatively pallid figures as Bassanio and Orlando—Benedick, the exception, is of interest precisely as a refuser of love—until in *Twelfth Night* male lovers come as close to disappearing as possible, given their comic function.

In accordance with this symbolic opposition of the sexes, each genre centers on a contrasted psychological motive and dramatizes the variations on a basic human drive. These are the paired energies described by Gibbon as "the love of pleasure" and "the love of action" (quoted in Storr 1968, Introduction). I cite the great eighteenth-century historian precisely because his terminology—standing as he does midway between Shakespeare and ourselves—is neither Elizabethan nor modern. Rather, it suggests a psychology that is perennial, even archetypal. Gibbon's love of pleasure and action looks forward to the libidinal and aggressive instincts of Freud and back to the concupiscible and irascible passions of the Elizabethans, which in turn derive from the appetitive and spirited parts of the Platonic soul. The contrast between these drives is everywhere in Shakespeare: it creates the tragic conflict in *Romeo and Juliet,* distinguishes the double plot in *King Lear,* and underlies the symbolic hierarchy of *The Tempest.* In *1 Henry IV* these rival powers of appetite and ire actually appear before us, personified in Falstaff and Hotspur. It is not surprising that the dualism which thus shapes individual plays should also inform the larger difference between dramatic genres.

Clearly these twin energies are central to Shakespeare's imagination. Whether we use the Platonic, the Elizabethan, or the Freudian names for them may depend on our critical approach or personal predilection: I am not sure that Shakespeare's psychology exactly matches any of these systematic distinctions. The Platonic terms may be the best: they were readily accessible to Shakespeare and they are broadly inclusive. Platonic appetite encompasses all forms of desire, and the spirited instincts are not limited to wrath and courage but include rivalry and the aspiration for glory and honor. Thus, in *Twelfth Night* there is a connection between erotic love and other, humbler appetites, between the high, romantic realm of Olivia and Orsino and the below-stairs realm of Sir Toby and Sir Andrew, the world of cakes and ale. The festive release of comedy includes jesting, eating, and drinking as well as making love: all the energies of desire are included in the freedom of its holiday. Similarly, the turbulent conflicts of the histories allow a release of aggression ranging from bitter rivalries and feuds at court to the brutal shock of battle. In these plays war is an extension of politics and politics is a covert form of war. Thus, when we turn from comedy to history, we find armed combats replacing masques and revels, quarrels and conspiracies instead of jests and wooings. The very balance between the two genres suggests that for Shakespeare rivalry, aspiration, and the will to power are motives as strong and basic as the yearning for sexual fulfillment— and, we may add, quite as dramatic. In theatrical terms violence may be as fascinating as sex, and nothing in the erotic comedies is as spectacularly direct as the bloodshed—murders, executions, duels—of the histories. Their dramatization of the aggressive drive to power still proves compelling to audiences who care nothing for Tudor doctrines of order and obedience. Even when monarchy has all but disappeared, the struggle to become king remains a perennial human theme.

III

What of Shakespeare himself? The exclusive emphasis of Tillyard and his school on order and hierarchy is misleading because it fails to recognize Shakespeare's imaginative involvement in the aggressive energies that threaten them. Indeed, this involvement helps explain why Shakespeare's sense of the need for order was so strong. My own stress on aggression, however, may seem contradicted by our image of the "sweet" and "gentle" Will Shakespeare whom contemporaries praised for his probity and civil demeanor. These traits were no doubt genuine, but they may also have served as defense or compensation, as ways of dealing with the more turbulent forces that found expression in his art. Citing his reputation for sweetness, C. L. Barber asks, "What did Shakespeare, by contrast with quarrelsome Marlowe and Jonson, do with his aggression?" (Barber and Wheeler 1986, 61). I would answer that he wrote history plays.

But sweetness and honesty may also have seemed ways of rising in the world: Shakespeare intended to be "gentle" in both senses of the word. The soaring ambition of the history plays may seem at odds with the solid bourgeois success of Shakespeare's actual career, yet some of his contemporaries glimpsed the fantasy behind the facts. In a teasing epigram John Davies of Hereford writes:

> Some say (good *Will*) which I, in sport, do sing,
> Had'st thou not plaid some Kingly parts in sport,
> Thou hadst bin a companion for a *King;*
> And, beene a King among the meaner sort.
> Some others raile; but, raile as they thinke fit,
> Thou hast no rayling, but, a raigning Wit.
> (Chambers 1930, 2:214)

The connections on which Davies touches between playing a king and wanting to be one are full of suggestion for the histories. As a common player, Shakespeare, like Falstaff, is an entertaining but dubious companion for royalty; at the same time his reigning wit makes him, like Hal, a prince among the meaner sort of actors and playwrights, his colleagues and competitors. Perhaps it was in this world of plays and playing, rather than in the larger social and political world, that Shakespeare pursued his kingly ambitions. Certainly if Hal is Shakespeare's ideal ruler, it matters that his right to the crown ultimately is based less on his lineage than on his own abilities. The rise of the house of Bolingbroke might be seen as a much displaced metaphor for the career open to talent. And it happens that our very first contemporary allusion to Shakespeare is as an "upstart," a pushing, conceited careerist, a mere actor assuming a playwright's power and privilege—in short, a usurper. Greene's famous gibe at the "Tygers hart wrapt in a

Players hyde" aligns Shakespeare with the ambitious York, who utters the line Greene parodies, and with the ferocious Margaret, whom it describes. It was this attack that produced Chettle's apologetic praise of Shakespeare's civility and honesty (Chambers 1930, 2:188–89). But the plays themselves show how York and Margaret are consumed by their own ambitions. If the upstart player was a literary usurper, stealing Greene's plumes—"the men that so Eclipst his fame," wrote one of Greene's admirers, "Purloyned his Plumes, can they deny the same?" (2:190)—and seizing upon Marlowe's crown, it is nevertheless true that usurpers do not fare well in Shakespeare's plays. Even Bolingbroke, who holds on to power to the last, suffers remorse of conscience inconceivable in Marlowe's Tamburlaine. It seems that ambition and ability do not suffice to make a king without some further legitimating sanction. We find what is needed in the Prince who purloins Hotspur's plumes and steals his father's crown—and yet is felt to have earned the right to both.

Thus the conflict between aspiration and order in the history plays is deep and real because it is rooted in Shakespeare's personality. In the perfect balance of *Richard II* he can side with both Bolingbroke and Richard and at the same time show the defects of each. No doubt there were psychic sources for this conflict, but it must have been reinforced by the facts of Shakespeare's family situation. Everyone will recall his father's rise from low estate to marriage with "a daughter and heir of Arden" and election to the highest civic office in Stratford, culminating in the coat of arms that would have entered the farmer's son into "the register of the gentle and noble" (Schoenbaum 1977, 38–39). Thus, the initial image and model that John Shakespeare presented to his little son was the kind of Tudor success story that an imaginative playwright might translate into grander political terms: the coat of arms that would have made John Shakespeare a gentleman is the real, though diminished, analogue of the crown that makes Bolingbroke a king. But the coat of arms was not conferred—at least not yet—and John Shakespeare, like the usurping Bolingbroke, fell on troubled times. His financial decline seems to have coincided with his son's early adolescence and may have impressed Shakespeare with the perils of rising in the world or instilled in him doubts that his father's early success was deserved and right. But its major effect was probably to fill the youth with dreams of coming to his father's aid by restoring the family fortunes. For Shakespeare, as for Prince Hal, aspiration became duty: his task was likewise to redeem the time, validating his father's uncertain claims by greater achievements of his own. The financial sense of "redeem" is pertinent here, for Freud explains how a child, yearning for independence, wants to repay the debt he owes his parents for the gift of life. This impulse becomes a dream of actually saving his father's life on some dangerous occasion, "and this phantasy is commonly enough displaced on to the Emperor, the King, or any other great man, after which it can enter consciousness and is even made use of by the poets" (Freud 1963b, 56). Shakespeare was able to act out this rescue fantasy both in life and in art. In 1596 John Shakespeare at last became a gentleman, thanks to his son's success. Almost simultaneously Shakespeare composed the scene, based on four lines in Daniel's *Civil Wars,* where Prince Hal dramatically saves his father's life at Shrewsbury.

If aggression is here raised to heroism, the psychological issues are not entirely simple. The desire to pay back the father is a way of being quits with him, according to Freud, and the impulse underlying the rescue fantasy may be more defiant than tender. Ultimately the wish to establish one's independence by rescuing one's father becomes the impulse to replace him. We recall that other scene in which Hal seizes the crown while the king is still alive. Both Shakespeare and his hero have surpassed their fathers, and both may be touched by the guilt that Freud also acknowledges—the guilt "attached to the satisfaction of having got so far. . . . It seems as though the essence of success were to have got further than one's father, and as though to excel one's father were still something forbidden" (Freud 1963a, 320).

On the whole, both his father's example and the wish to aid him probably encouraged Shakespeare's ambition to rise in the world by his own gifts and merits. Relations with his siblings, however, may have strengthened more traditional notions of hierarchy and the rights of primogeniture. Shakespeare was himself an eldest son with three younger brothers. The second, Gilbert, followed his father's bourgeois way of life as a respectable haberdasher while William went off to become a common player. The fourth son—almost young enough to be William's son and, significantly, named Edmund—followed William to London and likewise became an actor. In quite opposite ways both Gilbert and Edmund may have been threats and rivals to their elder brother. Of the third son we know almost nothing except the fact—again perhaps significant—that he was christened Richard.

Shakespeare's plays are, of course, full of fratricidal struggle: the drive to overgo the father is matched by struggles for supremacy among brothers. The romance pattern of *As You Like It,* where the youngest son is oppressed by his tyrannical elder brother, inverts the normal Shakespearean situation. Ordinarily an older or legitimate son and heir is threatened by a younger or illegitimate brother. Sometimes this relation is literal, as with Don Pedro and Don John, Edgar and Edmund, and Prospero and Antonio; sometimes it is figurative, as with Hamlet and Laertes. Both the key figures in the histories are involved in these fratricidal rivalries: Richard of Gloucester—himself a third son—climbs to the throne over the bodies of his elder brothers; Hal proves himself the son "nearest his father" and heir to the crown by slaying Hotspur. Note, however, that Hal defeats his rival on Hotspur's terms: it is valor, not birthright, that proves him Prince of Wales. We can appreciate the full significance of the choice of Falconbridge in *King John,* who surrenders to his pallid younger brother the secure status and property he inherits as the eldest son, embracing bastardy—and the name Richard!—to carve a career in a larger and more glamorous world by his own talents. Does Shakespeare here recall his own choice in abandoning Stratford for London and the theater? Certainly his and our sympathies are with this "mounting spirit," yet even here Shakespeare keeps the scales very evenly balanced: the bastard rises fast and far, but he can never become king.

I conclude that Shakespeare's attitude toward aggression is deeply ambivalent. But the persistence of the struggle of aspiration against order in his plays shows how strong were the aggressive instincts of their author. Even Tillyard recognizes in the great dramatist of ambition a profoundly ambitious dramatist. Shakespeare was not a bourgeois theatrical businessman, as the outer facts of his career might suggest, but a rising spirit typical of his contemporaries, the younger Elizabethans born in the 1560s, such as Raleigh, Essex, and Bacon. As Anthony Essler shows in his fascinating study (1966), this was a generation of aspiring minds. Unlike some of them, Shakespeare had not the birth, the fortune, the education, or the great connections needed for a career in public life. But if he could not be a king—or even the earl or duke Falstaff dreams of becoming—he could write plays about them, exercising in the collective fantasies of drama the sovereignty unattainable in fact. One thinks again of Prospero, that image of absolute power attained through the poet's control over the imagination of others. The realm Shakespeare ruled was the great Globe itself.

IV

At least in literature, the universal monarchy of wit, high ambitions were encouraged rather than proscribed. Indeed, the poet's career, like Virgil's, was supposed to scale a *gradus ad Parnassum,* rising from the lowest to the highest genres. Renaissance imitation of literary models, ancient or modern, regularly included the impulse to outdo or overgo them. So Ben Jonson, who himself clearly strove to surpass Shakespeare, praised him for surpassing others, for outshining Kyd and Lyly and even Marlowe's mighty line.

To a young dramatist coming up to London just before 1590, Christopher Marlowe—Shakespeare's exact contemporary and the spokesman for the aspiring mind of their generation—might have seemed the literary model both to imitate and to overgo. His immediate and sensational success with *Tamburlaine* promised that a career in the theater was indeed open to talent. In this play there is no slow evolution through the disciplines of lesser genres: doffing his shepherd's weeds to become an emperor, Tamburlaine moves in one leap from pastoral to epic. He is plainly a heroic projection of Marlowe himself, the base-born genius out to subdue his world. But Tamburlaine's triumphant career is more than the private fantasy of an individual. Such a hero's attainment of titles, riches, and power, observes David Riggs, reflects "the most important social phenomenon of the later sixteenth century, the rapid rise in social status of one whose claim to high worldly station is based on ability rather than birth" (1971, 63).

No wonder *Tamburlaine* was copied by so many dramatists: it articulated and enacted for its age a social myth at once deeply compelling and dangerously iconoclastic. We understand at once the fascination of Marlowe's play for the youthful Shakespeare. But it matters to my argument that Tamburlaine also embodies the very constellation of psychological drives so central to the histories. He is the incarnation of the will to power; his whole career is a display of unleashed aggression. Moreover, the world he conquers is made in his own image: the foes Tamburlaine conquers, like Cosroe and Bajazeth, are lesser Tamburlaines. In his most famous lines he invokes a "world picture" in which the very elements struggle for supremacy in men, and nature itself teaches them to have aspiring minds. This is hardly traditional doctrine. Indeed, much of the excitement of *Tamburlaine* derives less from the conflict on stage than from the play's resistless assault on the minds of the audience—it is we whom Tamburlaine must ultimately overcome. This is drama designed to challenge, and one way of understanding Shakespeare's histories is as a response to the challenge of *Tamburlaine*.

In this view it seems no accident that the first scene of *1 Henry VI* echoes in its opening lines the last scene of *Tamburlaine:*

THERIDAMUS: Weep, heavens, and vanish into liquid tears!
                   Fall, stars that govern his nativity,
                   And summon all the shining lamps of heaven
                   To cast their bootless fires to the earth.
                   (2 *Tamburlaine*, 5.3.1–4)

BEDFORD: Hung be the heavens with black, yield day to night!
                   Comets, importing change of times and states,
                   Brandish your crystal tresses in the sky.
                   (*1 Henry VI*, 1.1.1–3)

It is as if Shakespeare is carrying on where Marlowe leaves off. His aspiration to outdo his predecessor can be measured by the scale of his own undertaking. The conquests of Marlowe's hero override the structural limits of the five-act play just as they override the geographical and political boundaries of his world. It matters little for our present purpose whether part 2 of *Tamburlaine* was an unpremeditated addition to part 1; what Shakespeare had before him as a model both to imitate and to overgo was a vast historical drama in two parts. Hence his own *Henry VI* expands into three plays, and with the addition of *Richard III* this trilogy becomes a tetralogy, which is then matched by a second tetralogy to create a connected pattern of eight plays. The structure Shakespeare finally completes in *Henry V* is unmatched in Western secular drama. Essler argues that just such gigantic projects characterize the aspirations of Shakespeare's contemporaries: one thinks of *Magna Instauratio* or *The Faerie Queene* (1966, 165–201). Unlike Bacon and Spenser, however, Shakespeare finishes his heroic project—not, we shall see, without cost.

Thus, the expansive scope of the early histories expresses in literary terms the spirit of ambitious rivalry that is their political subject. But it was possible to outshine Marlowe by refuting as well as by outdoing him. If the form of these early histories emulates *Tamburlaine*, their

argument contradicts its basic premises. Riggs convincingly demonstrates the "continuing allusion" to *Tamburlaine* that runs through
Henry VI, beginning with outrageous parody in Shakespeare's treatment of the shepherdess turned conqueror, Joan of Arc. But this continuing allusion is also a running argument. Joan's demonic inspiration
inverts Tamburlaine's divine pretensions. In contrast, Talbot's example
persuades us that true glory belongs to loyalty and service rather than to
ambition and can be achieved in defeat no less than victory. Yet even
Joan is less dangerous than her captor, York, who turns his sword
against his countrymen. The big wars that make Tamburlaine's ambition virtue lose their glamor when fathers and sons must slay each other.
The expansive, outer-directed aggression of *Tamburlaine* turns inward
in *Henry VI* as England rends itself. Of this divisive civil strife Richard
of Gloucester is the emblem and the embodiment.

Richard is Shakespeare's anti-Tamburlaine. Already in *3 Henry VI*
Shakespeare gives his Richard lines that evoke the Marlovian ethos:

> And, father, do but think
> How sweet a thing it is to wear a crown,
> Within whose circuit is Elysium
> And all that poets feign of bliss and joy.
> (*3 Henry VI,* 1.2.28–31)

This eloquence and enthusiasm are not characteristic: in Richard's
soliloquies Marlovian energy is edged with quite un-Marlovian irony
and bitterness. Richard here plays the orator to persuade his father,
and psychologically "feign" is a key word—Richard no more believes
in "bliss and joy" than he believes in Elysium. If he makes his heaven
to dream upon the crown, it is as a displacement of other satisfactions
he is denied. The aspiration that seems so natural in Tamburlaine is in
Richard a symptom of profound distortion. Richard is Tamburlaine's
crooked shadow; his character exposes the dark side of heroic aggression, suggesting that such ambition to attain masks a compulsion to
destroy. Richard goes on after the lines just quoted:

> Why do we linger thus? I cannot rest
> Until the white rose that I wear be dy'd
> Even in the lukewarm blood of Henry's heart!
> (*3 Henry VI,* 1.2.32–34)

Both Richard and Tamburlaine seek to win crowns against what
seem insuperable odds. But whereas Richard is twisted and deformed,

Tamburlaine is "Of stature tall and straightly fashioned, / Like his desire lift upwards and divine" (*1 Tamburlaine*, 2.1.7–8). This physical contrast marks the difference in their relations to others and in their sense of self. Tamburlaine is the godlike hero who other men would wish to be, surrounded by followers who seek to imitate him and share his glory; Richard is the diabolic villain, marked off by the stigma of his deformity from other men, whom he uses, like Buckingham, and then discards. Both feel sexual love as a threat—Tamburlaine because he so desires beauty, Richard because he so loathes his own ugliness. Whereas wooing is another form of conquest for Tamburlaine, for Richard it is war to the death: he seduces in order to destroy. Tamburlaine hardly seems to hate even his enemies, whom he regards with contemptuous scorn, but Richard comes to hate everyone. Though he claims, pathetically, that "Richard loves Richard," this universal hatred extends to hatred of himself—rather, self-hatred is where it begins.

Marlowe grounds the will to power in an innate superiority. Tamburlaine fights to assert his natural right: he wants to rule others because he knows himself stronger and nobler than they. Shakespeare, as if in reply, grounds the will to power in a sense of radical defect. Richard fights to avenge his sense of wrong: he needs to rule others— "to command, to check, to o'erbear such / As are of better person than myself" (*3 Henry VI*, 3.2.166–67)—because he feels himself inferior to them. With this demonstration of the will to power as paranoia, aspiration as vengeful and compensatory, and competition as the impulse to destroy, Shakespeare would seem to have completed his demolition of the Marlovian dream. If the histories are only a refutation of *Tamburlaine*, they should stop here.

But Shakespeare goes on to write a second tetralogy, one that culminates in a hero who offers a different kind of contrast to Tamburlaine. In *Henry V* Shakespeare again produces a play that alludes to the first, epic part of Marlowe's *Tamburlaine*. Both plays focus on a single mighty protagonist; their episodic structure displays his heroic attributes and deeds, and the action of military conquest concludes in a marriage and a peace. But when one compares *Henry V* to *Tamburlaine*, one is struck by its sense of limit and restraint. Though Tamburlaine is also a historic figure, his career of Asian conquest has for Marlowe and his Elizabethan audience the boundless possibility of romance. In contrast, Henry is an English monarch; the facts of his story are already familiar and its meaning is largely determined. Tamburlaine is a shepherd who becomes an emperor, Henry a king who gains another crown; Tamburlaine sets out to conquer the entire world, Henry to recover France. Tamburlaine wins a series of escalating victories—a series which, as part 2 demonstrates, can go on indefinitely—whereas Henry wins just one. For Henry the end of war is peace, and he concludes his conquests with his marriage. Tamburlaine's marriage, in contrast, marks only a temporary truce, for war is his self-defining way of life, and nothing but death can stop him while any corner of his world remains unconquered. Henry, in short, sets limits to aggression. It is an irony of history that his death makes the peace at which he aims a truce as brief as Tamburlaine's.

The comparative restraint of Shakespeare's drama answers to the careful moralization of its hero. Tamburlaine seems a pagan or a pantheist, a being of passionate and tameless energies, whereas Henry is a Christian king "Unto whose grace our passion is as subject / As is our wretches fett'red in our prisons" (*Henry V,* 1.2.242–43). Tamburlaine is the transethical conqueror whose matchless force breaks through conventional limits and constraints as easily as political boundaries, a hero whose virtue is to go beyond morality. But Henry's virtues are the cardinal four—temperance, fortitude, justice, and wisdom—which, together with Christian piety, form the traditional qualities of the good king. Whereas Tamburlaine's claim to other realms is simply his power to subdue them, Henry scrupulously bases his right to France on hereditary and legal title. In contrast to Tamburlaine's impulsive and romantic challenge to Cosroe, Henry's declaration of war on France obeys all the protocol of formal diplomacy. When Tamburlaine finds Agydas pleading against him to Zenocrate, he sends the hapless courtier a dagger with which to destroy himself; when Henry discovers traitors plotting against his life, he punishes them as the laws and safety of his land require, but he also forgives and strives to bring them to repentance. Henry's lurid threats against Harfleur parallel Tamburlaine's attempt to terrify Damascus into submission. Both cities yield, but whereas Tamburlaine carries out his threats to slay the virgins of Damascus and sack the town, Shakespeare's Henry, unlike the historical king, spares Harfleur. Tamburlaine's courage—if that is the right word—goes with absolute certainty of success, and he delights in battle. Henry fights his greatest battle reluctantly, facing what seems certain defeat and death.

His only act of cruelty—slaying the French prisoners—is a necessary brutality committed under dangerous circumstances in the heat of battle. But Tamburlaine, not content with conquering Bajazeth, subjects the fallen emperor to torments that drive him to suicide and his wife to madness. Henry attributes the glory of his victory to God, whereas Tamburlaine, making Bajazeth his footstool and distributing crowns among his followers, all but claims divinity for himself. Tamburlaine seems indeed something both more and less than human, an avatar of force, but Henry is a king who knows himself to be a man.

These contrasts seem too systematic not to be deliberate. They operate to Henry's advantage but not always to Shakespeare's. Marlowe's imagination, in part 1, seems as expansive and unchecked as Tamburlaine's, whereas Shakespeare's is as subject to constraint as Henry himself. Tamburlaine has no need to appeal to an archbishop to justify his conquests, no need to forgive a traitor before putting him to death. The fierce and silent frown he turns upon Agydas is more eloquent and incomparably more dramatic than Henry's homilies to Scroop and his accomplices. To compare the two plays is to sense that Shakespeare finds the task he sets himself in *Henry V* no easy one, and at the same time to recognize what that task is. Shakespeare is reconciling morality and the will to power: the aggressive drives that make Richard III a villain become in Henry V attributes of the ethical hero.

The triangulation of *Tamburlaine, Richard III,* and *Henry V* offers a key to the overall pattern and argument of Shakespeare's histories. For these plays, in which Shakespeare presents such opposed views of Marlovian aggression, are the logical and dramatic termini of the two tetralogies. I have argued that the histories leading up to *Richard III* can be seen as continuations or extensions of *Tamburlaine* in their ambitious scope, in their central concern with aggressive aspiration, and in the wars and conquests that make up so much of their action, but at the same time as refutations of *Tamburlaine* in their exposure of the amorality and destructive consequences of aggression. Yet Shakespeare does not totally reject what he thus criticizes: he corrects, modifies, reformulates. Thus in the plays that lead up to *Henry V* he seeks to give moral and political sanction to his own version of the Marlovian dream. Shakespeare's project is to redeem ambition; his final exemplar of the will to power is the mirror of all Christian kings.

V

Shakespeare's ambivalent attitude toward aggression seems divided between the two tetralogies, negative in the first and positive in the second. This simple contrast matches the antithetical patterning of the two series. Edward Berry (1975) has convincingly demonstrated that the first tetralogy traces the systematic decay of political community. The second, I suggest, is planned to show its gradual restoration. One tetralogy moves steadily downward from loss of empire in France through civil war to tyranny at home; the other reverses this movement, evolving from despotism at home through civil war to conquest of empire in France. The double series illustrates one of the lessons regularly cited in the Renaissance to justify the study of history: the causes for the rise and fall of nations, "the means whereby they fall into decay and againe whereby they are re-established and restored" (Philippe de Comines, quoted in Campbell 1968, 46). Thus each tetralogy exhibits one of the recognized didactic purposes of the Elizabethan history play. The first is cautionary, employing negative examples to warn against the evils of conspiracy, rebellion, and civil war; the second is hortatory, using positive examples to inspire loyalty, patriotism, and noble deeds. One teaches what to shun, the other what to imitate; accordingly, the aggression that was so appalling in the first tetralogy becomes heroic in the second.

This contrast of negative and positive extends from structure to genre. The first tetralogy begins with epic in *1 Henry VI* and descends to tragedy in *Richard III*. The second opens with a tragedy in *Richard II* and rises to epic in *Henry V*—even the kingly titles are symmetrically opposed. That *Henry V* is meant as epic is obvious from its opening invocation of a "Muse of fire." But I would extend this epic analogy backward to include both parts of *Henry IV*, forming a trilogy whose counterpart in the first tetralogy is *Henry VI*. All three plays about Henry of Monmouth share a common action as well as a common hero, and I would reserve for them the name usually but less logically applied to the whole second tetralogy, the epic title "Henriad."

That we do not customarily think of any of these plays except *Henry V* as epic may be in part because we do not recognize their classical pedigree. Given the confusion in Elizabethan literary theory and practice—which blurs, for instance, any distinction between the "historicall" and the "heroicall"—the clearest mark of epic intent is resemblance to earlier epics. The youthful Shakespeare was acutely conscious of such classical precedents. Tillyard notes how ambitiously his earliest experiments in comedy and tragedy, *The Comedy of Errors* and *Titus Andronicus,* set out to emulate Plautus and Seneca (1964, 135–41). The generic triad is completed when we realize that Shakespeare's earliest histories likewise have an admired classical model, the *Pharsalia* of Lucan. The *Pharsalia* is that generic oddity, a negative epic; it traces the decline of Rome through civil war. In contrast, the epic precedent for the Henriad, the *Cyropaedia* of Xenophon, is positive and exemplary, showing the education of a young prince in virtue and his subsequent career of foreign conquest. Even though it is in prose, Sidney considers the *Cyropaedia* an "absolute heroicall poem," because in Cyrus it presents *"effigiem iusti imperii,"* an image or model of the good governor (1904, 1:160). This, I believe, is precisely what Shakespeare tries to do in the Henriad.

Wonder, or "admiration," is the emotion proper to epic. This is evoked not only by supernatural machinery and miraculous events, such as the devils who appear to Joan of Arc or the amazing victory that reveals God's hand at Agincourt. Admiration, in both the Elizabethan and the modern sense, centers on the epic protagonist and his heroism. The wonder in *Henry V* is Henry V, that "miracle of worth," as Daniel calls him (5.14.2). Such admiration inspires imitation both on stage and in the audience: the epic hero makes us want to be like him. Sidney's most striking example of this way of teaching bears directly on our present argument, for Hal's rescue of his father finds its epic precedent in the rescue of Anchises by Aeneas. Who reads of that heroic deed, asks Sidney, "that wisheth not it were his fortune to perfourme so excellent an acte?" (1:173). Shakespeare's fantasy becomes ours—if indeed it ends in mere fantasy. For by inciting others to imitation, Sidney argues, the poet's imaginings may be realized in fact: the maker of a Cyrus thus has the power to make many Cyruses (1:157).

We begin to sense the scope of Shakespeare's aspiration, as well as its moral justification. To attempt an epic was the highest reach of poetic ambition; as Dryden says, epic is the greatest work the soul of man is capable of performing, the only kind the Renaissance, in defiance of Aristotle, placed higher than tragedy. Yet such ambition was not purely selfish or merely personal. An epic conferred glory on the nation and the tongue as well as on the poet who produced it. So it was that in the flush of patriotism following the defeat of the Armada other Elizabethan poets—Shakespeare's models, rivals, and imitators—likewise strove to produce an English epic. As we have seen, such an achievement is more than literary in its power to shape virtuous character and inspire mighty deeds: the poet's aggressive energies find their expression in a form that is, in Milton's phrase, doctrinal and exemplary to a nation.

There is, then, some analogy between the tasks that confront Shakespeare and those that confront his hero. The problem of both men is to renew in the present a heroic past: Henry seeks to recreate at Agincourt the glories of Crécy and Poitiers, just as Shakespeare seeks to revive the spirit of Agincourt in his own day. To make this possible, each must fashion an image of human greatness that compels imitation—Shakespeare in his drama, and Henry in himself. We see why epic in the Henriad is an evolving form, for only in the last play of the series, as Henry attains his true royal identity, does the genre fully declare itself. Shakespeare at last feels ready to ascend the "brightest heaven of invention" (*Henry V*, Pro. 2). It would be a sorry critic who failed to respond to his heroic purpose. But we must still ask ourselves: does Shakespeare succeed?

VI

Both the structural pattern of the two tetralogies and their analogy to epic support, indeed demand, a positive reading of *Henry V*. So does their psychological argument, which demonstrates the wrongful use of aggression in the early plays and its rightful use in the later ones. But what justifies this radical reversal? The ambivalence we sense in Shakespeare's attitude seems grounded in the very nature of aggression itself. As the British psychoanalyst Anthony Storr reminds us, aggression can lead to cruelty, war, and murder; but it also fuels the drive to independence so essential to growing up, the will to overcome obstacles and master one's world, and the aspiration to all high endeavor (1968, Introduction). In short, the same energies can produce a Richard of Gloucester or a Prince Hal, and the lack of them can be disastrous, both psychologically and politically. In Henry VI the first tetralogy has a Mycetes to match its many Tamburlaines. The weakling king is as much a psychological extreme as his hunchbacked nemesis: all but devoid of aggression and ambition, Henry can neither fight nor rule. And no English monarch, not even Richard III, causes more harm to his people and his land. Thus, from their very inception the histories show us that a king without the will to power lacks the primary and essential quality that makes a king.

The problem, no less political than psychological, is how to deal with energies at once so necessary and so perilous. Though we have noticed the stress on ethical restraint in Shakespeare's portrayal of Henry V, discipline and control alone are not enough: there is more to Shakespeare's psychopolitical argument than the familiar opposition of passion versus reason. Here the analogy between comedy and history is useful. Certainly Shakespeare never suggests that the erotic and aggressive drives can be suppressed or eradicated—at least, as Pompey would say, until eating and drinking are put down. But if the comedies do not teach orthodox lessons of chastity and self-control, neither do they celebrate an unleashed eroticism. Festive release of the libidinal permits its evolution and refinement, until in the hero and the heroine it becomes a love we feel to be both romantic and real, an ideal that is a human possibility. A similar process of release and refinement, I suggest, is at work in the later histories. As the comedies evolve an ideal of romantic love that fulfills and legitimates the erotic impulse, so these plays develop an ideal of heroism and virtuous rule that fulfills and legitimates the energies of aggression.

Neither project was easy. Despite the cultural values the Elizabethans placed on beauty, love, and marriage and on patriotism, fame, and honor, the cultural prohibitions against desire and ambition remained very strong. So, I believe, were the corresponding prohibitions in Shakespeare's imagination. His is an essentially ethical vision of life; it affirms the sexual and aggressive drives by idealizing them. I hazard the guess that he found the forces of aggression more deeply threatening. Though the comedies reveal every nuance of inhibition and hostility, the attitude toward sex in these plays seems essentially—and joyously—affirmative. In contrast, the whole first tetralogy, as we have seen, is an extended indictment of aggression. Only in the second does Shakespeare seek to redeem it by working out an ethic for the will to power and by directing aspiration toward higher ends.

What are these higher ends? What goals do politics have beyond order or power? Again the comedies may be our guide. There the sexual impulse in the individual leads to mutuality and relationship, and these in turn lead to a larger, more inclusive sense of community. Eros, Freud tells us, strives to connect, to draw life together in ever larger unities. This is why the marriages at the end of Shakespeare's comedies are so often multiple and why the lovers thus united form the center of a society renewed in charity. At the same time what distinguishes the hero and especially the heroine from other characters is their greater intensity and refinement of feeling, a love that manages to be at once ardent and intelligent, self-giving and self-aware. This distinction implies what we may call an erotic ethic, which informs the symbolic hierarchy of couples in such comedies as *The Merchant of Venice, Twelfth Night,* and *As You Like It.* For our purposes it is important that this ethic turns not on self-control or self-restraint but on a notion of human excellence, a kind of erotic *areté*.

We find both these values, the communal and the ethical, as political goals in the history plays. At this point we can no longer associate politics exclusively with aggression and the will to power. That side of political behavior was as obvious in Shakespeare's day as it is in our own; there is little need to ground it in political theory with citations from Machiavelli. But to understand the political ideals of virtue and community means turning back to a tradition older than Machiavelli, to a conception of politics the Renaissance inherited from Cicero, Aristotle, and Plato. For Aristotle and Cicero the impulse to community that Freud sees as erotic is also political: indeed, these are differing aspects of the innate social instinct that evolves from the family to the state and ultimately embraces all humanity. The human creature is thus by nature a political, no less than a sexual, animal. But this drive to community, Aristotle insists, aims not just at life—security, order, exchange—but at the good life, which is the life of virtue. Ethics and politics thus share a single purpose: to make the individual or the whole state "good and capable of noble acts" (1941, 1099b). Thus, we arrive back at Plato's simple and astonishing definition of political science as "the knowledge by which we are to make other men good" (1937, 1:292b).

To make others good is the task of a king. Here politics and literature converge, for kings, like epic heroes, were thought to inspire imitation. It is above all by his own example that a ruler makes his people good: hence the political import of the ethical development that is Hal's princely education in *Henry IV.* The pattern in Part I reflects the dual psychology with which we are by now so familiar. In leaving

Falstaff's tavern Hal abandons the pleasures of appetite; in conquering Hotspur he overcomes the aggressive impulses toward wrath and violence—or, rather, he shows their proper use, for what began as personal rivalry takes on higher meaning for the prince. Whereas Hotspur fights for himself, for his house, and for fame, Hal fights for his father, for England, and for the honor of the deed itself. This is aggression in the service of community as well as of ethics.

But in Part II there remains a test harder for one born to command and rule. Aggression here is the will to power typified by King Henry and symbolized by his crown. When Hal takes the crown, he symbolically repeats his father's usurpation; when he surrenders it, he surrenders his father's personal ambition. And as one Henry dies, something in the other dies too. Thus, when Hal banishes Falstaff, he is renouncing the Pauline "old man" that is his former self, the egoism that instinctively claims pleasure, honor, and power. The tyrant, Aristotle tells us, seeks his own good; the true king seeks the welfare of his subjects. Hal has not been dehumanized, as so many critics contend, but he has been in this sense depersonalized. In becoming king, Henry V becomes the man for others, the potential center of a new political community, the robed monarch who tells his astonished counsellors and kin, "I'll be your father and your brother too" (*2 Henry IV*, 5.2.57).

Henry's epic task in *Henry V* is to create this new community and to bring about some likeness of his own conversion on a national scale. For the Elizabethans, as we have seen, the irascible instinct is a primary and indestructible element in human nature. Throughout the history plays the choice is whether this aggression is to be directed inward or outward, against fellow Englishmen or against foreigners. Shakespeare implicitly, and Samuel Daniel (in his *Civil Wars*) explicitly, shows the Wars of the Roses as caused in part by factious energies denied outlet after peace with France. Conversely, both poets, again implicitly and explicitly, see Henry V as dispelling these turbulent humors by turning them against the French; once more we have aggression in the service of community. If this is a just war, like the crusade that for such different reasons haunts the imagination of John of Gaunt and his heirs, then it demonstrates aggression in the service of the ethical. The justice of Henry's war is open to question—indeed, both Shakespeare and Henry question it—but the issue is decided by an authority higher than the Archbishop of Canterbury. Agincourt is the last of the trials by combat that run through the whole tetralogy, beginning with the abortive duel between Mowbray and Bolingbroke. In *Henry V,* as in *Richard II,* the appeal is to divine justice—"how thou pleasest, God, dispose the day!"—and in the almost miraculous outcome, the divine verdict is clear.

Henry V creates his new England on the fields of France. He turns his quarreling international army into a brotherhood of blood, inspiring in others a courage like his own. That York and Suffolk die for Lancaster speaks eloquently to one who remembers what those names portend in the first tetralogy. But we do not see these nobles actually fighting, just as we do not watch the archers sharpening their stakes or witness the king's hand-to-hand combat with Alencon. Henry's victory is of the spirit, and virtually all he does at Agincourt is make a speech. But what a speech it is! The king talks to his followers in language that both aristocrat and yeoman can understand. He incites his peers to rivalry for honor and promises to "gentle" the condition of his common soldiers. But the nobility they do achieve is no mere social status, even as the honor to which Henry aspires is not for himself: he has become what the French king calls him, "Harry England." Thus, Shakespeare and Henry, each for his own time, renew the vision of a heroic England. This vision is patriotic, but we may feel it is something more than that: the band of brothers united in their courage against overwhelming odds remains an image of the heroic valid always and everywhere, from "this day to the ending of the world" (*Henry V,* 4.3.58).

Such, I think, is Shakespeare's intention. That it does not quite work out I have no need to demonstrate: the strains, uncertainties, and skeptical countercurrents in the play have been exposed by many a more expert hand. One illustration will suffice: the massacre of the French prisoners. It occurs in Hall and Holinshed but not in Shakespeare's dramatic source, *The Famous Victories.* Shakespeare did not have to include the massacre, but he did. It is as if something in his imagination requires Henry's epic triumph to be splashed in blood. The reason should by now be clear: Shakespeare's ambivalence toward aggression, so neatly divided between the two tetralogies, has not been thereby dissipated. Indeed, it deepens as he approaches his tragic period, and this change is reflected, almost against his will, in *Henry V.*

I have argued that *Henry V* is not a play that springs into being *de novo* at the time of its composition; rather, it is the culmination of a long-laid plan. Just when that plan was first conceived it is impossible to say. Nothing in my argument requires a date earlier than the inception of *Richard II*, when Shakespeare, having successfully completed the first tetralogy, undertook a second that would be its reverse image. I suspect, however, that already when Shakespeare wrote *Richard III*, he intended a contrasting drama on the ideal king who is Richard's antitype, the Christian conqueror who offers a moral corrective to Tamburlaine. Indeed, such an intention may have developed earlier still. I like to think that it is natural for young and ambitious poets to dream of great works yet to be. Is it unlikely that as he dramatized the catastrophic career of Henry VI, Shakespeare already had the idea of someday dramatizing the very different career of Henry's great progenitor? *The Famous Victories of Henry V*, which became Shakespeare's model for the Henriad, is almost the only vernacular chronicle history still extant that antedates *Henry VI*. And Shakespeare's first trilogy is haunted by the figure of "That ever-living man of memory" (*1 Henry VI*, 4.3.51). Indeed, the eight major histories, in order of composition, begin and end with Henry V, and I think it possible that from the start Shakespeare intended to conclude these histories with the king whose spirit is ritually invoked in their first scene. The circle is the figure of perfection, not of accident, and the contrast between beginning and ending, Henry's funeral and his marriage, perfectly typifies the contrast Shakespeare draws between his two tetralogies.

To Shakespeare in the early or even the middle 1590s the famous victories of England's hero king was an epic subject whose validity must have seemed guaranteed. It seemed so to Daniel, in whose *Civil Wars* the ghost of Henry himself appears to demand an epic about his deeds: "O what eternall matter here is found / Whence new immortall *Illiads* might proceed!" (5.5.1–2). It also seemed so to Drayton, who actually produced a brief epic entitled *The Battle of Agincourt*. But it did not turn out to be so for Shakespeare in 1599. He was no longer the youthful author of *1 Henry VI*: ruling the French perhaps no longer seemed an Englishman's natural right, nor killing them a proof of his heroic virtue. Other plays written within about a year of *Henry V*—*Julius Caesar*, *Hamlet*—take quite a different view of all our impulses to aggression. But the whole pattern of his preceding histories committed Shakespeare to produce a dramatic epic, not a riddle of multiple perspectives or balanced ambiguities. It says much for Shakespeare's honesty that he included so many of his doubts and questions. It says even more for his artistic tenacity and courage that he remained true to his major vision. Literary history is littered with uncompleted epics; to finish such a project requires a power of aspiration that allies the epic poet to his hero. Precisely because it acknowledges and overcomes so many reservations, *Henry V* achieves a heroism of statement. Like his embattled king, Shakespeare wins against great odds—not the least of which is our own view of war and conquest, a view hardly conceivable to an English contemporary of Essex, Drake, and Raleigh. Yet even today—and even without cuts—*Henry V* works as heroic drama in the theater. Can anyone suppose that Henry's Saint Crispin speech is meant to inspire only Westmoreland and Salisbury? He speaks it to his audience on stage, but Shakespeare directs it to us. We find ourselves included in Henry's heroic brotherhood and capable—if only in imagination—of "noble acts." At the play's end the actors put off their splendid costumes, and we of the audience shuffle out into the common streets and back to our average lives. But perhaps we have learned how heroism feels.

VII

Let me end as I began, with Prospero. He is the image of absolute power; he is also by common consent an image of Shakespeare himself. The magic he exerts over the other characters is the dramatist's mastery of theatrical illusion, the ability to make us see visions and dream dreams. We have observed his will to power: the aggressive instincts so fatally absent in Henry VI are strong in Prospero. If he is a type of wisdom, it is not because he is without desire or anger but because he is finally able to govern these unruly passions. The psychology of Shakespeare's final romance includes the concupiscent and irascible drives of comedy and history, which are figured in the drunken clowns and courtly conspirators and joined in Caliban. Prospero must surrender these impulses in himself, but it seems even harder for him to give up his revenge than to give away his daughter. The Prospero who raises a storm to wreck his enemies is initially, like Lear, a figure of wrath in age. Through the long scene that follows, this stormy anger emerges in different forms against Ariel, Caliban, and Ferdinand—even, at moments, against Miranda: "Thou attend'st not!" (*The Tempest,* 1.2.87). It is easy to see why Caliban or Ferdinand should mistake him for a tyrant. But in fact Prospero is—or becomes—the true prince. Thus, he exhibits with special clarity the paradox of aggression redirected to the communal and the ethical.

The tempest that gives the play its title expresses Prospero's wish to destroy his enemies, but the very act of expression enables Prospero to transcend and move beyond it. In the scenes that follow, he works through his anger by Shakespeare's dramatic method, acting out his aggressive impulse in fictive form, overpowering and tormenting his enemies in the process of bringing them to knowledge of their sins. Never has Prospero consciously intended anything but their good, yet at first the need to punish seems stronger than any purpose to forgive. But gradually anger yields to a sense of mastery, which in turn leads to a desire to teach and change. What finally enables Prospero to forgive at the play's moral crisis is of course Ariel's speech describing the sufferings of Gonzalo and his companions. Finding in this spirit of air a touch of human feeling, Prospero is moved to find an answering tenderness in himself. This is the sense of community which reconciles ancient enemies and unites Naples and Milan. But Prospero has a further motive for forgiveness: "The rarer action is / In virtue than in vengeance" (5.1.27–28). Prospero forgives Antonio not because Antonio earns forgiveness by repentance or a change of heart but because it is the "rarer action." Prospero has not ceased to aspire, but the object of his aspiration is now higher and more difficult: it is the "virtue" he has taught by learning and attaining it.

Prospero's transforming art is not entirely illusion, for by its dramaturgic working Alonso repents, Ferdinand learns, and even Caliban is impelled to seek for grace. But it is not limitless, either: it cannot violate the inner freedom of those it rules any more than can the omnipotence it imitates. Antonio chooses to resist it and remains unchanged. So we may do, as well. For of course the transformation Prospero would effect includes the audience whom he addresses directly in the epilogue. Never is his real power over us greater than here, as he surrenders its last fictive vestiges and places himself at the mercy of those who have been so long his willing subjects, teaching us our need for forgiveness by asking it himself. By now it should be clear that the power Prospero has so desired is exercised for the good of others, so that rule becomes a form of service. It is a final political lesson from the good and wise magician who would teach us, could we but learn, how to be wise and good.

Sons and Substitutions: Shakespeare's Phallic Fantasy

Norman N. Holland

The theme I shall develop in this essay risks being embarrassingly obvious. I see a pattern in Shakespeare's fathers and sons: the father is the social and moral superior, the son the lower and lesser being. But the son acts on behalf of the father as his agent or deputy—his *locum tenens,* to be precise. He does for the father something that the father, for whatever reason, does not or cannot do for himself. He *substitutes* for the father, a word to which I shall return.

In a way, I am simply restating an aspect of such classic ideas about Shakespeare as Tillyard's and Spencer's "Elizabethan world-picture" and Lovejoy's "great chain of being." Because the pattern so closely coincides with the general principles of Elizabethan hierarchy, you could even read "father" here in Lacanian terms as the superior law— the *nom,* or *non,* a cultural given.

Surely this father-son relationship is quite obvious, yet Shakespeare complicates the relation so as to make it richly his own. First, the fathers are of the old-fashioned kind, individual, like the actual father that we might confront on the couch or in the clinic. (Hence I do not read Shakespeare's "father" as a Lacanian abstraction.) Second, this father-son pattern serves only as a frame within which Shakespeare paints more detailed plots. Moreover, I find this masculine pattern worked out against Shakespeare's gradual and literally mysterious accommodation to the feminine. The creative power of woman grows quantitatively and qualitatively more important for him as the psychological vassalage of son to father becomes less so.

That is the ending. At the beginning, though, come "brave Talbot, the terror of the French," and his son John, who may be Shakespeare's first fully drawn portraits of a father and son. Talbot spells the pattern out as he mourns his son in the last scene. The doughty father had begged and ordered the boy to flee the battle, but his son stayed. Then the father was downed, and his son stood over him and guarded him. Finally,

> Dizzy-ey'd fury and great rage of heart
> Suddenly made him from my side to start
> Into the clust'ring battle of the French;
> And in that sea of blood my boy did drench
> His overmounting spirit; and there died
> My Icarus, my blossom, in his pride.
> (*1 Henry VI*, 4.7.11–16)

Then Talbot himself dies.

The pattern is as follows: the father leads; the son is loyal; the son acts outward from the father, assuming the risk of action (as Icarus flew away from Daedalus). I visualize it as an L-shaped pattern, in which the father's power extends downward from the top, like God's, along the vertical bar of the L, and the son acts outward along the horizontal bar.

Once I begin looking for it, I find this L-shaped father-son pattern pervasive, most strongly and clearly so in the early plays. In *1 Henry VI*, besides the various Yorkist and Lancastrian dynasties, there is the example of the master gunner of Orleans, who aims his cannon but then leaves, putting his young son in charge of the gun. It is the boy who fires it and kills the mighty Earl of Salisbury.

The Henry VI plays offer a cluster of father-son relationships—the Talbots, the Cliffords, and the Yorks. Lord Clifford, for example, in *2 Henry VI* vows to spare none of his enemies once his father has been killed. In *The Comedy of Errors* Egeus's son acts outward for him, going in search of his missing brother. The four Lancastrian histories provide further variations on the theme. Prince John, the good son, is of course true to his father, King Henry IV, throughout the drama, as his father had been to John of Gaunt when he was Henry Bolingbroke, in *Richard II*. By contrast, Hal, in *1 Henry IV*, images right and wrong versions of the son's vassalage to a father—right to his kingly father, wrong to Falstaff.

Hamlet works out this L-shaped pattern, or its violation, in its many father-son relations. The Ghost wants his son to act on his behalf against his enemies, as young Fortinbras does. Even Claudius says,

"Think of us / As of a father" (1.2.107–8), but then he parodies the pattern when he insists that Laertes show himself his father's son by acting outward against Hamlet in the treacherous duel.

The pattern occurs again in *Macbeth* with old Siward and young Siward, the son risking himself in single combat with the villain. Old Siward mourns him by saying he was fighting not only for his real father but for the Father in heaven:

> Why then, God's soldier be he!
> Had I as many sons as I have hairs,
> I would not wish them to a fairer death.
> (5.9.13–15)

The son has simply exchanged fathers. Moreover, Siward's imagined sons (heirs?) grow like hairs from their father's body, as Talbot's son started from his father's side.

We could go on tracing the pattern between literal fathers and sons throughout the canon, but if we allow our category to include father figures and son figures as well, we can see many more versions. In *Richard III* Henry Tudor emerges as the agent of God, as Richard himself may have been in the first four acts the aggressive scourge of God, on the model of Marlowe's Tamburlaine. In *1 Henry IV* Falstaff asks Hal to bestride him if he falls in the battle, as young Talbot had done his father. In *2 Henry IV* the imaging of right and wrong father-son agencies continues, and Falstaff's followers in *The Merry Wives of Windsor* show what it is like to be vassals of a preposterous lord. In *Henry V* Shakespeare trumpets the father-son relationship, as King Henry gathers all the different peoples and accents of Great Britain as vassals to himself, at the same time as he acknowledges his own vassalage to God.

The pattern frames the action of *Julius Caesar;* it appears at the opening when Antony touches Calpurnia for Caesar and at the end when he has revenged Caesar's murder. It opens *Macbeth,* when Macbeth and Banquo, the psychological sons of Duncan, act for him against those who rebel against the father figure. It informs *Othello* as long as Iago remains Othello's loyal ensign. Indeed, the L-shaped pattern admits any relationship between a loyal retainer and a ruler— Falconbridge and King John, for example, or Kent and Lear; and on the side of evil, Buckingham and Richard, or the murderers and Suffolk, Richard, and Macbeth. Titus Andronicus acts on behalf of Saturninus the same way, but the reversal of the old-young pattern signals something is amiss.

The L-shaped father-son pattern also images the relation between a master (psychologically a father) and a servant, particularly a younger servant (who would be psychologically a son): Orsino and Viola-Cesario or Timon and Flavius, Oberon and Puck or Prospero and Ariel (the good son) and Caliban (the bad, rebellious son). As Peter Laslett puts it, servants "were subsumed in exactly the way that all children were subsumed by their fathers" (1971, 20–21; see also Pearson 1957 and Stone 1977). *As You Like It* opens with a series of these male Ls, when the Duke acts through his wrestler or Oliver. So does *A Midsummer Night's Dream,* when Oberon acts through Puck and Theseus through courtiers; it does not matter to the pattern that one L is natural and the other supernatural.

Romeo and Juliet doubles the pattern. One L faces an opposite L, as the servants who are the lower members of the Montague hierarchy thrust and parry at the servants at the bottom of the Capulet hierarchy. In the same way, Rome and Menenius are the fathers at the top for whom Coriolanus acts outward aggressively, while the rival son figure, Aufidius, acts outward for *his* paternal figures, the city of Corioli and its elders.

In combining the prince and the general, the general and his soldiers, the master and his servants, the father and his sons, into one L-shaped pattern of vassalage, I am pointing to commonplace Elizabethan principles of social organization. Primogeniture kept noble estates in one piece, and in many other ways this kind of father-son loyalty warded off anarchy. Even so, I do not find the same preoccupation with this theme in Marlowe, Jonson, or even Webster. Kyd and Heywood do more with it, although not, I think, as much as Shakespeare. He, moreover, gives it a special coloring.

Socially and psychologically the Shakespearean son is the father's vassal. He is to be loyal, he is to obey, and he is to act for the father. Metaphorically we could say he is the father's right hand or his sword. More precisely we could say the son acts for his father as a hound or a hawk does for a hunter. The gentleman hunter claims the absolute loyalty of the beast. The beast acts outward on the world, doing exactly what the gentleman hunter would do if he were acting for himself. Whatever the beast wins belongs to its master.

Part of Shakespeare's special coloring of the theme is that the son's aggression outward on behalf of the father often takes specifically oral forms, like Orlando's demanding food for starving old Adam. The master gunner's son fires just at the moment when "it is supper-time in Orleance" (1.4.59). Talbot describes his son as acting like a "hungry lion" (*1 Henry VI*, 4.7.6–7). Like a hawk or hound, these vassal sons seem ready to bite or eat on behalf of their father masters.

Further, the good Shakespearean father gains his son's loyalty orally (in the psychoanalytic sense) by giving him the food and shelter that a kind master gives his hawk or hound. This oral father-son relationship can fail if the father neglects to give correctly. Shakespeare devotes two whole plays precisely to such errors in giving. Lear and Timon err in sequence: both give their bounty *before* the hawk becomes obedient instead of after.

Shakespeare gives another special quality to this pattern of the son as hawk or hound, agent or vassal to the father. The task of the son—of maleness itself—is to go out along the horizontal of the L. Hence Shakespeare develops a recurring motif: leaving home. The young man is to go out into the world. The opening lines of *The Two Gentlemen of Verona* contrast Valentine setting out in the world with Proteus "dully sluggardiz'd at home" (1.1.7): "Home-keeping youth have ever homely wits" (1.1.2). Proteus looks at his friend and remarks, "He after honor hunts, I after love" (1.1.63), and the word "hunts" sets the motif of leaving home within the hawk-hound symbolism. Valentine's father speeds him on his way, as Proteus's father will later. The young man's destiny is to go out into the world and win fortune on behalf of the father who sends him. Even Julia must go forth in this male-male way, and she must go with a horizontally projecting codpiece ("Out, out" [2.7.54]). Conversely, in *Hamlet* Claudius insists that the prince stay in Denmark and not return to Wittenberg, and that behavior contrasts with proper fatherhood.

In the first scene of *As You Like It* Orlando complains of his brother's neglect, "He keeps me rustically at home" (1.1.7), and he resorts to an emblem almost as favored by Shakespeare as hawks or hounds for the right role of males in the hierarchy—horses: "They are taught their manage, and to that end riders dearly hir'd; but I (his brother) gain nothing under him but growth" (1.1.12–14). From under this vertical domination Orlando wants to spring free: "The spirit of my father grows strong in me, and I will no longer endure it" (1.1.70–71). He wants to leave home, as Hamlet and Laertes want to leave the court in the opening scene of *Hamlet*. In another usurped realm Rosalind has to leave, and she dresses as a boy to do so.

Cymbeline's missing sons also demonstrate this Shakespearean pattern. They are sons who have been (they think) kept at home, a home which therefore is

> A cell of ignorance, travelling a-bed,
> A prison, or a debtor that not dares
> To stride a limit.
>
> (3.3.33–35)

On hearing this, their foster father comments, "How hard it is to hide the sparks of nature!... Their thoughts do hit / The roofs of palaces" (3.3.79–84). He says that when he sits and tells his warlike feats, the boy's "spirits fly out / Into my story" (3.3.90–91). They start from his side, like young Talbot; like Icarus, they fly.

I have mentioned the oral failures in this father-son relationship. It admits also, of course, a phallic (aggressive, striving) failure, which seems to have been a particularly important kind of outrage and betrayal for Shakespeare. For example, when he wants to convey the horror of civil war in 3 *Henry VI*, he shows a father who has unknowingly killed his son and a son who has unknowingly killed his father. Lord Clifford in 2 *Henry VI* vows to spare none of his enemies once his father has been killed. The two Henry IV plays build entirely on the idea of a son who is failing his father as a warrior or is acting for the wrong father, Falstaff, and who finally betrays that father as well. Particularly outrageous are Northumberland's failure to support his son Hotspur and King John's attacks on little Arthur.

Another kind of failure in the male-male pattern occurs when an ineffectual, impotent king-father fails to rule strong sons. Henry VI is an obvious example, as are Richard II and King John. Such figures work out Yeats's statement of a personal myth for Shakespeare, "a wise man who was blind from very wisdom, and an empty man who thrust him from his place, and saw all that could be seen from very emptiness." Yeats gives Hamlet and Fortinbras as examples, but Richard II and Bolingbroke might serve even better. The same pattern occurs in *King John*, where John is like Bolingbroke and Arthur like Richard II. In *Richard III* little Prince Edward is the ineffectual, true monarch to that rampaging boar, Richard. Edward is a prototype of other witty boys whom the plays threaten, torment, or kill. These sons, who fail by giving out words instead of acting for their fathers, or who are witty and suffer (for it?), suggest some of Shakespeare's feelings about writing plays, but that would be a different and much larger topic than this essay's.

Rebellion is my present theme. Sons or son figures directly attack fathers or kings in the first two of the major tragedies (*Julius Caesar* and *Hamlet*) and in the histories of 1590–1600, which are called tragedies in the quartos (*Richard III* and *Richard II*). Failures of sons to be good vassals continue to be central for all the tragedies up to 1606, but the tone of the plays changes. Henry Ebel writes that "*Julius Caesar* eliminates or qualifies heterosexual or familial relationships in order to channel all emotional intensity into the particular drama of Oedipal rebellion with which it deals" (1975, 118). "Oedipal" is the key word here. As Shakespeare moves from Brutus's rebellion against a father figure to Hamlet's and those in the later tragedies, villainy becomes more sexual, and the issues between "fathers" and "sons" become more sexually colored. Claudius's attack on the king-father has a sexual element, but the ghost-father has to caution Hamlet against extending his revenge to his mother in the very sexual bedroom scene. Hamlet's nonaction suggests an ambivalence in his action on behalf of his father, a covert rebellion. The tragedies after *Hamlet* have darker ways of attacking the king or father. Iago betrays his general-father by the play of language. In this same way in *King Lear* Edmund betrays his father, Gloucester, who has in turn betrayed his son Edgar. Macbeth secretly murders his king-father.

In these phallic or oedipal rivalries good sons (and often the bad ones, before they go bad) are their fathers' right hands, their swords, their hawks, their horses, their hounds—all symbols for the father's phallic power. I think, for example, of the extended equation in *2 Henry VI* of the "Lord Protector" and his ambition to his hawk and its "climbing high" (2.1.7). The Dauphin in *Henry V* boasts of his horse, "When I bestride him, I soar, I am a hawk," and goes on to equate his horse's to his mistress's bearing him (3.7.15, 46). Read Sonnet 91, and listen with a psychoanalyst's third ear. The speaker notes that others take pride in hawks, hounds, or horse, "a joy above the rest," but to him

> Thy love is . . .
> Of more delight than hawks or horses be
> And having thee, of all men's pride I boast:
>> Wretched in this alone, that thou mayst take
>> All this away, and me most wretched make.

The loved young man is like "a joy above the rest." He is "all men's pride," whose loss would make the one who possesses him (it) most wretched. In *Lucrece* the symbolism becomes even more explicit. Before the rape Tarquin threatens his victim:

> he shakes aloft his Roman blade,
> Which like a falcon tow'ring in the skies,
> Coucheth the fowl below with his wings' shade,
> Whose crooked beak threats, if he mount, he dies.
>
> (505–8)

Nicely ambiguous. If he (the falcon) rise, he (the fowl) dies, but in another sense, he (the falcon) does too. Be that as it may, after the rape Tarquin is "the full-fed hound or gorged hawk" (694).

In this symbolism, hound, sword, and phallus act sexually and aggressively outward from and for their male owner. Indeed, in the famous Sonnet 20 Shakespeare spells this motif out still more explicitly, defining masculinity purely by the presence of a penis. Nature "prick'd thee out" with the horizontal, outgoing member in the L-shaped pattern. In the same way, *The Two Gentlemen of Verona,* like the other early comedies, contains lots of phallic jokes, as when Julia dresses up as a boy—again, the horizontal member defines masculinity and male-male relations.

What I am describing in the father-son pattern are Shakespeare's phallic fantasies, in which, it seems to me, the son becomes almost literally the father's genital. That transformation perhaps is not surprising in a man's fantasy about serving another man. What is surprising to me is that the son is sometimes the sexual as well as the aggressive agent for the father figure. That is indeed unusual vassalage.

The Sonnets make the most obvious example of a son's acting sexually for a father figure. In Sonnet 37 Shakespeare makes the father-son pattern quite explicit:

> As a decrepit father takes delight
> To see his active child do deeds of youth . . .

He goes on to say that in the son's virility the father's is restored. The father's lameness and other lacks will be cured by "my love ingrafted to this store" so that "I in thy abundance am suffic'd" (as a hunter receives what hawk or hound captures).

The older poet urges his young friend to go out into the world, to have sex, and to become a father himself. The youth of the Sonnets is like Bassanio in *The Merchant of Venice,* who is sent off by the older Antonio to woo Portia (to bring back the golden fleece and the power of mercy); like Fleance in *Macbeth,* who will supply the offspring for the line of Banquo to become kings of Scotland; or like Antony in *Julius Caesar,* who is to touch Calpurnia and thus trigger her fertility. The complicated wooing at the beginning of *Much Ado About Nothing,* in which the prince woos Hero for himself and then gives her to his loyal vassal Claudio, sets up a situation in which Claudio is to act sexually for his general-father. That substitution contrasts with the feared substitution of a midnight lover for the legitimate betrothed.

Consider again Talbot's eulogy of his son in *1 Henry VI:* "Fury and great rage of heart [desire?] / Suddenly made him from my side to start [to spring out]." He rushed into "the clust'ring battle of the French," who are associated in this play and in later plays with women and effeminacy; then "in" a sea of blood he drenched his "overmounting" spirit, and he died in his pride. Recall Mercutio's phallic puns on "spirit," Romeo's on "dying," and Shakespeare's in *Lucrece* on "pride." The sea of blood might thus hint at an enclosing, feminine— and deadly—container. I grant that I am reading the passage closely and with sexual meanings in mind (like those elaborated in early psychoanalysis), but I hear a very deep level in the Shakespearean father-son relation: the son is the father's phallus. Talbot wants his son to escape so that the Talbot line ("our household's name") will survive; that is, for generative ends. "In thee thy mother dies"; that is, when you die, your mother dies.

The son substitutes for the father. The etymology of *substitute* fits this phallic fantasy: *sub-* (under) + *statuere* (to cause to stand). A substitute is one that is caused to stand under—here, to stand under the father. Interestingly, the other word I have been using, *vassal,* comes from the Celtic equivalent: **wasso-* (one that stands under). There may be a similar fantasy involved in the word *deputy.* The verb *depute* comes from *de* (off) + *putare* (to prune or cut, as in *amputate*). To make Angelo in *Measure for Measure* a deputy is perhaps (in fantasy) to start a phallus off on its own.

I hesitate to offer so crudely Freudian a reading, but it does enable me to guess why the Lovejoy-Tillyard-Spencer version of Elizabethan hierarchy occupies so central a place in the psychology of Shakespeare's plays and poems. To question the great chain of being is to threaten castration. To restore it is to restore virility itself.

More than any other plays, the problem comedies test this sexual vassalage. *Troilus and Cressida* works out the pattern in both military and sexual spheres. The fathers—Agamemnon, Ulysses, and Nestor— try to get a reluctant Achilles to do their fighting for them, as Hector fights on Priam's behalf and as others fight on Hector's behalf. At the same time, Pandarus urges Troilus on to sex, trying to get him to act out the older man's sexual wishes. The younger man would then sexually parallel Hector's military vassalage to their father, Priam. Ulysses is trying to bring Ajax and Hector together, and Pandarus is trying to bring Troilus and Cressida together. She escapes Troilus's and Pandarus's control, as Achilles escapes Ulysses's, with shameful results. The shame comes about because of substitution—exactly the relationship that the normal father-son agency established. The Myrmidons substitute for Achilles, making him a bully and a coward, and Diomede substitutes for Troilus, making him a cully.

All's Well That Ends Well and *Measure for Measure* are likewise plays where key substitutions produce startling, if not shameful, results. It is as though Shakespeare wanted to test the world-view that had sustained him up to the 1600s. *All's Well* again tries the agency of son for father. The cure of the king comes in erotic terms: "Your dolphin is not lustier" (2.3.26). "*Lustick,* as the Dutchman says. . . . He's able to lead her a coranto" (2.3.41–43). Sexually restored, the king orders his vassal Bertram to marry Helen. To keep his word, he makes Bertram his sexual agent. Bertram refuses that relationship and chooses to be a martial agent instead, leaving to fight for the Duke of Florence. In this pattern it is all right for a son to act for a father figure aggressively, but the father's delegating him as a sexual agent leads to trouble. Later, when Bertram chooses for himself in a sexual situation—it does not seem to matter that he chooses wrongly—the plot can work itself out.

Measure for Measure begins with Shakespeare's usual father-son pattern: the Duke appoints Angelo a political deputy to act aggressively for him. Angelo, however, makes himself his sexual deputy as well, attempting to seduce the very woman whom the Duke, at the end of the play, somewhat improbably singles out as his own. The trouble in the comedy begins when the son figure begins to act sexually in the father figure's stead.

In short, I can read the problem comedies as Shakespeare's distrust of the sexual possibilities in a father-son pattern that had served him well psychologically until he ceased to have a father. The problem plays test the father-son ideal: What is authority with its agency through sons? I am echoing Barber and Wheeler's observation, in their essay in this book, that Shakespeare did not make the father-son crisis the subject of tragedy until he had himself surpassed his own middle-class father. In my reading of the problem comedies he would be working out guilts for some earlier sexual rivalry. Possibly this is the reason *Troilus and Cressida* contains the definitive speech on the Shakespearean and Elizabethan conception of degree—definitive, yet spoken by a rambling, scheming, Polonius-like old man and undercut by both the circumstance and manner of its delivery.

Among the tragedies only *Othello* tests this sexual delegation as intensely as do the problem comedies. Iago's famous confusion of motives stems from his imagining permutations of the play's possible sexual substitutions. None of these erotic imaginings seem real, however, compared to the solid delegations of authority, the military chain of command, against which the tragedy plays its sexual uncertainties. "Why is it," asks Madelon Sprengnether, "that Othello is more inclined to trust the word of Iago than that of Desdemona?" (Gohlke 1982, 164). Because, I would answer, the masculinist norm dictates trust in male-male delegation, and Iago acts within that norm. Delegation works when the Venetian senate entrusts its aggressive power to Othello, and indeed that action allows him to evade Desdemona's father's claims. Delegation continues with Othello's agency through Cassio and through Iago and even with Iago's through Roderigo. As William Kerrigan notes in his essay, the shared vows of Iago and Othello, whose relationship has long been regarded as a kind of marriage, subordinate the heterosexual marriage of Othello and Desdemona to the marriage of a senior to a junior male. Othello's tragic mistake is that the danger comes, not from the feminine sexuality he fears, but from the theatrics of a son figure.

What I find most surprising about this pattern of the son as substitute for the father is that Shakespeare uses the L-shaped male-male relation as the paradigm for woman. At least he does so at the beginning of his career, before he has started the long accommodation to the feminine that seems to me the keynote of his psychological growth.

Central to my reading of Shakespeare's transfer of the L-shaped father-son pattern to the relation of man to woman is *The Taming of the Shrew*. Consider the Induction, which makes *The Taming* an extended play within a play. In it a dominant man acts through his hounds, hawks, servants, and a "son"—the beggar Sly. A lord comes in with his hounds, finds Sly asleep, and has the idea of playing a joke on this drunken tinker. He will dress him up, wine him, dine him, and have his servants persuade him that he is the lord himself. In effect, Sly the beggar will be fed and housed in the father-son "oral" pattern, and he will act for the lord as the hounds do. The lord makes almost as much a point of feeding his hounds as of feeding Sly. He even supplies Sly with a wife, in the person of his page dressed as a lady, an action that contains that odd Shakespearean hint that the substitute is to act for the lord sexually as well as aggressively.

This "Lord"—he is not otherwise named—rules a world, as Petruchio does in the main play, which the Induction frames. If Petruchio says the sun is the moon or an old man is a young virgin, Katherine agrees, as dutifully as any servant of the lord of the Induction would. Petruchio announces, "It shall be what a'clock I say it is" (4.3.195). Petruchio controls what she shall eat, how she shall dress, and when she shall sleep. He acts out with Kate the lord's business of feeding someone who substitutes for you, making just the comparison I would expect:

> My falcon now is sharp and passing empty,
> And till she stoop, she must not be full-gorg'd,
> For then she never looks upon her lure.
>   (4.1.190–92)

He goes on to say that another way "to man my haggard" is to keep her awake as one does with hawks that "bate and beat and will not be obedient" (4.1.193, 196).

Because of this training, by the end of the comedy Kate is behaving just like a hawk or a hound. In the finale Petruchio bets on her in a contest of wits with the widow that seems very much like a dogfight; then he bets again in a contest of obedience in which Kate is to fetch the other two wives, as a retriever would fetch a duck:

> Twenty crowns!
> I'll venture so much of my hawk or hound,
> But twenty times so much upon my wife.
>
> (5.2.71–73)

It is in these terms that I understand Kate's speech about the proper role of a wife. The wife Kate idealizes (and Shakespeare, too, I am sorry to say) is like a hawk or a hound—or, strangely, a son to a father.

We are touching here on a more interesting theme than the obvious one of the father-son relationship: the suppression of the feminine or, to use Shakespeare's own phrase, the taming of the shrew. Interestingly, it is for his one unquestionably false woman that he revives the harsh images of Petruchio eight years before. Pandarus says to Cressida, "You must be watch'd ere you be made tame" (3.2.43), as though he were training a hawk, and adds, "[if] you draw backward, we'll put you in the fills," that is, the shafts of a wagon (3.2.45), as though Cressida were a horse that had to be trained to obedience.

With Cressida, as with Katherine and many of the women in the early works, I see Shakespeare trying to convert a rebellious or tempting femininity into the relationship of a loyal, obedient son to a loyal father, or a favorite hawk or hound to its master, or even (I hesitate to say) an obedient phallus to its owner. As Sprengnether suggests, structures of male domination and control serve to allay anxieties for Shakespeare about treachery or betrayal by women, particularly in their function as procreators or mothers (Gohlke 1980b). Hence, as I read him, Shakespeare avoids the danger by making woman over into man. I could, in the manner of Freud, state, and perhaps overstate, the fantasy I surmise: women do not dangerously lack penises if they *are* penises. At the beginning of *The Taming of the Shrew* Katherine is behaving like a man, and that is bad. At the end she is behaving like a man's hawk or hound. She becomes a mere appendage of Petruchio, and that sort of masculinity is permissible for a woman.

That partly obedient, partly rebellious masculinity is the only kind permitted the maidens in the early and middle comedies. Viola, Rosalind, Julia, and Portia can dress up as boys and go out into the world, either away from the father figure or acting on his behalf, because they exemplify a femininity reduced to obedient boyishness. While they are in the world as men or boys, they have to follow the male ethic of obedience to a master. Conversely, the young women in *A Midsummer*

Night's Dream do not dress up as men, and the ensuing Green World of mad mistakings in the woods images what happens when the female principle is not controlled by a father or male ruler, or even a male costume.

In general, the romantic comedies play with the sharp division of male from female, undoing the division and restoring it, in the fantasy Sprengnether suggests in her essay in this book. These women (acted by boys) both are and are not women. In *As You Like It* Rosalind begins dressed feminine but soon dresses masculine; later she partially undoes her masculinity by pretending to be Orlando's beloved. In this context I recall that Shakespeare's favorite defenses are splitting, isolation, and projection (Holland 1966, 135, 338), all ways of making one thing into two. In *Twelfth Night* Orsino treats the masculinized Viola—Cesario—in the usual way a master treats a servant or a father treats a son, but Shakespeare has the girl-boy act as Orsino's sexual agent as well, in order to attract Olivia. Shakespeare solves the problem by psychologically splitting Viola into male and female. Then he can allow the male Sebastian his prerogative as husband, but subordinate the female Viola to her mate Orsino.

The history plays broach yet another feminine complication of father-son delegations. Henry V, for example, urges on his troops this way:

> Dishonor not your mothers; now attest
> That those whom you call'd fathers did beget you.
> (*Henry V*, 3.1.22–23)

When Talbot tried to dissuade his son from staying for the fatal battle, the son replied:

> Is my name Talbot? and am I your son?
> And shall I fly? O, if you love my mother,
> Dishonor not her honorable name
> To make a bastard and a slave of me!
> The world will say he is not Talbot's blood
> That basely fled when noble Talbot stood.
> (*1 Henry VI*, 4.5.12–17)

Essentially, both King Henry and young Talbot are saying that the proper relation of father to son, the right vassalage of brave subordinate to superior, ensures that the son is indeed the father's son and therefore guarantees the honor and chastity of the mother.

In effect, the father-son bond controls the sexuality of women. *King Lear* illustrates the opposite: the failure of a son's fealty or a father's care leads to unchastity, the freedom of women, and the untaming of the shrew. This release of the sexual can work itself out tragically (as in *Titus Andronicus* or *King Lear*), comically (as in *A Midsummer Night's Dream*), sourly (as in *Troilus and Cressida*), or violently (as in *Henry V* with the king's threats of rape).

Because of this linkage the straightforward phallic rivalry of son-subject against father-king yields, around 1600, to something more sexual. Cuckoldry, or the possibility of cuckoldry, Coppélia Kahn points out, becomes a theme—in *Hamlet,* for example, or, most of all, in *Othello* (1981, 123). In that pivotal tragedy the woman, not the man, is trustworthy, and the male pattern of subordination and substitution is the deception. The turnabout marks for me a change in Shakespeare's development.

I think we can read the group of tragedies that follows *Hamlet* as beginning Shakespeare's reconciliation to the feminine, a reconciliation that will bear full fruit in the romances. Peter Erickson writes of Shakespeare's fashioning, in the late plays, "a benign patriarchy." He moves "from a brutal, crude, tyrannical version to a benevolent one capable of including and valuing women" (1985a, 148).

In *King Lear* two of the daughters amply justify all Shakespeare's earlier fear of the feminine and his need to tame the shrews. The third, however, suggests a new view of woman. Her final reunion with her father opens up a transcendent vista, as does no previous death in Shakespeare, allying her to those gods whom Lear has so vainly been invoking in the main body of the play. We have come back to someone like the Abbess in *The Comedy of Errors,* with supernatural powers of recuperation, or Hero in *Much Ado About Nothing,* with magical death and rebirth. Shakespeare is complicating his allegiance to the father-son principle. He is about to retreat from controlling the feminine and instead begin worshipping it, enclosing king- or fatherpower in womanpower. A father's love for and from a daughter will replace a father's pride in a son.

In many ways *Macbeth* would seem to be the purest statement of Shakespeare's masculine ideal, echoing the male-male relationships of the Henry VI trilogy. At the opening of the play we have Macbeth and Banquo, good son figures, fighting on behalf of the father figure Duncan against bad sons who rebel against the king-father. Woman, in the person of Lady Macbeth, disturbs this all-male arrangement. Later, when crime yields to punishment, the male-male pattern reimposes itself. Malcolm, the good son, rebels against Macbeth, the bad father. Once Macduff's wife and babies have been killed, Macduff and Malcolm are completely separated from woman, whereas Macbeth, still tied to his mad and sinister wife, despairs and dies.

What I find different in the male-male battles of *Macbeth* from those in *Richard III* or the Henry VI plays is the dominating presence of the witches. Shakespeare has introduced supernatural influences into plays before, but because he presents the witches apart from their prophecies to Banquo and Macbeth, they seem to have powers above and beyond their tempting Macbeth and fulfilling their prophecies through him. Banquo's sons *will* be kings, even though Banquo does nothing about it. An ambiguously female supernature surrounds the main (male) events, influencing them, surely, but perhaps also governing and dominating them. Being womanly but also partly male, the witches are for Shakespeare doubly duplicitous. We cannot tell the extent of their dangerous power, both male and female, but the visions they conjure up have to do with birth and death and the cycling of generations, as well as with the traditional Shakespearean concern, kingship. This mysterious duplicity of woman is both inside and outside the L of male hierarchy.

I imagine Shakespeare's patterns in geometric terms—the father-son, master-servant, falconer-hawk, or hunter-hound L that frames the action. Sometimes, as in *Macbeth*, what is thus framed is the disturbing doubleness of woman. In the early plays supernature took the form of prophecies and curses, some of them by women, notably the three cursing queens in *Richard III* (Kahn 1981, 55). Such women were inside the action, however, impotent to change the events being created by the dominant men. Supernature took the form of the conventional male god of the final dreams in *Richard III,* an avenging god of justice. Later, in *Macbeth,* a womanly aura (not Lady Macbeth's, but the witches') also surrounds the L.

Cleopatra has that same mysterious quality. In the male world she disrupts Antony's Roman valor. Like Cordelia or Lady Macbeth, her ranking alongside Antony means defeat in military matters. In another mode, outside the male-male L, she surrounds the action with celestial music and strange, fertile gods; in the transcendent ending she and Antony become stars and gods, and death itself is birth. Like the witches in *Macbeth* Cleopatra seems charged with the glories of fertility and the generations—birth, death, and rebirth.

Pericles moves further toward the transformation of Shakespeare's L-pattern into the romances' version by changing the relation from father-son to father-daughter. As in all the late plays, a theophany reveals a surrounding supernatural order. However, these new gods are not the legalistic father-gods of Shylock or Hamlet but family-gods (as in *Cymbeline*) or mother-goddesses, like Diana. *Pericles* tests female virtue in painful detail. Because Marina, even in a brothel, retains her virginity against every kind of pressure, she acquires the same kind of healing power as does Helen in *All's Well That Ends Well*, after "meditating on virginity" (1.1.110): she can heal the father figure. Then, like Cordelia, she allies herself with the gods to nurture that father. Her sexual restraint evokes Diana, who with her maiden priests restores Pericles's wife.

Pericles risks his daughter by separating from her, and she richly rewards his venture. Antiochus, by contrast, has bound his daughter to him through incest. He fails to risk her or send her away from home, like those fathers in the early plays who will not let their sons risk themselves in the world at large.

Cymbeline does not go so far as *Pericles* in giving women power. The first and last lines of the play speak of obedience to male powers in the most traditional Shakespearean terms, and much of the play deals with the disobedient daughter on the model of Hermia, Juliet, or Anne Page. Imogen disguises herself as a boy, and here, as in the early plays, a woman who disguises herself as a man shows she can function in the male world, adopt male values, and submit to the male hierarchy. She is Fidele—faithful as a dog, and she says of her disguise:

> This attempt
> I am soldier to, and will abide it with
> A prince's courage.
>
> (3.4.182–84)

Cymbeline wants to keep Imogen home. Like other rulers in the late plays, he acts the part of an evil or misguided father: Leontes, Antiochus, the rebels in *The Tempest* and even Prospero himself, Henry VIII, or Creon. Now, however, Imogen's womanliness supports the male hierarchy, even as she gets outside it. Only the queen represents the earlier duplicitous femininity, threatening from within the male order. Once she is exposed, traditional male hierarchy returns. In effect, the chastity of Imogen guarantees the justice of Jupiter.

In *The Winter's Tale* Leontes's failure to believe in his wife's chastity costs him all his male loyalties. Eventually he reconciles himself to the feminine, even to being ruled by a woman, Paulina. Magically, through "th'adventure of her person" (5.1.156), Perdita brings back substitutes for those lost male relationships, and the powerful crone Paulina brings back the almost divine feminine principle embodied in Hermione's statue.

With Prospero in *The Tempest* we come full circle to the man of great power, whose words order a world into being, as do Petruchio's or the lord's in *The Taming of the Shrew*. The symbol of Prospero's power is, as in the early plays, hounds and hunting: "A noise of hunters heard. Enter divers SPIRITS in shape of dogs and hounds, hunting them [the rebels] about; Prospero and Ariel setting them on" (4.1.255, stage direction). At the end of Shakespeare's career, however, the finale is not the victory of one male over another or the taming of femininity in marriage but forgiveness and the cycling of the generations. It is not a son whom Prospero sends outward but a daughter, "this my rich gift" (4.1.8). In cautioning against breaking "her virgin-knot" before the marriage ceremony, he repeats the old Shakespearean worry that feminine chastity is needed to guarantee what Ferdinand calls "quiet days, fair issue, and long life" (4.1.24). One can read Prospero's freeing of Ariel as a sign of Shakespeare's release from the old pattern of father acting through son—and one can read the fact that he only reluctantly lets Ariel go by fits and starts as Shakespeare's ambivalence at writing *finis* to this pattern that had guided his writing and, perhaps, his life.

At the end, as at the beginning, I think we can see pervading Shakespeare's works a relationship between a father figure and a son figure like that between a gentleman and his hawk or hound. The father trains the son by artfully meeting the son's needs, though not too much and not too soon. The father figure then sends the son figure out into a risky world. The son is supposed to do the father's business, typically to achieve and bring back some prize—riches, a wife, revenge, glory on the battlefield, a child.

The pattern changes in tone and feel as Shakespeare ages. In the early histories and the first tragedies, he tests the pattern by having sons rebel against fathers. Father figures and son figures relate around aggression and the hierarchy of men. In the early comedies women are made to submit to these values, often by dressing up as boys.

In the middle tragedies and the problem comedies, Shakespeare explores more and more the fears and distaste associated with the father's delegating sexual functions to the son or the son's usurping or manipulating the father's sexual prerogatives. At first the son can act for the father in sexual ways, but Shakespeare becomes increasingly uneasy with this option.

At the same time, this father-son relation colors Shakespeare's writing about women. Initially the ideal woman is like a son, playing a tamed hawk or hound to a dominant male. Gradually Shakespeare discovers other ways of coping with a femininity he finds duplicitous and dangerous. The woman can be the loyal son without being so demeaned: she can be a Cordelia, a Perdita, a Miranda.

Gradually, too, the balance changes between the male and female patterns. At first males guarantee the chastity of females by loyally acting out this father-son pattern. Failures in the father-son relation prove the inconstancy of women. Gradually this pattern is reversed: the chastity of women in an almost supernatural way guarantees the world's order and the loyalty of sons to fathers.

Where in the earlier plays supernature takes the form of a powerful, revenging male god of law, justice, and revenge, in the late plays deity takes the form of gods or goddesses of life, who guarantee the natural rhythm of the sexes and the generations. Whereas in the early plays it is the business of the kings and fathers to make themselves like gods of justice, in the late plays the kings and fathers must attune themselves to nature, procreation, and the feminine. In the late plays men act out the mercy and forgiveness that had earlier been woman's province.

At the deepest level, we are seeing in the late plays quite another kind of sexual substitute, vassal, or deputy. In the early form of Shakespeare's phallic fantasy a son acted as the father's phallic power—sometimes amplifying it, sometimes destroying its originator. In the late form of that fantasy a daughter can substitute for, or amplify, masculinity. In a sense Shakespeare, who in this reading began with a great fear of losing his manhood, learns to accept, indeed love, an absence as a substitute for a presence. The final substitution is of a woman for a man.

I imagine a Shakespeare who began his writing career with a need to become—ultimately to be—an extension of his father. This trait curiously combines passivity with activity—the passivity of total submission with the activity (both aggressive and, more ambiguously, sexual) that that submission authorizes. Such a person could be bisexual. Such a person could act in an assertive, even macho, way toward others but lapse into abject obedience to the father figure. He could be cruel if authorized (as Prospero is with Caliban, as Bernard Paris shows in his essay in this collection). Mostly, though, he would be a "gentle" man, in the one adjective for Shakespeare his contemporaries bequeathed us. The passive (if you will, homosexual) possibilities at the beginning of Shakespeare's career made possible the feminine substitution at the end.

"I imagine a man . . ." Is that what I am doing? Not quite. I am trying to do for many plays what C. L. Barber so eloquently did for the Sonnets: "We can turn our backs on the unanswerable questions of fact, and read the poems not as tantalizing clues but as *expression* of a man's experience. When we do so, we find that, though they do not tell a story, they do express a personality" (1960, 8).

Since the early days of the New Criticism it has been traditional to read the plays in terms of ideas or themes (and, more recently, "the free play of language" or signifiers signifying signifieds). Many Shakespearean critics find this concentration on language valid, satisfying, and popular. Indeed, in reading the works for a father-son pattern I am doing something the same, in that I am looking for consistencies and contrasts in the language.

I am also doing something different, though, in that I am myself substituting (which is not without its element of fantasy). I am replacing abstract meaning with traits, which collect into an imagined person. I am construing what Shakespeare wrote, much as I might interpret a conversation with you by imagining the kind of person you are. "Shakespeare" becomes a way of representing his works to myself and thus of evoking a human truth rather than a quasi-metaphysical meaning. I imagine such a Shakespeare, but he is not *the* Shakespeare, who never was available to us anyway. He is *a* Shakespeare, *my* Shakespeare, Shakespeare as I realize him, a gambit, a try—finally, the opening to a conversation.

Love, Death, and Patriarchy
in *Romeo and Juliet*

Kirby Farrell

I

Recent criticism has tended to depict patriarchy primarily as an au-
thoritarian institution for the regulation of society. Where Elizabethan
theorists praised the system for its order, we now have difficulty seeing
beyond its flagrant injustices and limitations, especially its misogyny.
Yet repression is not the whole picture. What made patriarchy tolera-
ble, even valuable, to so many Elizabethans? No one in Shakespeare's
Verona, for example, openly rebels against patriarchy. Like Romeo,
Juliet blames fate that she "must love a loathed enemy" (1.5.141); she
desperately tries to placate her father with "chopt-logic" (3.5.149).
For all their touchiness about being thought slaves, even the servants
are willing to fight for their houses. Why would individuals consistently subordinate their desires to the will of a patriarch?

   The answer I read from the play is that like religion, patriarchy
provides crucial symbols which validate the self and enable people to
imagine that they can transcend death. Anxiety about death pervades
Romeo and Juliet. The word "death" itself shows up more often here
than in any other work in the canon. In the lyrical balcony scene
(2.2.53–78) no less than in the ominous Prologue, love is "death-
mark'd." Yet even before his first glimpse of Juliet, Romeo worries that
"untimely death" will overtake him (1.4.111). This "black and porten-
tous" dread, I shall be arguing, dramatizes the breakdown in Verona of
patriarchy's ability to control anxiety about death and unconsciously
anticipates the dangerous consequences of that breakdown.

From *Play, Death, and Heroism in Shakespeare*, by Kirby Farrell. © 1989 The University of North Carolina Press. Reprinted by permission.

Patriarchy itself evolved from ancient systems of social order based on heroic leadership and strength. Insofar as he became a symbol of personal vitality and mythologically the progenitor of his people, the hero objectified the will to life and its opposition to death. As the term *hero-worship* itself implies, such a figure was usually invested with supernatural powers. Renaissance patriarchy combined ancient heroic models with forms drawn from Christianity, which revered "the Lord" and projected a heroic drama in which the heavenly father and his son triumph over a rebellious servant, Lucifer, and confer eternal life on the obedient children who identify with them.

Like Christianity, in which priestly fathers commonly exercised worldly as well as spiritual influence, patriarchy gave a local master superhuman sanction. Elizabethan theorists associated the father with the king and with God himself: it was he who created, defined, and validated his child's personality. He granted and guaranteed the psychic life of all who depended on him. The faithful servant or child could share in the father's righteous potency with a heightened sense of vitality and invulnerability tantamount, as Ernest Becker would say, to a conviction of immortality (Becker 1973). Tasso reveals the underlying premise in reporting that he confided in his patron "not as we trust in man, but as we trust in God. It appeared to me that, so long as I was under his protection, fortune and death had no power over me" (Bradbrook 1980, 73).

In early modern England "no one in a position of 'service' was an independent member of society. . . . Such men and women, boys and girls, were caught up, so to speak, 'subsumed' is the ugly word we shall use, into the personalities of their fathers and masters" (Laslett 1971, 20–21). Dependents necessarily cultivated the worshipful self-effacement psychologists call transference: living vicariously through a master who reciprocally lived through his house. The father's strength energized the entire family. In this perspective patriarchy was a process that consolidated diverse wills into one extraordinary will and generated a communal feeling—in effect, a spell—of immortality.

At the same time, like God's majesty, patriarchal potency included powers of annihilation as well as of love. The prince seeks to control his "rebellious subjects" by threatening their lives (1.1.97). Old Capulet roars a murderous curse at the uncooperative Juliet: "Hang, beg, starve, die in the streets" (3.5.192). More than mere discipline is involved here, for he who commands death seems to transcend it. In

Otto Rank's words, "the death fear of the ego is lessened by the killing, the sacrifice, of the other; through the death of the other, one buys oneself free from the penalty of dying" (Becker 1973, 99). In Verona the fathers' command over death remains symbolic. Nevertheless, even a child's unconscious anxiety about a rejection akin to death must have reinforced identification with the father.

In such a system only self-effacement brought a share in the father's power. Autonomy equalled rebellion and meant a rejection tantamount to death. In theory, either one identified with one's master and vicariously shared his power by lording it over inferiors (as Sampson and Gregory would dominate rival servants and women) or one was dominated. Dreading to be thought slaves—"That shows thee a weak slave, for the weakest goes to the wall" (1.1.13)—the Capulet servants associate aggression on behalf of their master with escape from the nullity of servitude. Yet their inferiority is the creation of their masters and produces volatile ambivalence in them. They summarize their situation with an ambiguity too dangerous to be consciously faced: "The quarrel is between our masters, and us their men" (1.1.19–20)—not merely between houses but between masters and servants.

In seeking to dominate, the servants act out the submerged values of their masters. Since patriarchy is founded upon the promise of security to dependents such as women, Sampson imagines humiliating his enemy by violating his women. Likewise, he appropriates the patriarch's role of godlike judge when he fantasizes that he "will be civil with the maids—I will cut off their heads" or maidenheads (1.1.24–25), equating rape with execution. By contrast, Romeo acts out patriarchy's benevolent generativity when he first approaches Juliet, assigning her an identity (the sun) and commanding her to arise and claim her rightful place in the order of things (2.2.3–9). These examples reflect one of the crucial paradoxes of the play's imaginative world: that even those who seemingly oppose patriarchy internalize patriarchal values.

The marriage old Capulet would make for his daughter helps to explain the willing self-effacement of dependents. By meekly wedding the paternally sanctioned Paris, thereby making him a patriarch in his own right, Juliet would fulfill her father's will and also transform herself. Lady Capulet fetishizes Paris as a book of spellbinding value that "in many's eyes doth share the glory" (1.3.91). By marrying him, Juliet too would be glorified and would share in "all that he doth possess, / By having him, making [her]self no less" (1.3.93–94). With its connotations of worship, "glory" exactly expresses the religious assumptions underlying the patriarchal system. By compelling admiration from others, Juliet's marriage would exalt her and by extension / her parents. For a dependent deference can be a means to vicarious triumph.

In Verona, however, patriarchy is under stress. The prince envisions himself protecting the city's declining "ancient citizens" from the turmoil of "rebellious subjects" (1.1.82, 97). At the same time romance has begun to rival patriarchy as an alternative mode of love and deliverance. As a result, the fathers' demand at the least for deference and at the most for total self-sacrifice or death sets off a violent chain of events. Social patterns and preoccupations inherent in the patriarchal system create conflicts that make rebellion inevitable.

In patriarchy the conviction of well-being depends on mystification, since in the end a master's strength is finite and people do helplessly die. Any threat to that spell jeopardizes the community's sense of security. The principal threat, however, is succession (Farrell 1984, 87–93). Sooner or later a son must take his father's place. As a result an aging father may become apprehensively tyrannical, or his child disenchanted and rebellious. Withdrawing his strength from the father, weakening their shared identity, the child cannot help but evoke dread.

Since the system polarizes roles into extremes of dominance and submissive identification, the moment when those roles at last reverse may be terrifying. Having made mothers of his daughters, as the Fool protests, King Lear suddenly becomes as powerless as a child who is subject to whipping and utter effacement. Hence the potential violence of paternal retaliation. Acting the righteous judge, a father can pronounce doom on an unruly child and thereby—however painfully—make the child's loss confirm his own vitality.

One solution to the problem of succession splits the conception of power. The father becomes an unmoved mover, as it were, a conscience-figure or judge who controls a seemingly static house or kingdom by directing his powers of life and death inward in the form of blessings and executions. By contrast, the annihilation of enemies acts out the heroic mastery of death, and that power may be delegated to sons and followers. In this way the potency of the father remains incontestable.

Since Verona has no outside enemy, however, heroic aggression is turned inward. When old Capulet calls for his broadsword, for example, he is about to assault old Montague, who is tacitly his "brother" in relation to the patriarch who governs them, the prince. In this context the otherwise peculiarly gratuitous feud is a device that allows males to seek forbidden self-aggrandizement by scapegoating rivals, and each house kills in the name of righteousness. Although the feud helps to preserve the illusion of immortality essential to patriarchy's survival by providing a safety valve for aggressive feelings against masters, it only postpones the inevitable crisis of succession.

Hence the need to glorify the submission of the child while elevating the father to "be as a god" (*A Midsummer Night's Dream*, 1.1.47). The model for that submission is Christianity, in which the central action is the atonement of the son with the omnipotent Father. Christ resists Satan's temptation to personal dominion over the earth and by self-sacrifice earns eternal life for humankind. While God remains the unmoved mover, his son struggles in the world and earns through his faithful death a resurrection that transforms him from lamb to fatherly shepherd, from victimized mock–King of the Jews to the militant warrior who will harrow Hell and rout Antichrist in the last days. In this arrangement the shepherd/warrior ambiguously shares in the identity of the Father without threatening his preeminence as everlasting judge.

In a fallen world, however, as Renaissance sectarianism made plain, the urge to rebellion remained strong. Reformers repudiated the patriarchal pope and feuded with each other, seeking to dethrone each other's "false" god and win the eternal life afforded by the true Father. The English, typically, construed their own rebellion as the rescue of true faith from Antichrist. The patriarchal analogue to religious schism is Verona's feud. Like rival dispensations, each house kills in the name of righteousness. Cursing Benvolio, for example, Tybalt cries, "I hate hell, all Montagues, and thee" (1.1.71). In psychoanalytic terms fanaticism such as Tybalt's suggests a reaction formation, a means of suppressing one's own taboo impulses by killing off the devilish enemy of authority one might otherwise become.

In Verona as in Christianity the patriarchal role is split between incontestable control and heroic expansiveness, yet the reconciliation of roles is repeatedly subverted. Prince Escalus functions as conscience and judge, commanding obedience "on pain of death" (1.1.103). But the prince seems weak, and his unruly "sons" deviously aggressive; although they profess obedience, they repeatedly maneuver for power.

Instead of suffering abuse, as Christ did, they perpetuate a rivalry in which every little indignity contributes to a rising spiral of violence. The rivalry itself ambivalently allows "sons" to challenge and curry favor with their lord. Capulet, for example, insists on Juliet's marriage to the prince's kinsman, Paris, which presumably would give him an edge over his rival, Montague. His scheme not only expresses the mentality of the feud but also signifies an effort to identify with the supreme source of strength in Verona. Not surprisingly: for in a larger context these "sons" are themselves fathers covertly challenged from below.

Within his own house a lord such as old Capulet is himself a weakened conscience, his role as warrior being appropriated by actual or surrogate sons, such as Tybalt, and below them by unruly servants. Tybalt, after all, boldly usurps the role of warrior lord. Wishing to assault Romeo at the ball, he tests his surrogate father's authority to the limits, provoking old Capulet to roar: "Am I master here, or you?" (1.5.78).

As a potential son-in-law Romeo himself is tacitly a rival son with Tybalt, competing to inherit Capulet's power. Like old Capulet and old Montague, Tybalt and Romeo displace their resentment of superior authority onto one another. Furthermore, Romeo scales the patriarch's orchard wall to steal his daughter's heart and thereby his posterity, yet he denies all hostility in himself and others: "There lies more peril in thine eye / Than twenty [Capulet] swords" (2.2.71–72). Eventually, as Verona's sons destroy one another, Romeo will join Mercutio, Tybalt, and Paris in the graveyard.

As the means of producing new life and one means of mediating the child's eventual appropriation of the parent's position, marriage becomes the object of intense parental control. As old Capulet insists, "[all] my care hath been / To have [Juliet] matched" (3.5.177–78). Ideally, such intimate control compensates the father by corroborating his will even as it guarantees an undying line of posterity. Hence the tragic nature of the parental dread that spurs Juliet's defiance. Lamenting Tybalt's death and prevented by the prince's edict from taking comfort in the usual fantasies of triumphal revenge, old Capulet keenly feels his own mortality: "Well, we were born to die" (3.4.4). Promptly he makes a "desperate tender / Of my child's love" to Paris (3.4.12–13). For a moment he loses faith in his own ordained mastery and tries to secure the future by force. Bullying his daughter to wed

Paris and thereby fatally alienating her, the old man brings on the horror he seeks to dispel.

Let me emphasize that we are looking at a system of behavior. Without imputing Machiavellian motives to Prince Escalus, for instance, it should be noted that the feud actually serves to protect his limited power from expansive ambitions from below. By blaming the fathers, he can exercise his threat to execute troublemakers and thus "maintain his posture as a decisive ruler" (Brenner 1980, 50). Until the night of the ball at least, the fathers have similarly profited from the distressing competition between feisty sons impatient for power.

The feud presupposes, then, that one "son" may kill another to identify with the father's strength as warrior-hero. With the emphatic symmetry of "Two households, both alike in dignity" (Pro. 1), Capulet and Montague are virtual alter egos, as are Tybalt and Romeo and, in the opening brawl, the opposed servants. Externalized, the doubling plays out fratricidal rivalry. Fully internalized in a vulnerable character, patriarchal conflicts may produce self-murder. And that, I maintain, is what finally destroys Romeo and Juliet.

II

For all their lyrical tenderness, Romeo and Juliet create their love out of the tragically conflicting materials of their own culture. In Romeo's changing desires, for instance, the chorus sees a struggle to inherit a father's position: "Now old desire doth in his deathbed lie, / And young affection gapes to be his heir" (2.Pro. 1–2). The lovers attempt to evade the world of the feud, yet in making love they unwittingly act out patriarchal and Christian forms. Construing love as worship and substituting the beloved for father and God, they seek apotheosis in each other. Out of the resulting turmoil comes death and "a glooming peace" (5.3.305): an equivocal vision of redemptive destruction that resists any ready evaluation.

In an imaginative world where children grow up transfixed in the aura of a protective lord or else face terrifying nullity, we should not be surprised that love may reproduce in a beloved the engulfing, life-giving power of godlike parents. Insofar as the polarization of power in Verona requires either continual submission or the devious homicidal assertiveness of the feud, love's mutual worship answers profound needs. For if individuals become disenchanted with absolute security and heroic aggression, as Romeo and Juliet do, they need alternative convictions to sustain them. Love is therefore counterphobic not only as any system of immortality must be but also as a defense against the anxious demands of an ideology whose spell is no longer wholly efficacious.

Romeo envisions Juliet as a supernatural being, a masculine "bright angel" and "winged messenger of heaven" who overmasters awestruck "mortals" so that they "fall back and gaze on him" (2.2.26–32). At the same time, Romeo's vision expresses the infantile wish to be chosen by, and identified with, a majestic father, as is shown by the gender of the angel. His imagination finds fulfillment in the paradox of empowering self-effacement at the heart of patriarchy. The fantasy's completion comes in Romeo's dream that Juliet has awakened him from death and ordained him an emperor, the paramount patriarchal role (5.1.9).

Juliet participates in the same fantasy when she equates orgasm and immortality in her cry,

> Give me my Romeo; and when I shall die,
> Take him and cut him out in little stars,
> And he will make the face of heaven so fine
> That all the world will be in love with night.
>   (3.2.21–24)

Like "all the world," Juliet will be subsumed as a worshiper in Romeo's apotheosis. If his transformation into stars alludes to Caesar's apotheosis as a "goodly shyning starre" in Ovid, as one editor has suggested (Gibbons 1980, 170), then Juliet is envisioning an analogue to Romeo's dream that sexual love (her kiss) can revive him from death to become an emperor. By "dying" through sexuality "are happy mothers made" (1.2.12). By the same means, reciprocally, may a woman make a youth an immortal lord. In its imagination of power this fantasy is profoundly patriarchal. Like Romeo's vision of the angel, however, this celebration of all the world absorbed in the face of heaven also suggests a worshipful infant's concentration upon the all-important, life-giving face of a parent.

The lovers' mutual worship expresses a generosity, subverted or repressed elsewhere in Verona, that balances their self-destructiveness. In their lovemaking, for example, Romeo and Juliet repeatedly fantasize that deathlike self-effacement can lead to apotheosis. Repudiating their own names (2.2.34–57), loving in darkness, they try to be invisible in hopes of escaping patriarchal control. They imagine innocent self-nullification that excuses their actual defiance of their fathers even as each casts the beloved in the role of life-giving lord. When Juliet wishes Romeo were her pet bird, a "poor prisoner" (2.2.179) whose liberty she would be "loving jealous of" (2.2.181), Romeo eagerly assents. Yet Juliet declines to dominate him, protesting that "I should kill thee with much cherishing" (2.2.183).

Finally, however, their behavior is equivocal, and that doubleness makes their self-effacement perilous. Confronted by Tybalt after his secret marriage, Romeo tries to play possum and placate him. Yet Romeo's passivity allows Tybalt to use him as a screen, thrusting under his arm to kill Mercutio (3.1.103). Immediately guilt and anger overwhelm Romeo. His will released, Romeo first turns against Juliet—"Thy beauty hath made me effeminate," he cries, "And . . . soft'ned valor's steel" (3.1.113–15)—and then, murderously, against Tybalt.

In this crisis actual uncontrollable death breaks the spell of symbolic immortality, and the underlying patriarchal structure asserts itself. Defeated by Tybalt's "triumph" (3.1.122), called a "wretched boy" (3.1.130), Romeo feels overwhelmed by "black fate" (3.1.119–20). In reaction he tries to reassert heroic control over death by levying a death sentence on Tybalt (3.1.129). Rebelling—against the emasculating "angel" Juliet as well as against the would-be master Tybalt—Romeo discharges his rage at a rival "son" and alter ego. In the complex of motives that produces the lovers' suicides this process is important. For there the part of the self that identifies with the patriarch and demands mastery finally punishes with death that part of the self that for the sake of love would suffer enemies and surrender all claims to worldly power in the hope of deferred rewards. The internalized father slays the weakening child.

Because the basic patriarchal structure governs even rebellion, desires for autonomy tend to call up opposite roles organized around fantasies of death and omnipotence. When Gregory and Sampson jest about breaking the law, for instance, they promptly fantasize about slavery and execution, and then, in reaction, about annihilating their enemies. Similarly, the Juliet who would make Romeo outshine Caesar is also the paralyzed child who helplessly hears her parents wish her dead. Exposed in his rebellion by the murder of Tybalt, the Romeo who would be an emperor (5.1.6–9) abases himself, feeling himself put to death by the mere word "banishment," with which the friar, like a patriarchal judge, "cut'st my head off" (3.3.21–23). Taunted as a slave by Tybalt (1.5.55), Romeo goes to his doom with grandiose defiance of slavery, vowing to "shake the yoke of inauspicious stars" (5.3.111). Death and omnipotence are two faces of the same fantasy. Their dissociation contributes to the irrational violence of the feud as well as to the lovers' "mad scenes"—Romeo's tantrum on the floor of the friar's cell and Juliet's near hallucinatory collapse as she dispatches herself with the sleeping potion.

It happens that we can glimpse the origins of this polarization of the self in Romeo and Juliet. Heading toward the Capulets' ball, Romeo worries about "some vile forfeit of untimely death" that may overtake him before he can redeem the "despised life clos'd in my breast" through some heroic act (1.4.111, 110). His imagery implies that he has mortgaged his life and will lose it since the term will "expire" before he can pay. Punning, he fears an untimely debt as well as an untimely death, one that will "forfeit" his "despised life." A sense of guilty inadequacy makes him expect the punishment of death or foreclosure.

In patriarchy, however, the child owes the godlike father a death inasmuch as he or she holds life at the father's will. In Theseus's summary of the doctrine, the child is "imprinted" by the father, and it is "within his power / To leave the figure or disfigure it" (*A Midsummer Night's Dream*, 1.1.50–51). What is more, the child owes a debt of obedience or self-effacement, in which guilty wishes for autonomy are repressed in a symbolic death. Where patriarchy splits into the roles of the father who is a judge and the son who is a warrior, the son additionally owes this conscience-figure a debt of heroic glory, which may have to be paid by risking his life. Such a debt produces the self-hate in Romeo's "despised life" and helps to explain his desperate reassertion of lost valor in the murder of Tybalt.

Juliet's behavior also reveals an underlying psychic debt, the origin of which surfaces in the nurse's account of Juliet's weaning (1.3.16–57). Though physically capable, the child angrily resisted her own independence. Her first efforts at autonomy led to a fall, and the fall brought not parental support and further self-assertion but a surrogate father's queasy joke that a woman lives to fall: "Thou wilt fall backward when thou hast more wit" (1.3.42). Yet Juliet's fall produced "a perilous knock" and implied a threat of death, especially for a child whose alter ego Susan is "with God" (1.3.19).

In falling, Juliet gave her "brow" "a perilous knock," the same injury she imagines inflicting on herself upon awakening in the monument. Trapped in the suffocating family tomb—within reified patriarchy itself—she fears she will be overcome by guilty rage and destroy her brain, seat of the self and forbidden autonomy. In turn she would punish herself by means of a "great kinsman's bone" (4.3.53), metonymic parental force. As in the anecdote about weaning, a venture toward autonomy produces (in her mental life) first a fall toward death, then trauma.

The nurse's husband's joke tacitly proposes a patriarchal solution to counter the fall toward death. A "fall backward" into sexually submissive marriage and motherhood will rescue the child from the terrifying fall toward autonomy at the cost of being able literally to stand on one's own two feet. Juliet consents to pay a debt/death through a marriage that will at once efface and exalt her. Girls must fall sexually to be redeemed by a new lord and win posterity for the family and themselves, even as young males must be willing to fall in battle to win immortalizing glory.

In this imperative of self-sacrifice lies the germ of the idea of a play-death such as Juliet acts out by means of the friar's potion. Her fall in a death-counterfeiting sleep would appease an outraged parental judge and lead to a lordly resurrection from the family tomb with the banished Romeo. Making Verona new in amity, Juliet would be fulfilling a patriarchal fantasy comparable to Romeo's dream of love awakening him from death as an emperor. The play dramatizes the pervasiveness of this fantasy in Verona. In engineering Juliet's resurrection, the ostensibly humble friar gives himself a godlike role—he plans literally to raise her from the grave. Uniting the lovers and aspiring to atone for all Verona, he parodies old Capulet's marriage plans, implicitly correcting them, as if to prove himself "the best father of Verona's welfare" (Brenner 1980, 52). "Ghostly sire" (2.2.188) and worldly father are implicitly competitors in the larger system of patriarchal rivalry.

III

Reconstituting patriarchal forms to serve their own desires for autonomy, Romeo and Juliet never openly defy their parents. Yet with the wish for autonomy comes a veiled recognition of the suffocating claims their parents make on them. Their parents' will to subsume each child's identity comes unconsciously to seem to the lovers like cannibalism. The monument that embodies her family in Verona becomes to Juliet an imprisoning mouth (4.3.33–34) and to Romeo a devouring "maw," womb, and mouth (5.3.45–47). Just as the mother becomes an expression of the father's will, and the father expresses ideologically the life-giving and potentially life-withholding generativity of the mother, so the tomb conflates the parents into one ravenous orifice.

As in Lear's fantasy of the savage who "makes his generation messes / To gorge his appetite" (*King Lear*, 1.1.116–18), the threat is not merely of parental wrath or incestuous desire but also of cannibalistic self-aggrandizement, a frantic hunger to incorporate more and more life in order to overcome death. Such aggrandizement is the more terrible for being sharply felt by the child and yet invisible. In effect, the lovers fear an infantile voracity such as a once-subsumed child, having at last come to dominate, might release against its own offspring. Since monuments objectify a claim to transcend annihilating time, the "hungry" tomb expresses patriarchy's deepest and most primitive drive, the drive for survival.

We need to remember that the father's claims to mastery over death are corroborated in his role as judge and even executioner. If the father is a god, as Theseus decrees, he is also always potentially death himself. In this respect the prince's struggle to contain the feud is a struggle—echoed in the world outside the Elizabethan theater—to reserve for a supreme patriarch the right to command death.

At its most benign this power thrillingly confirms the lord's generosity. By conspicuously sparing the child's life, the father (or monarch) makes the love between them incalculably valuable. Thus, in his amorous submission to Juliet, Romeo exults, "O dear account! my life is in my foe's debt" (1.5.18). At its most terrifying, when internalized by the child, such power generates intolerable insecurity, as in Romeo's dread of the hostile stars and his suicidal sense of doom.

From this standpoint, the lovers' suicides reflect the dynamics of patriarchal control. To master her fate, Juliet would play a lordly role ("myself have power to die" [3.5.242]) as Cleopatra does to escape Caesar. Unconsciously, however, the introjected imperatives of the parental judge can make suicide a form of execution in which an alienated conscience destroys a rebellious self, as in Juliet's vision of dashing out her own brain with an ancestral bone, the objectified will of the father. Likewise Romeo's conscience punishes him with suicidal self-hatred. Banished for his defiance, he "[falls] upon the ground . . . / Taking the measure of an unmade grave" (3.3.69–70). Angry at Juliet for his own defiance in slaying Tybalt (3.1.113–15), he turns his anger against himself, fantasizing that his own name has murdered her (3.1.102–5). With Juliet he calls down punishment on himself, as Elizabethan noblemen routinely did in speeches from the scaffold professing love for the queen: "Let me be put to death. / I am content, so thou wilt have it so" (3.5.17–18); "Come, death, and welcome! Juliet wills it so" (3.5.24). Ambiguously, however, he calls Juliet "my soul" (3.5.25), so that this execution is also internalized.

As patriarchy's internal conflicts become intolerable, its radical connection with death threatens to surface in consciousness, most equivocally in the personification of death by parent or child. Old Capulet envisions death as a young, rivalrous inheritor who has "lain with" Juliet and usurped his control over her (4.5.36). His description of his adversary exactly fits Romeo. In the Capulets' monument Romeo himself, in turn, personifies death as a rival. Death is a warrior-king whose "pale flag" has not yet fully "conquered" Juliet (5.3.93–96). Then the rival becomes an "amorous . . . lean abhorred monster" (5.3.104), who will make Juliet his "paramour." Romeo imagines Juliet sexually enslaved in the palace of a monster who is also a warrior-king.

This fantasy projects the long-denied dark side of the patriarchal forms in which the lovers have construed each other. Romeo dissociates from himself as Death the part of him that would be made an emperor by Juliet's kiss. In this final moment of tenderness he rejects the devouring triumphalism latent in all patriarchy. He repudiates the death that "hath suck'd the honey" of Juliet's breath. Otherwise Juliet, by loving such an emperor Romeo, would be submitting to rape, like the women Sampson fancies "ever thrust to the wall" (1.1.16). Sampson identifies with patriarchal tyranny, the same tyranny that Romeo at last projects on death and vows to resist to the end of time.

Giving his own life with chivalric honor to rescue Juliet from a monster, Romeo finally plays out the sacrificial, warrior's debt of the son to his father. Even as he sacrifices himself in part for patriarchal values, he would "shake the yoke of inauspicious stars" (5.3.111) in a final repudiation of the fathers. This is the fatal paradox at the heart of patriarchy: when rebellion against a myth is insidiously possessed by that myth, it serves the myth. In taking his own life to defend Juliet's sexuality against the rival warrior-king Death, Romeo gives new life to Verona's feud.

At the end of the play benevolence takes disturbing form in the funerary statues the fathers decree. Still thinking in terms of demands, Capulet vows, "This is my daughter's jointure, for no more / Can I demand." To this Montague replies, "But I can give thee more." Thereupon he boasts that he will make Juliet the golden cynosure of all true lovers: "There shall be no figure at such a rate be set / As that of true and faithful Juliet" (5.3.296–304). The fathers' economic vocabulary and competition call to mind the psychic debts felt by the children and the ominous economic term Romeo associates with death—"engrossing" (5.3.115). In addition, such greedy possession calls to mind Romeo's imagery of the tomb as a "detestable maw," a womb of death (5.3.45). The metaphors place the young in an engulfing parental womb that would suffocate, not grant, life. The womb and the sexually enslaving monster express the parents, whom the lovers love and fear and also, unknowingly, hate.

Now that marriage and the sword have failed, the fathers would reconstitute their conviction of immortality by re-creating their children as holy martyrs to love, "poor sacrifices of our enmity" (5.3.304). As icons the children will be fabricated into exemplary types. Yet there must be a difference between the golden statues and the poignant individuals we have seen. That difference is of course the basis of the play's critique of patriarchy. In the end it also measures the dramatist's need to honor the structure of power outside the Globe Theater and no doubt in his own upbringing, while onstage—and in the sympathies the play evokes—it enacts a challenge to that power.

Audiences have often interpreted this challenge as a justification of romantic exaltation, even as various critics have taken it to legitimate the lovers' aspirations to autonomy. By contrast, at least one historian maintains that the original Globe audience would have felt obliged to condemn the play's disobedient children (Stone 1977). However, if we understand patriarchy as a system of beliefs evolved to control anxiety about death, these contradictory responses to the play appear in a new light. Seizing on a limited truth, each tries to protect the illusion of security at stake in the play, either by revaluing the social order (for example, by postulating its reform through love) or, more often, by repudiating patriarchal values on behalf of a substitute system of beliefs. Like the voices onstage, we too need to fortify ourselves against the prospect of annihilation.

Because of the danger of offending an audience, especially an audience of Elizabethan patriarchs, the play does not forcibly disenchant its myths. Instead it creates conditions in which imagination might discover itself as a tissue of beliefs. Such a recognition would at least momentarily turn the imagination against itself, showing the triumphal verities onstage and off to be as compulsive and insubstantial as dreams. In such a moment of alienation the self could begin to appreciate its dependency, even (to echo Sampson and Gregory) its enslavement. In that dizzying moment lies the possibility of change and, perhaps, a new ground for love.

Although *Romeo and Juliet* seems to me deeply disenchanted at its core, it dramatizes the imagination's resilience in the face of annihilation. As London, and Shakespeare himself, survived devastating plague in the early 1590s (a catastrophe echoed in 5.2.8–12), so the play registers the shock of mortality to a privileged system of belief. The final lines show Verona turning blasted life into art ("never was a story of more woe" [5.3.309]), as Shakespeare himself, having sensed the darkness beyond the bright dreams of culture, would go on generating fictions that engage that darkness, including the flagrantly dreamlike late romances.

IV

The quality of disenchantment in *Romeo and Juliet* suggests a Shakespeare who was radically equivocal about authority and creativity. As the son of a modestly eminent father of declining fortunes, Shakespeare may have discovered early in life that patriarchy could no longer make good—if it ever had made good—its promises and demands. Perhaps, as in *Romeo and Juliet,* a disenchanted son used his obligatory self-effacement to evade an ineffectual father. Making himself invisible, "an artificial night" (1.1.140), Shakespeare may have cultivated a poetic passion through which he pursued his own destiny. After all, Romeo's daring imagination wins him the prized daughter of a lord and, belatedly, the admiration of an entire city that has misjudged him. Analogously, Shakespeare forsook his father's world and sought his fortune in the theater—a psychic orchard, so to speak—

where he could influence the hearts of some of the most important people in England while earning fame and the place of a gentleman.

Let me develop this fanciful metadramatic analogy a bit further. Himself an agent and beneficiary of change, the young artist must have sympathized with the Romeo who steals Juliet—old Capulet's posterity—by his imaginative passion. Yet Romeo can find no way to reconcile this poetic autonomy with the harsh daylight world of the city; and since it may tragically internalize patriarchal values, poetry's intoxicating power may be untrustworthy or even fatal. Shakespeare's own solution was to use poetry to lure the city, London, into the theater of the Capulets' tomb where exaltation could be gloriously expended again and again for profit, insight, and mutual pleasure.

Shakespeare's was a personality, then, that learned to transform its own aggression and aspirations into vicarious heroic forms that could bind the sympathy of others, at least for one intense, profitable moment, and then be ambiguously relinquished. Rather than endorse or repudiate the world's verities in art, as conventional writers did, Shakespeare dramatized their natural irrationality—their status as fantasy. He presented not the doctrine of patriarchy, for example, but the network of veiled assumptions about death and heroism that the doctrine implied. He put that elusive psychic reality before audiences as a mystery or a dream ("or did I dream it so?" [5.3.79]). To be sure, he let an onstage chorus of conventional wisdom interpret the dream ("All are punish'd" [5.3.295]) in order to escape retaliation for arousing wishes and fears presumably repressed (or banished) by many in his audience since early childhood.

Recognition that people live by strategic fictions such as patriarchy opens up all aspects of behavior for negotiation and therefore provides a basis for consensual relationships and, not incidentally, the artist's own creativity. Disconnected from underlying physical forces and appetites, by contrast, a cultural fiction may be a terrifying illusion, a candle lighting fools the way to dusty death. If disenchanted, Shakespeare saw, human behavior may reduce to a fierce appetite for domination and nurture tenuously held in check by ruthless strategy: in Verona a feud, or in the imagery of the history plays a dialectical struggle between a king and ravenous wolves.

Hence Shakespeare's equivocation. Like the strong-willed yet famously slippery Queen Elizabeth, whose regime revived old forms such as chivalry to disguise its innovations, he survived public life in a world of homicidal religious and political rivalry by honoring venerable cultural forms while re-creating them. In one sense his genius lay in devising ways of making disenchantment healthy. His own *Romeo and Juliet* appears simply to echo Brooke's familiar, lifeless *Romeus,* although in fact it functions as a sort of pun on Brooke's story, producing a new meaning. Such a quibbling imaginative stance permitted devious self-assertion in the ostensible service of deference. As a result, although Shakespeare retired to the outward life of a country patriarch in Stratford, his actual relationship to that role is a mystery.

With its tendency to loosen the self's desperate attachments to the world and make reality dreamlike in moments of crisis, Shakespeare's style of equivocation must have helped control the dread of death, as had patriarchy. In addition, it enabled him to devise new forms of authority for experience: for example, to reconstitute patriarchy in the theater itself, where he vicariously commanded "his" spellbound audience's sympathies even as he urged spectators to exercise their own autonomy ("as you like it," "what you will"). For as he wittily deferred to the spectators, the dramatist was implicitly redefining them and directing their fantasies toward a new vision of life. Invested with ambiguous cultural authority ("the Lord Chamberlain's Men," "the King's Men"), Shakespeare created a surrogate, provisional family that could console for death by encouraging imaginative sympathy in the spectators and clarifying relationships in the world outside the theater that were already evolving beyond the drastic bonds of patriarchy.

Shakespeare and the Bonds of Brotherhood

Marianne Novy

Brothers appear in Shakespeare's plays of all genres and at every stage in the playwright's career (Fineman 1980; Montrose 1981; Garber 1981, 30–51). His representations of both brotherly love and brotherly conflict diverge from psychological realism. If the plays reveal an ideology of brotherhood, it is a strangely polarized one.

Sometimes brotherly love seems a magnetic force. In *The Comedy of Errors* such a force leads Antipholus of Syracuse away from his father in search of Antipholus of Ephesus, the brother he lost in infancy, even though the chance of success seems only that of "a drop of water, / That in the ocean seeks another drop" (1.2.35–36). Later, in *As You Like It,* this bond leads Orlando to save the life of the brother who has plotted against him.

Yet neither Antipholus speaks directly to the other, even at their reunion. Similarly, the reconciliation of Oliver and Orlando is narrated in an emblematic mode, not dramatized. Literal brotherly harmony as evoked on stage is often removed from realism and associated with childhood, as in the description of the two little princes Richard III has murdered, or the pastoral idyll of Guiderius and Arviragus among the Welsh caves.

At other times conflict, rather than love, binds brothers. Rivalry appears in five of the six pairs of brothers in the comedies alone, yet it is seen as anomalous: Adam, Orlando's old servant, calls Oliver "your brother—no, no brother" (2.3.19). Conflict dominates the three groups of sisters in Shakespeare even more: Adriana and Luciana, Kate and Bianca, and Goneril, Regan, and Cordelia.

Inheritance laws penalizing sons who are not firstborn (Richard III) or who are illegitimate (Edmund in *King Lear,* Don John in *Much Ado*

About Nothing) sometimes partly motivate enmity between brothers. Even so, the hostility often seems to defy or exceed reason. Oliver, Orlando's older brother, declares, "My soul (yet I know not why) hates nothing more than he" (*As You Like It*, 1.1.165–66). In *The Comedy of Errors*, though brotherly love has motivated one Antipholus to seek the other, the plot sets the twins in competition for an identity.

More frequently than any other familial relation in Shakespeare, brotherhood poses the question of the nature of Nature. Is it natural behavior toward a brother to save his life, as Orlando does, or to plot against him, as does Oliver? Is the bond of brotherhood more like the golden chain that the goldsmith gives Antipholus of Syracuse or the ropes that chasten and restrain Dromio and Antipholus of Ephesus? These two views usually appear as discrete alternatives, with few suggestions of a psychological connection between hostile and loving brotherhood.

What the plays hardly ever show directly are ambivalent brothers. Oliver tells us that when Orlando saw him in danger from a lioness, he hesitated ("twice did he turn his back" [4.3.127]) before saving Oliver's life. But once Orlando commits himself to follow "kindness, nobler ever than revenge, / And nature, stronger than his just occasion" (4.3.128–29), the relationship is transformed. Early in the play they fight each other; now they love each other. Initial suggestions of love mixed with anger are limited to Oliver's pretense: "I assure thee (and almost with tears I speak it) there is not one so young and so villainous this day living. I speak but brotherly of him; but should I anatomize him to thee as he is, I must blush and weep" (1.1.153–57). Orlando protests against Oliver's injustices to him and restrains himself because of his brotherhood—"Wert thou not my brother, I would not take this hand from thy throat till this other had pull'd out thy tongue" (1.1.59–61)—but his anger seems simple and uncomplicated.

By contrast, in *The Tempest*—and I believe only there—a Shakespearean brother confronts painful ambivalence in fraternal conflict. Not only does Prospero marvel that Antonio's behavior goes against the nature of fraternity ("that a brother should / Be so perfidious!" [1.2.67–68]) but he also feels a personal hurt because, as he tells Miranda, Antonio was "he whom next thyself / Of all the world I lov'd" (1.2.68–69). In *As You Like It* images of brotherhood move from conflict to harmony and thereby minimize the dissonance of including both kinds in the same play. In *The Tempest* fraternal harmony, set in a narrated past, is retrospectively revealed as deceptive, but Prospero still suffers from longing for its return. Later I will discuss further complexity in the presentation of brotherhood in this play. Before that discussion, and before exploring more of the historical and biographical context of Shakespeare's treatment of brotherhood, I want to give some examples of how often the plays make brotherhood structurally important without making it psychologically complex.

A character's attitude toward his brother seems almost a simple code for his degree of social integration. Characters who are at odds with, or unknown to, their brothers often seem emotionally alienated in other ways as well. Antipholus of Syracuse, just arrived in Ephesus, begins his first soliloquy, "He that commends me to mine own content, / Commends me to the thing I cannot get" (*The Comedy of Errors*, 1.2.33–34). At the beginning of *As You Like It* Oliver feels "altogether mispris'd" (1.1.170–71) by his own people, and Orlando says, "Only in the world I fill up a place, which may be better supplied when I have made it empty" (1.2.191–93). In both of these plays reconciliation accompanies the brothers' commitment (or recommitment) to marriage.

By contrast, in *Much Ado About Nothing* Don John's "sadness . . . without limit" (1.3.4) refers not only to his illegitimacy but also to his hostility toward his brother, Don Pedro, which Shakespeare juxtaposes with the harmonious, though comic, alliance between Leonato and his brother Antonio. At the end of the play John is still hostile and Don Pedro also, in his own way, is an outsider among the happy couples, if we believe Benedick: "Prince, thou art sad" (5.4.122). Richard of Gloucester anticipates the monstrosity he will show as Richard III when he says:

> I have no brother, I am like no brother;
> And this word "love," which greybeards call divine,
> Be resident in men like one another,
> And not in me: I am myself alone.
> (*3 Henry VI*, 5.6.80–83)

He subsequently makes these words true by planning the deaths of his brothers one by one to get the crown; then he keeps his crown safe by ordering the murders of the little brothers who are his nephews, a kind of symbolic murder of brotherhood.

Prince Hal, Richard's opposite in many ways, makes a point of reassuring his brothers that he will not kill them, as Amurath, the Turkish Sultan, killed his. Rather, he says, "I'll be your father and your brother too" (2 *Henry IV*, 5.2.57). Part of his power as a leader lies in his ability to extend his concept of brotherhood. Sundelson points out how important brotherhood imagery is in Hal's speech to his soldiers at Agincourt on the feast of the twin brothers Crispin and Crispian (1983, 62–65):

> We few, we happy few, we band of brothers;
> For he to-day that sheds his blood with me
> Shall be my brother.
>
> (*Henry V*, 4.3.60–62)

Later, to confirm the union of their countries, Hal, now Henry V, and the French king, his former enemy, address each other as "brother France" (5.2.2) and "brother England" (5.2.11).

Why is brotherhood so important in Shakespeare's plays and yet so often, even in *The Tempest,* presented in polar terms of absolute love or hate? Louis Montrose has shown the relevance of primogeniture to *As You Like It.* The Elizabethan sense of the younger son as typically aggrieved no doubt added to the topicality of that play, especially if, as he suggests, the Globe audience drew heavily on groups, such as students and shopkeepers, that were mainly peopled by younger brothers (Montrose 1981, 33; Thirsk 1969; Harbage 1941, 80). Through pursuit of the crown, as narrated in *Hamlet* and presented on stage in *Richard III*, the aggrieved younger brother of a king acts out his revenge on an even larger scale.

Primogeniture, however, is not the only social practice involving brothers for which Shakespeare's plays might serve, in Montrose's words, as "a theatrical source of social conciliation" as well as "a theatrical *reflection* of social conflict" (1981, 54). Primogeniture and its discontents fail to explain, for example, Oliver's hostility or the ease with which the Antipholus and Dromio twins escalate their attacks on each other. Nor does primogeniture fully explain why Shakespeare often alludes to two Biblical stories in which the younger son is favored: the story of Cain and Abel, in which the elder son kills the younger out of envy for the divine reception given to his offering, and the story of the prodigal son, in which the elder son envies the celebration prepared for the younger upon his return home. Why is the younger son favored in these stories and in much of our folklore? Montrose argues that "cultural fictions of the triumph of younger siblings offer psychological compensation for the social fact of the deprivation of younger siblings" (1981, 47). Another answer, however, comes from the time before children notice any division of the family's financial resources and when they care most about emotional resources. In childhood most older brothers feel that the younger is favored, because forgetting how they themselves were treated as infants, they resent the care and attention he requires. These stories might serve to compensate the younger brother, but for the elder they might very well reflect the emotional reality he felt in childhood.

William Shakespeare was himself an eldest brother. Before he was born, his parents had one and probably two daughters who died in infancy. Gilbert was born in 1566, two years after William. Three years later came Joan, and in another two years Anne, who died at three. When William was ten, another brother, Richard, appeared, and six years later the last, Edmund. These facts may throw some light on the origins of what we might call Shakespeare's personal mythology. C. L. Barber and Richard Wheeler have hypothesized that his early infancy would have been idyllic, because he was the long-awaited and only son. When Gilbert was born, his mother's attention would have been divided, and as other children appeared, one by one, maintaining belief in her love for him might have required a considerable imaginative effort.

Shakespeare never wrote directly about brothers competing for a mother's affection. I suggest, however, that several aspects of his plays are his imaginative response to his family situation. First, Shakespeare's plays frequently include a figure whose situation is rather like that of an elder brother who feels replaced in his mother's affections: the man who worries about his wife's or lover's fidelity. Themes of brotherhood and cuckoldry converge in a number of the plays, often with imagery that explicitly suggests conflict over a mother (Fineman 1980). This convergence is not surprising if we accept Dorothy Dinnerstein's theory (1976) that the intensity of masculine anxiety about cuckoldry comes from the infant's anxiety about losing the mother, who is his whole world.

The struggle between brothers for the wife of one of them appears tragically in *Hamlet* and farcically in *The Comedy of Errors,* where the right husband is locked out of his house at dinnertime. In *The Winter's*

Tale Polixenes and the jealous Leontes call each other "brother" frequently and reminisce about being raised together in childhood. Posthumus's jealousy of Imogen, in *Cymbeline*, explodes after Iachimo describes her in terms that vividly evoke a mother-infant relationship. Iachimo saw "under her breast . . . a mole" (2.4.134–35), which, when kissed, gave him "present hunger / To feed again, though full" (2.4.137–38). Even in *As You Like It* Oliver's hired wrestler Charles greets Orlando by saying, "Come, where is this young gallant that is so desirous to lie with his mother earth?" (1.2.200–201). Furthermore, this play full of brothers is also full of cuckoldry jokes.

Triangles and adultery abound in literature; distinctive in Shakespeare is the focus on the mistakenly self-styled cuckold, who generates a triangle by imagining his wife's adultery. From a sociological point of view Shakespeare may have been criticizing his society's suspicion of women, but his obsession with this configuration hints at a profound personal involvement that has psychological roots in his family position. The wrongly self-styled cuckold shares with the eldest brother the experience of being an insider in a relationship while feeling like an outsider. No matter how loving his mother is, an elder brother can still feel betrayed when she has a new baby to care for. By the time Shakespeare was sixteen and his youngest brother was born, he might have seen the irrationality of such a sense of betrayal even as he experienced it again. An attempt to control his feelings by taking his mother's point of view might be one origin of Shakespeare's ability to identify with female characters.

The Sonnets, where Shakespeare comes closest to expressing feelings in his own voice, show some other ways family images are important in his work. When he writes about a betrayal that is not merely fantasy, he uses an image of a mother-child relationship even more explicitly. The simile in Sonnet 143, where the poet tries to accept the woman's interest in another, is so much outside the usual decorum of Elizabethan poetry that it seems especially close to Shakespeare's personal mythology.

> Lo as a careful huswife runs to catch
> One of her feathered creatures broke away,
> Sets down her babe and makes all swift dispatch
> In pursuit of the thing she would have stay;
> Whilst her neglected child holds her in chase,
> Cries to catch her whose busy care is bent
> To follow that which flies before her face,

Not prizing her poor infant's discontent;
So run'st thou after that which flies from thee,
Whilst I, thy babe, chase thee afar behind,
But if thou catch thy hope, turn back to me,
And play the mother's part, kiss me, be kind.
    So will I pray that thou mayst have thy *Will,*
    If thou turn back, and my loud crying still.

Though the conflict in the poem is between child and chicken, from the point of view of the temporarily neglected child it is immaterial whether the rival is animal or human. However, although in his own family Shakespeare was older and thus more mobile than the baby his mother was caring for, here he places himself in that infantile position. Similarly, the plays show his ability to identify with both elder and younger brothers.

I believe Sonnet 143 hints at how Shakespeare learned to deal with being replaced by younger brothers. As Conrad van Emde Boas has suggested, according to Holland's summary, he developed a capacity to identify with other members of his family (see Holland 1966, 85; Wheeler 1972). The Sonnets burst with evidence of a highly mobile sensibility, and they show many other traces of such identifications (see Barber 1960). One sees him imaginatively taking a mother's position when he writes to the youth, "Thou art thy mother's glass, and she in thee / Calls back the lovely April of her prime" (Sonnet 3), or when he promises to keep the youth's heart "so chary / As tender nurse her babe from faring ill" (Sonnet 22). Elsewhere he claims a father's eye:

As a decrepit father takes delight
To see his active child do deeds of youth,
So I, made lame by Fortune's dearest spite,
Take all my comfort of thy worth and truth.
                    (Sonnet 37)

If this image comes from Shakespeare's memory of seeing his own father with a younger brother or sister, it recalls another transcendence of rivalry through identification.

The Sonnets are full of claims of identification in situations of potential rivalry: "My friend and I are one; / Sweet flattery! Then she loves but me alone" (Sonnet 42); "Thou art all the better part of me" (Sonnet 39); " 'Tis thee (myself) that for myself I praise" (Sonnet 62). As Barber has noted, such love seems the heir of familial love even when familial metaphors are not explicitly used (1980, 190–93). Shakespeare seems able to imagine the feelings that come from every position in the family, and then from every position in the sonnet triangle:

> Beauteous thou art, therefore to be assailed;
> And when a woman woos, what woman's son
> Will sourly leave her till [she] have prevailed?
> (Sonnet 41)

Such an ability to identify with others is one basis for the range of imaginative sympathy in Shakespeare's plays (Holland 1966, 135).

Shakespeare goes beyond the degree of identification required by dramatic form and explicitly makes identification a subject in his theater. His characters often try to get others to feel empathy. In *Twelfth Night* Viola pleads with the Duke:

> Say that some lady, as perhaps there is,
> Hath for your love as great a pang of heart
> As you have for Olivia. You cannot love her;
> You tell her so. Must she not then be answer'd?
> (2.4.92–95)

Isabella uses a similar strategy with Angelo in *Measure for Measure:*

> Go to your bosom,
> Knock there, and ask your heart what it doth know
> That's like my brother's fault.
> (2.2.136–38)

Role playing within the plays often functions in the same way. Prince Hal, for instance, understands his father's attitude better by taking his role in the improvisation with Falstaff. As Barber and Wheeler point out, in *1 Henry IV* the confrontation with father-son conflict is limited: identification defuses it (1986, 11). Perhaps one may make a similar argument that Shakespeare's interest in identification between brothers kept him from imagining brotherhood, until very late in his career, with the psychological complexity that he gave to his portrayal of relationships between men in plays like *Othello, Hamlet, Macbeth, Julius Caesar,* and *Coriolanus,* and even to idealized male friendships in *Two Gentlemen of Verona* and *The Merchant of Venice.*

In *The Tempest,* the last play he wrote without a collaborator,

Shakespeare treats brotherhood in the greatest depth and acknowledges its ambivalence in a way the magical resolutions of early plays did not. Prospero expresses the pain he feels at Antonio's usurping the dukedom Prospero had given him to manage. Antonio's behavior poses for Prospero the question of how good can lead to evil and casts doubt on parent-child relations as well as on fraternal ones, as Prospero explains to Miranda:

> My trust,
> Like a good parent, did beget of him
> A falsehood in its contrary, as great
> As my trust was, which had indeed no limit,
> A confidence sans bound.
>
> (1.2.93–97)

Many critics have wondered why in this scene Prospero repeatedly asks Miranda whether she is listening. Stagecraft may require interruptions to break up a long speech, yet these questions all appear during his description of Antonio's behavior. Perhaps the memory of Antonio's betrayal makes Prospero insecure about Miranda. When he asks her to respond to the challenge that Antonio, like all false brothers, presents to the whole system of family loyalty, her answer develops his own earlier simile:

> PROSPERO: Mark his condition, and th' event, then tell me
>   If this might be a brother.
> MIRANDA: I should sin
>   To think but nobly of my grandmother.
>   Good wombs have borne bad sons.
>
> (1.2.117–20)

As Prospero earlier affirmed the goodness of his own quasi-parental and fraternal trust, Miranda rather literal-mindedly reaffirms the goodness of Prospero's mother and by implication the general goodness of family attachments. As if she had passed an examination with this answer, her father never again asks if she is listening.

Convinced as Prospero is that his brother is evil, he still attempts, though incompletely, to see his position. He suggests that Antonio "did believe / He was indeed the Duke, out o' th' substitution" (1.2.102–3). The move out of rivalry to identification, which is mediated by Ariel, becomes explicit when Prospero announces his willingness to forgive the court party:

> Hast thou, which art but air, a touch, a feeling
> Of their afflictions, and shall not myself,
> One of their kind, that relish all as sharply
> Passion as they, be kindlier mov'd than thou art?
>   (5.1.21–24)

It is essential to the theatrical effect that Prospero expresses his hurt and his willingness to forgive not in soliloquy but in dialogue with two other characters, neither of whom are adult males. The cultural context of Shakespeare's presentation of brotherhood includes the Elizabethan code of emotional control, which associates expressions of love and loss with women and restraint of all emotions except anger with men (Novy 1984, 8–18, 190–98). A wronged brother like Orlando or old Hamlet follows this code when he speaks of his brother with straightforward anger, uncomplicated by a sense of loss or betrayal. Many male characters in his plays find they must transgress this code, but it is usually because of a relationship with a woman. The code, I believe, is one reason the Antipholus twins hardly speak to each other upon their reunion in *The Comedy of Errors,* even though their prototypes, the Menaechmi, greet each other enthusiastically in Plautus's text (1960, 5.9).

The reunion of the brother-sister twins Sebastian and Viola in *Twelfth Night* is much more articulate. Though formal, it suggests great love. Such a difference seems to correspond to a difference in the cultural context for brother-sister relations. Even Lawrence Stone, whose general view of Elizabethan emotional life is bleak, believes that brothers and sisters were often close (Stone 1977, 115). By contrast, in Shakespeare's earlier scenes of reunion between brothers, the formal qualities that signal ideological importance coalesce with the demands of masculine restraint. With Ariel's definition of sympathy as human and Prospero's association of it with "nobler reason 'gainst my fury" (5.1.26), *The Tempest* hints at an ideal of reason in feeling that transcends simple links of the first with men and the second with women. When the brothers meet, however, Antonio shows no repentance and Prospero is no model of reasoned sympathy.

Yet Prospero seems to accept that his humanity both limits his control over others and links him to them. His brotherhood to Antonio stands for both these aspects of his humanity. He emphasizes the physicality of his bond with Antonio and announces his forgiveness even as he names Antonio's sins and declares them acts against nature:

> Flesh and blood,
> You, brother mine, that [entertain'd] ambition,
> Expell'd remorse and nature, . . .
>
> . . . .
> . . . I do forgive thee,
> Unnatural though thou art.
>
> (5.1.74–79)

Antonio may be, as Prospero says later, one "whom to call brother / Would even infect my mouth" (5.1.130–31), but by his very saying of "brother" he acknowledges that he does in some sense share the infection. "This thing of darkness I / Acknowledge mine" (5.1.275–76), he later says of Caliban; and he is close to saying the same thing here about Antonio. As he must accept the ineradicable weaknesses and impulses of his own body, so he must accept the fact that Antonio, whom he can never reform, is still his brother.

Prospero's words "flesh and blood" allude to the physical bond of brotherhood, in melancholy contrast to the physical reference in the final scene of *The Comedy of Errors* when the Dromio brothers at last reconcile: "We came into the world like brother and brother; / And now let's go hand in hand, not one before another" (5.1.425–26). Rather than touch his brother, Prospero asks in the epilogue for the help of the audience's "good hands" (Epi. 10). He confirms his understanding that humanity involves both connections and limitations when he asks for applause that is a prayer and an acknowledgement of his listeners' similar need for forgiveness. "As you from crimes would pardon'd be, / Let your indulgence set me free" (Epi. 19–20). Prospero shows his resilience as he moves beyond the desire to take vengeance on his brother and seeks instead other bonds, which he gains in part by relinquishing Miranda, Ariel, and his magic. Coming to terms with his brother becomes a metaphor for accepting his own life.

By the time Shakespeare wrote *The Tempest* he was expert at showing how intense rivalry could involve love and how intense love could turn into a sense of betrayal. It is no coincidence that in writing his most articulate expression of betrayed brotherly love, he gave Prospero a female listener. He made Prospero emotionally complex partly by representing through Miranda a transformed image of the mother, whose distant presence shadows most of the fraternal relationships of his plays. This image persists, I think, not only because potential competition for the mother is implicit in brotherhood but also because

Shakespeare seems to have been able to identify both with his mother's love of a younger brother and with the younger brother's love of her. Consequently when Prospero tells Miranda that Antonio was "he whom next thyself / . . . I lov'd" and is reminded that "good wombs have borne bad sons," the play hints at a connection between his love for Antonio and his love for his mother, which, like Miranda's love, he had inevitably to sacrifice to another.

In tragedy, Stanley Cavell suggests, the inevitable separation between actors and audience mirrors the ultimate isolation of the characters, and all of us, from one another (Cavell 1969, 338); in comedy, Northrop Frye observes, as the ending usually celebrates the solidarity of the characters, it may appropriately move toward communion with the audience (Frye 1969a, 164). In *The Tempest* the importance of Prospero's acknowledgment of his brother and of Caliban suggests a third attitude toward human relationships: they are inevitable, but they are difficult and uncontrollable. One side of the inevitability and uncontrollability, in the romance vision, is that those we think lost forever may return, as Alonso, Pericles, and Leontes discover; the other side is that those we would like to lose forever may also return. Analyzing another romance, *Cymbeline,* Meredith Skura suggests that in Shakespeare "the child can leave his family behind, but he cannot escape its influence" (1980, 206).

Barber and Wheeler find that to Shakespeare's temperament "all relationships are provisional, contingent because they replace others. At the core is the original loss of the parental objects and the possibility of its recurrence" (1986, 47). The other side of this formulation is that the apparently lost relationships themselves keep reappearing. Shakespeare wrote about one aspect of this explicitly in Sonnet 31:

> Thy bosom is endeared with all hearts
> Which I by lacking have supposed dead;
> And there reigns love and all love's loving parts,
> And all those friends which I thought buried.

In the world of the romances, because of the return of past hurts, forgiveness is necessary; because of the return of past loves, forgiveness is possible. Thus the relationship Prospero asks of the audience in the epilogue is neither the easy fellowship of comedy nor the pain in separation of tragedy, but a forgiveness—a bond of acceptance despite acknowledged difficulties—analogous to the forgiveness he has given Antonio, if less harsh. Once again the relationship between brothers is paradigmatic for social integration, but here the difficulties and ambiguities involved are explicit.

Prospero is the older brother in Shakespeare who most articulates emotions toward a younger brother in a way that invites us to share them. *The Tempest,* which critics have called more directly autobiographical than Shakespeare's other plays, does focus on a character who was the oldest son, as was Shakespeare. This autobiographical element may link with others. As a member of an acting company Shakespeare worked with colleagues who were figuratively in a fraternal relation to him. As the company's author and one of its longer-standing members, who, according to tradition, had often played the roles of older men, such as the Ghost in *Hamlet,* Shakespeare could have played a fatherly role toward his colleagues, if we speculate with Barber and Wheeler about the parental nature of his work in "creating parts to realize and nurture the talents of his fellows" (1986, 61). Although his own son had died at eleven, in regard to some of his fellow actors Shakespeare, like Henry V and Prospero, could have seen himself as both father and brother.

Shakespeare had one brother who was almost young enough to be his son, the brother who followed him to London and also became an actor. Edmund Shakespeare was born only three years before William's daughter Susanna. Why did Shakespeare give Edmund's name to the character who in *King Lear* (written in 1605–6) exclaimed against an older brother and plotted to get that brother's territory? We cannot tell. It appears that Edmund was buried on December 31, 1607, a few months after the burial of his illegitimate son. His funeral was expensive, with a tolling of the great bell of the church of St. Mary Oveny, near the Globe, and was held in the morning, unlike most funerals at the time. Scholars have speculated that Shakespeare paid for the funeral and arranged to have it held in the morning so that theater people, performing in the afternoon, could attend (see Schoenbaum 1977, 28–29). Was Edmund an unsuccessful Antonio, trying to play his brother's role? Is his death one reason Antonio is silent at the end? Or did Edmund feel a hero-worship rare among the brothers in Shakespeare's plays? Whatever the case, it is appropriate that the brother of the man who created so many theatrical celebrations of brotherhood had more than maimed rites.

Shakespeare's Women:
Historical Facts and
Dramatic Representations

Carol Thomas Neely

On January 21, 1638, Madame Anne Merrick wrote to a friend in London that she could not come from the country for a visit but must "content herself with the study of Shakespeare and the 'History of Women.'" Many other women since this "first recorded student of Shakespeare" (Stopes 1901, 85) have been interested in both Shakespeare and women's history, including Charlotte Carmichael Stopes, a passionate and indefatigable genealogist and scholar, author of a number of books on Shakespeare and other Elizabethan figures, who unearthed and reprinted Merrick's comment. Following in this long-standing tradition, I will juxtapose the profile of the women in Shakespeare's extended family that emerges from the Stratford documentary records to the characterizations of women in Shakespeare's plays in order to shed light on the status of Renaissance women, the representations of women in the plays, and the discontinuities between the two. Indirectly the study illuminates Shakespeare, the man and artist who exists in the gap between them and transmutes—perhaps—his perceptions of the one into his creations of the other. But I approach Shakespeare as man or as author obliquely through the women who formed him and the women he created. This is the inverse of the more common attempt to approach the question of women obliquely through Shakespeare's representations of them. Because my aim is to illuminate the "history of women" as well as the "study of Shakespeare," I look at characteristic patterns, not specific influences, making use of evidence drawn from Shakespeare's extended family not only during his lifetime but also earlier and later. My information comes from biographies of Shakespeare, especially Charlotte Stopes's *Shakespeare's Fam-*

ily (1901), Edmund K. Chambers's *William Shakespeare: A Study of Facts and Problems* (1930), Mark Eccles's *Shakespeare in Warwickshire* (1961), and Samuel Schoenbaum's *Shakespeare: A Documentary Life* (1975). In these books much information is present in the background to fill out the sparse outlines of Shakespeare's life. I bring this information into the foreground and marshall it for new purposes.

I will explore contrasts between the "social relations of the sexes" (Kelly 1984, 1–18) in the documentary records and the plays, examining demographic figures, family structures, economic and legal power, marriage patterns, control of sexuality, cultural influence, and memorialization after death. The documentary records give us information about women's active participation and influence in marriages, wills, property settlements, and litigation of all kinds. In the plays, where women's economic and legal power is invisible or severely constrained, we see women's emotional responses, the responses of others to them, and their cultural power and social and sexual confinement. The discontinuities suggest that it is difficult to use the plays in any straightforward way to tell us something about Shakespeare the man (as nineteenth-century critics wished to do) or to tell us something about the status of women in the period (as twentieth-century feminists have wanted to do). These discontinuities tell us something about the nature of representation, the conventions that shape it, the ideologies that necessitate it, and the desires that fuel it. They may help us better to understand one kind of material out of which Shakespeare constructed his plays.

Shakespeare in Stratford was surrounded by women of considerable longevity. Most of them outlived their brothers and husbands; many had long widowhoods or remarried. Although Shakespeare only knew one step-grandparent, he had lots of sisters and cousins and eight aunts, one on his father's side and seven on his mother's; five of these married and two remarried. His Aunt Agnes married twice, his Aunt Joan outlived her husband, Edmund Lambert, by seven years, and his Aunt Margaret on his mother's side, after her first husband, Alexander Webbe, died with their sixth child an unbaptized infant, lived for forty-one more years; she died in her seventies two years before Shakespeare died. Shakespeare's mother, Mary, likewise outlived John Shakespeare; he died in 1601 in his seventies, and she died seven years later, probably in her late sixties (Eccles 1961, 22; Stopes 1901, 36). Shakespeare's sister, Joan, also outlived her husband (who died the same year as Shakespeare) by thirty years. Anne Hathaway's stepmother lived almost twenty years longer than her father (Schoenbaum 1977, 81). Anne herself outlived Shakespeare by seven years. His daughter Susannah outlived her husband; Judith, another daughter, probably did too, and her mother-in-law Quiney was a widow. Shakespeare's granddaughter Elizabeth outlived her first husband by twenty-three years, whereas her male cousins, like many male children in all branches of the family, died before they reached maturity. Shakespeare's mother died in her late sixties, his wife at sixty-seven, and his stepgrandmother, Agnes Arden, his sister Joan, and his daughter Judith all at seventy-seven.

This longevity is not atypical for the period, given the fact that in spite of the number of children these women had, none seems to have died in childbirth (Laslett 1984, 108–10; Thompson 1974, 33–35). Shakespeare's mother, one of eight children, herself had eight children, one every two or three years from 1558 to 1580. Shakespeare had at least twelve cousins. His Aunt Margaret had six children, and her son, Robert Webbe, the cousin who gradually acquired Mary Shakespeare's inherited property, had seven. Judith's husband Thomas Quiney was one of ten children. Shakespeare's sister Judith, his only married sibling, had four. Shakespeare, of course, had three children: Hamnet died young, Judith's three sons died without heirs, and Susannah's only child, her daughter Elizabeth, though twice married, had no children. The number of children surviving infancy in earlier generations is somewhat greater than the norm for the period, which seems to have been about four (Laslett 1984, 116), and much greater than the norm in the plays, which is about two.

The Stratford environment is rich in women with children and women without—or between—men. But the plays are replete with men without wives, children without mothers, and single men. In them there are few older women: there are almost no grandmothers, not many mothers, and only a handful of widows and aunts. Women rarely have more than one child and almost never outlive their husbands, although husbands often outlive their wives. There are fathers without wives present in *The Taming of the Shrew, The Two Gentlemen of Verona, Love's Labors Lost, A Midsummer Night's Dream, The Merchant of Venice, Much Ado About Nothing, As You Like It, Henry IV, Othello, King Lear, Cymbeline,* and *The Tempest;* and the mothers in *Comedy of Errors, Pericles,* and *The Winter's Tale* are absent—apparently dead—for most of the action of the plays. There are, however, a few exceptional older women, mostly widows with children: the powerful chorus of women in *Richard III,* the countess in *All's Well,* Volumnia (a mother and grandmother) in *Coriolanus,* Cymbeline's queen in their second marriage, Paulina in *The Winter's Tale,* and Mistress Quickly in *The Merry Wives of Windsor.* In this play Mistress Quickly—widowed, and attached to men only as Caius's housekeeper—is more central, powerful, and sympathetically represented than in the Henry IV plays, where, also widowed, she runs a tavern and hopes to marry Falstaff, although she is exploited by him.

The pattern of marriages and the nature of women's participation in marriage is also quite different in the documentary records and in the plays. Mercantile marriages in Stratford (and in London), like Shakespeare's own marriage, had three salient features: (1) middle-class couples seem usually to have taken the initiative in entering into matches, which parents subsequently acceded in; (2) licenses seem often to have been needed to comply with the complicated restrictions of ecclesiastical courts or secular authorities; (3) marriage ages varied considerably, although marriage at a late age was the norm. Agnes Hill, a widow with four children, paid five shillings to secure a license from Basall Manor to marry Robert Arden, a widower with eight children and also a manor copyholder (Chambers 1930, 31; Eccles 1961, 16). Judith Shakespeare and Thomas Quiney (married February 10, 1616) were required to get a license from the Bishop of Worcester in order to be married during the prohibited Lenten period from January 28 to April 7. Because they failed to do so, Quiney was ordered to appear in court; when he did not appear, he was excommunicated. Although Judith may also have been excommunicated, their first child, who was given the name Shakespeare, was christened November 23, 1616, ten months later (and eight months after William Shakespeare died). More famously, William Shakespeare was required to get a license to waive the asking of the banns three times so he could marry Anne Hathaway before a long prohibited period. Since, depending on the church calendar for the year, it was often true that much of the period between November and April was prohibited, and since many marriages were performed during those months, obtaining licenses perhaps was a nuisance rather than the scandal Shakespeare's biographers like to imagine. William and Anne would seem to have entered into marriage at their own initiative, as apparently did Shakespeare's mother, whose mother and father were both dead when she married; Anne Hathaway's mother and father were also dead when she married, and Shakespeare's daughters seem to have initiated their own matches.

The obtaining of a license, Anne's pregnancy, and her age (twenty-six, eight years older than Shakespeare) seem, in the context of custom, demographic statistics, and the Stratford documentary records, typical for the period. (See Peter Laslett [1984, 82, 112, 161] on mean marriage ages and Keith Wrightson [1982, 66–88], who notes that "it is clear that bridal pregnancy was widely tolerated" [80].) The dismay long voiced by moralizing or sexist scholars and biographers at the irregularities of the match seems partly the result of the wish to impose on Shakespeare's life the idealized or prescriptive pattern made familiar by his representations in the plays. Although marriage ages for women seem to have varied considerably in Stratford, they tended to be late rather than early—quite comparable to Laslett's statistics from different sets of parishes on mean marriage ages for women in this period: 23½, 24, and 25 (Laslett 1984, 82, 112, 161). Mary Arden was probably between eighteen and twenty-one when she married John Shakespeare, who was a few years older. Shakespeare's sister Joan's first child, named William, was born in 1600, when she was thirty. Given what appears to have been her normal fertility (her subsequent children were born in 1603, 1605, and 1608) and the normal pattern for Stratford families, whereby the first child of a fertile woman was born within a year or two after marriage, Joan was probably close to thirty when she married. Susannah, 25, married John Hall, 32, and Judith, 31, married Thomas Quiney, 26. Elizabeth Hall, 18, married Thomas Nash, who was fifteen years older than she. The only example of marriage at a young age comparable to those ages specified in a few of the plays is, predictably, aristocratic: Thomas Lucy at 14 married a bride of 13. In the context of this variety of marriage ages it seems worse than misleading to characterize Anne Hathaway at 26 (as Schoenbaum does) as "by the standards of those days, growing a bit long in the tooth for the marriage market" (Schoenbaum 1977, 82).

There is no evidence about Shakespeare's participation in the marriages of his daughters. However, his depositions and those of others in the Belott-Mountjoy suit not only show his involvement in marriage negotiations but also provide detailed documentation of what would seem to be representative proceedings leading to middle-class marriage. Shakespeare was living in London in the house of Christopher Mountjoy, a French Huguenot and a maker of ladies' headdresses, during the period that preceded the 1604 marriage of Mountjoy's only child, Mary, to his former apprentice, Stephen Belott. In 1612 Belott sued Mountjoy for the dowry, or portion, he claimed to have been promised in connection with the marriage; the depositions in the case (included in Chambers 1930) delineate the process leading to marriage. A "shewe of goodwill betweene the plaintiff [Belott] and defendantes daughter Marye, which the defendantes wyffe did geue countenaunce unto and thinke well of" (90), was the catalyst to the match. Mountjoy and his wife then sent Shakespeare to Belott: "The said deffendantes wyeffe did sollicitt and entreat [Shakespeare] to move and perswade [Belott] to effect the said marriadge" (92). At some point Belott sent his representative, Daniell Nicholas, "to goe with his wyffe to Shakespe⟨are⟩" (91) to find out what Mountjoy would promise as a marriage portion. (The amount promised was never paid and was the issue of the trial and the subject of Shakespeare's depositions.) Nicholas testified that Shakespeare claimed Mountjoy would pay "about the some of ffyftye poundes in money and certayne houshould stuffe" (91) and that Shakespeare had witnessed the couples' betrothal: "In regard Mr. Shakespeare hadd tould them that they should haue a some of monney for a porcion from the father, they weare made suer by Mr. Shakespeare by geuinge there consent, and *agreed to marrye,* ~~geuinge eache others hand to the hande~~ and did marrye" (93).

The negotiations leading to the marriage seem conventional although the supposedly promised portion of fifty pounds seems high; it was reduced by the court to the conventional portion of £16 13s. 4d. (twenty nobles, or ten marks), but Mountjoy never paid that either. This same sum, the conventional portion, was bequeathed to Anne Hathaway by her father to be paid on her wedding day (Stopes 1901, 62) and was left by Robert Webbe to his daughters to be paid at age twenty-one, although Webbe's father, Alexander, left his daughters only five marks to be paid at age eighteen (Fripp 1929, 98, 95). Shakespeare, having risen above his contemporaries in the family, paid Judith £100 at marriage, £50 more on the condition that she give up her claims to property that was to go to Susannah, and another £150 of which she was to have the interest for three years, after which it would pass to her, to her living heirs, or to her husband on condition that he settled land on her equal in value to the money.

In contrast to this substantial dowry are the wildly exaggerated ones of some middle-class daughters in the plays—Anne Page's £700 inheritance from her grandfather and additional "possibilities" (*The Merry Wives of Windsor*, 1.1.64) of a generous dowry from her father and Kate's dowry of twenty thousand crowns or £5,000. The heavy traffic in suitors in Padua and Windsor is not surprising! In other respects, too, marriage is a very different matter in the plays, although tensions surrounding it and conflicting stakes in it are still present. In the plays marriages are accomplished not by prolonged negotiations but by a father's fiat or by children's elopements. Mothers rarely participate even when they are present, as they are in *Romeo and Juliet* and *All's Well That Ends Well*; an exception is Mistress Page's attempt to determine her daughter's marriage partner in *The Merry Wives of Windsor*. Legal technicalities are minimized, except in *The Merchant of Venice* and *Measure for Measure*, and even there neither the father's will nor the "true contract" (*Measure for Measure*, 1.2.145) turns out to be the most important legal question. The plays often represent marriage as a clean break, a decisive separation of children from parents and a decisive resolution of generational conflict; they subordinate marriage's function of providing the institutionalized transfer of title, line, property, and money through generations.

Because such transfer is an issue in Stratford and because the women in the family are numerous and long-lived, these women, though technically rendered by marriage *femmes couvertes* who are controlled by the law, also exercise power through it. They are parties to property litigation and are central to wills as legatees, executrices, devisors, or claimants. When Robert Arden made his will in 1550, he bequeathed the largest share of his property (valued at £77 11s. 10d.) to his unmarried daughters, especially to Mary, the youngest, who received "all my lande in Willmecote cawlide Asbyes and the crop apone the grounde sowne and tyllide as hitt is" (Eccles 1961, 17), and ten marks (the conventional Stratford dowry). The rest he divided among his seven other daughters. Agnes, his second wife, was left £6 13s. 4d. or ten marks "upon this condysion that she shall sofer my dowghter Ales quyetly to ynjoye half my copyhold in Wyllincote during the tyme of her wyddewoode; and if she will nott soffer my dowghter Ales quyetly to occupy half with her, then I will that my wife shall have but £3 6s. 7d. and her gintur [jointure] in Snytterfelde" (Stopes 1901, 38). When Agnes Arden made her will in 1578, she, just like her husband, left her goods and property to her children by her first marriage (to her son and son-in-law in trust for her grandchildren). In 1580, when a challenge was made to her grandnephew's claim to the Arden property, she testified on his behalf—at home, because she was too "aged and impotent" to travel to London to do so (Eccles 1961, 18).

Margaret Webbe, Agnes's brother's wife (and also her stepdaughter), was executrix and residuary legatee of her husband's will, in which Robert Webbe required her "to see my children vertusly brought up" (Eccles 1961, 21). In contrast (and infamously) Shakespeare, in his will, leaves no general bequest to his wife but leaves his property to Susannah, their older daughter, nine years married and with a child, and his money to Judith, just married and childless; both property and portion are stipulated to devolve on male heirs, the property to pass after Susannah's death "to the first sonne of her bodie lawefullie yssueing & to the heires Males of the bodie of the saied first Sonne lawefullie yssueing," and so on through the sons of the seventh son, or, lacking male issue, to Elizabeth Hall, Shakespeare's granddaughter, and her male heirs (Chambers 1930, 173). Although there were no surviving male children, Susannah and her daughter Elizabeth successfully fought to keep the Shakespeare property, which mother settled on daughter in 1639. Thomas Nash, Elizabeth's first husband, treated Elizabeth's property as his own in his will, which bequeathed all of it, including New Place, to his kinsmen, Edward Nash and his son, Thomas. When he died, Susannah and Elizabeth, executrix and residuary legatee, refused to follow the provisions of the will and reconveyed the property for their own use and that of future heirs (Chambers 1930, 179–80; Stopes 1901, 101–3). They won, perhaps by an out-of-court settlement, a lawsuit brought by Edward Nash to get the will enacted as written. Elizabeth apparently argued the case herself in Chancery, refusing to produce some papers as ordered. "She was brave in her determination that her own rights and her mother's should not be assailed, and she was perhaps prudent in her opinion that the fewer papers that were produced, the shorter time the suit would last," says Stopes (1901, 103). When Elizabeth died childless after the death of her second husband, her will directed her trustees to sell New Place, stipulating that "my loving cousin, Edward Nash, Esq., shall have the first offer or refusal thereof, according to *my promise formerly made to him*" (Stopes 1901, 103).

Although the aristocratic women in the plays have potential access to far more money and property than the women in Stratford do, their connections with it are de-emphasized. It merely passes through them from their fathers to their husbands. Some are disinherited; others lose property by marriage or their own generosity. Desdemona and Cordelia are disinherited. Portia at her betrothal gratuitously gives up all her inheritance to Bassanio. When the "potent dukedom" (5.4.169) is restored to the Duke senior at the end of *As You Like It,* he immediately bequeathes it to his son-in-law, Orlando, erasing Celia's fantasy that she would make Rosalind her heir (1.2.19). Even aggressive, strong-willed Regan in *King Lear,* a powerful widow who has just won a battle to protect her inheritance, extravagantly grants it all to her lover, Edmund:

> General,
> Take thou my soldiers, prisoners, patrimony;
> Dispose of them, of me; the walls is thine.
> Witness the world, that I create thee here
> My lord and master.
>
> (5.3.74–78)

We do not know if Isabella in *Measure for Measure* is moved by the Duke's offer of shared possessions: "What's mine is yours, and what is yours is mine" (5.1.537). Only Jessica in *The Merchant of Venice* looks out for her own economic interests, stealing Shylock's ducats as a kind of dowry and spending them on herself. The women in the plays never have even the minimal amount of power in connection with property and the law that women in Stratford had. Since the men in the plays have considerably more political, economic, and legal power than the men in Stratford had—absolute power to exchange money, goods, lands, and women—the relative power of the women in the plays is further circumscribed. This may be because of their aristocratic status, which makes their property more valuable than that of the women in Stratford.

Finally, neither the women in Stratford nor the women in the plays are found to engage in the cultural and religious activities that seem to have allowed self-expression and enhanced status to some women in the period. We do not see Shakespeare's women being genuinely educated or educating children like some of their aristocratic counterparts. Bianca's abortive lute and Latin lessons in *The Taming of the Shrew* and Katherine's bawdy English lesson in *Henry V* might almost be read as parodies of the decorative function of education for Renaissance women. With the notable exception of Isabella in *Measure for Measure* and Katherine in *Henry VIII*, we do not see female characters translating texts, committing themselves to religious beliefs, or taking part in charitable activities. I have not found evidence of Stratford women educating others or furthering religion, either, except as godparents or in bequests to the poor in their wills; but they may have done so.

Likewise we have no evidence that Stratford women exercised control over their households, as the prescriptive literature requires women to do; some must have done so during long widowhoods or if, as was the case for both Anne Shakespeare and Susannah Hall, their husbands were away most of the time. (John Hall was an eminent physician who traveled widely.) In the plays men often make household arrangements, as do Baptista, Leonardo, and Prospero. Even in *Romeo and Juliet*, with his wife present, Juliet's father both negotiates the marriage and oversees the details of the wedding preparations. Almost the only job for women in Shakespeare's plays is the oldest profession: Mistress Quickly, Mistress Overdone, and the Bawd in *Pericles* are bawds, and Doll Tearsheet and Kate Keepdown are prostitutes. Mistress Quickly also runs a tavern (as did Judith Shakespeare's mother-in-law). There are some exceptions: Olivia and the Countess in *All's Well That Ends Well* are nominally in charge of households; Mistress Quickly is a housekeeper in *The Merry Wives of Windsor*, and the wives control their households, as they control everything else in that play.

There is, however, one cultural resource the women in the plays have that is not, for the most part, available to the Stratford women: literacy. Susannah could sign her name, and Judith signed with a mark, as did John Shakespeare. Whether any of them could read or write is uncertain, but it seems unlikely that the daughters could (Schoenbaum 1977, 295, 321). Cressy (1980) says that "women were almost universally unable to write their own names for most of the sixteenth and seventeenth centuries" (145) and puts female literacy at under 10 percent (119–21, 128, 144–49). Perhaps Shakespeare's granddaughter Elizabeth Hall, who may have argued her case in Chancery, could read and write.

Virtually all of the women in the plays, however, can read and write. It is amazing, in fact, how many of them onstage read poems or letters, write them, or are recipients of them; an incomplete list includes Julia in *Two Gentlemen of Verona,* Bianca, the women in *Love's Labors Lost,* Portia, Beatrice, Rosalind, Viola, Ophelia, the wives in *The Merry Wives of Windsor,* Helena, Cordelia, Lady Macbeth, and Volumnia. Such literacy is, of course, effective dramatically; even the clown in *The Winter's Tale* can read his shopping list. The literacy, learning, and verbal power of the women in the plays is the result of their existence in a verbal medium. But perhaps this power, extraordinary for Renaissance women, is part of the reason why these representations of women constrain them in other ways. Silence was the virtue most often and most stringently required of Renaissance women, and women's verbal self-assertion was almost invariably associated with sexual self-assertion and promiscuity (Jardine 1983, chap. 4). Hence the chastity of the highly literate and verbal women in the plays may require especially stringent protection and extravagant affirmation.

For whatever reason, the women in Stratford are the object of less rigid prescriptions regarding their sexuality than are the women in the plays. Although vulnerable, they can frequently defend themselves against slander. Shakespeare's wife Anne was pregnant when she married. His married daughter, Susannah Hall, it was reported rather bawdily by one John Lane, Jr., "had the running of the reins [i.e., venereal disease] and had been naught with Rafe Smith at John Palmer" (Schoenbaum 1977, 289); she sued Lane for slander, and when he did not appear in court, he was excommunicated. Thomas Quiney confessed to getting Margaret Wheeler with child (the incident occurred before his marriage to Judith Shakespeare, the trial for it six weeks after); his penance to wear a white sheet in front of the church was remitted, and he was only fined five shillings. He may have drawn this mild conventional punishment because mother and child died in childbirth, sparing the community economic responsibility for the illegitimate child. These irregularities are comparable to those G. R. Quaife chronicles among peasants in Somerset in the early seventeenth century, and they do not seem to have resulted in ostracism by the family or the community. In the plays such incidents occur only among lower-class characters, such as Jaquenetta or Kate Keepdown. When Juliet, in *Measure for Measure,* dowerless and without family, is pregnant with an illegitimate child, the play does not concern itself, as the period would have done, with the welfare of the child, either as an

economic or an emotional issue; the pregnancy exists only to dramatize the illicit sexuality of the parents.

In the plays female sexuality is not expressed variously through
courtship, pregnancy, childbearing, and remarriage, as it is in the period. Instead it is narrowly defined and contained by the conventions
of Petrarchan love and cuckoldry. The first idealizes women as a catalyst to male virtue, insisting on their absolute purity. The second fears
and mistrusts them for their (usually fantasized) infidelity, an infidelity
that requires their actual or temporary elimination from the world of
men, which then re-forms itself around the certainty of men's shared
victimization. Both ideologies suppress female sexuality and subordinate women to male bonds and male fantasies (Neely 1985, 5–7). The
contingencies of everyday life in Stratford clearly did not require or
permit this degree of control.

After women's deaths, when their control is no longer an issue,
idealization of them flourishes. Good deaths were an appropriate,
acceptable, and achievable ideal for women in the period and a subject for idealized representation in the plays. It is, therefore, after
death, in memorials for them, that the women in Stratford and those
in the plays draw closest together, and the period's conventional
gender polarization becomes most explicit. Shakespeare ends his life
in Stratford as he lived it, surrounded by family—by women. To the
left of his grave is that of Anne, "Wife of William Shakespeare." Her
Latin epitaph, apparently commissioned by her daughters, reads (in
translation):

> Thou, my mother, gave me life, thy breast and milk; alas! for such great
> bounty to me I shall give thee a tomb. How much rather I would entreat
> the good angel to move the stone, so that thy figure might come forth, as
> did the body of Christ; but my prayers avail nothing. Come quickly, O
> Christ; so that my mother, closed in the tomb, may rise again and seek
> the stars.
>
> (Stopes 1901, 90)

To the right of Shakespeare's grave is that of his daughter, Susannah,
"Wife to John Hall, Gent: Ye daughter of William Shakespeare,
Gent." Her epitaph reads:

> Witty above her sexe, but that's not all,
> Wise to salvation was good Mistris Hall,
> Something of Shakespeare was in that, but this
> Wholy of him with whom she's now in blisse.

> Then, Passenger, hast nere a teare,
> To weepe with her that wept with all;
> That wept, yet set her self to chere
> Them up with comforts cordiall.
> Her love shall live, her mercy spread,
> When thou has't ner'e a teare to shed.
> (recut from copy in Dugdale's *Warwickshire*,
> quoted in Chambers 1930, 12)

The epitaphs of Anne and Susannah are similar in that each places the dead woman in a conventional female role and praises her nurturing capacities. Anne is remembered as a mother giving birth to children and nursing them, Susannah as a daughter who has her father's wit and, more important, is compassionate and merciful. (Interestingly, neither is identified as a wife in the epitaph proper, perhaps because their husbands died before them. John Hall's epitaph remembers him both for his healing skill and his faithful wife [Chambers 1930, 11].) Anne's generative capacity makes her analogous to Christ, who came forth resurrected from his tomb and is asked likewise to bring Anne forth from her tomb that she, having given life, "may rise again and seek the stars," gaining eternal life. Susannah, because she is her father's daughter and, like him, both "witty" and "wise to salvation," is now with him "in blisse." She too is represented as nurturing and Christ-like; she is characterized by her compassionate tears, "comforts cordiall," mercy, and love. One cannot fail to be reminded of Cordelia, Shakespeare's representation of a loving daughter whose father wishes to be "in bliss" with her (*King Lear*, 4.7.45).

In striking contrast to the epitaphs of the women are those on Shakespeare's grave and monument:

GOOD FREND FOR JESUS SAKE FORBEARE,
TO DIGG THE DUST ENCLOASED HEARE:
BLESTE BE Ỹ MAN Ỹ SPARES THES STONES,
AND CURST BE HE Ỹ MOVES MY BONES.

JUDICIO PYLIUM, GENIO SOCRATEM, ARTE MARONEM:
TERRA TEGIT, POPULUS MAERET, OLYMPUS HABET
STAY PASSENGER, WHY GOEST THOU BY SO FAST?
READ IF THOU CANST, WHOM ENVIOUS DEATH HATH PLAST,
WITH IN THIS MONUMENT SHAKSPEARE: WITH WHOME,
QUICK NATURE DIDE: WHOSE NAME DOTH DECK Ỹ TOMBE,

FAR MORE THEN COST: SIEH ALL, Y̌ HE HATH WRITT,
LEAVES LIVING ART, BUT PAGE, TO SERVE HIS WITT.
(Schoenbaum 1977, 306, 310)

Shakespeare, like Susannah, is remembered for his "witt," but it is specifically connected to his vocation, and he is not placed in family roles. Both his inscriptions are aggressive and imperative; their firm commands are directed not toward family and friends but toward anonymous future visitors who know the work, not Shakespeare the man, and are repositories of his fame. They remember "what he hath writt," and it is that that is transcendent; the man is dead (with whom "quick nature dide"). Jesus is invoked to insure the efficacy of the curse on the living, not to promise the salvation of the dead. The survival of the bones is secured by this curse, and the art, which overgoes "living art," assures its own survival. Neither nurturing nor "bliss" is an issue here.

Like the Stratford women, the women in the plays are eulogized after their deaths as exemplary models of female perfection. But the dramatic eulogies are somewhat different from those for Anne and Susannah. Whether the play is Christian or pre-Christian, tragedy or romance, laments for dead women focus on their irrevocably dead bodies, their capture by death or return to nature, rather than on any possibility of Christian resurrection or salvation. This is especially true of laments for the women in the tragedies: "Shall I believe / That unsubstantial Death is amorous, / And that the lean abhorred monster keeps / Thee here in dark to be his paramour?" (*Romeo and Juliet*, 5.3.102–5); "And from her fair and unpolluted flesh / May violets spring!" (*Hamlet*, 5.1.239–40); "When I have pluck'd thy rose, / I cannot give it vital growth again, / It needs must wither" (*Othello*, 5.2.13–15); "She's dead as earth" (*King Lear*, 5.3.262). Even in the romances the more formal eulogies for the dead mothers, Thaisa and Euriphile, emphasize their incorporation into nature rather than their bliss in heaven. In *Pericles* Thaisa is cast into the sea, "Where, for a monument upon thy bones, / The [e'er-]remaining lamps, the belching whale / And humming water must o'erwhelm thy corpse, / Lying with simple shells" (3.1.61–64). In *Cymbeline* Euriphile is likewise returned to nature: "All lovers young, all lovers must / Consign to thee and come to dust. . . . Quiet consummation have, / And renowned be thy grave" (4.2.274–75, 280–81). The inscription on Marina's pseudomonument in *Pericles* depicts her as "withered in her spring of year," seized by the earth: "Therefore the earth, fearing to be o'er flowed, / Hath Thetis' birth-child on the heavens bestowed" (4.4.35, 40–41). In *Much Ado About Nothing* Claudio's somewhat pat eulogy for Hero does claim, "So the life that died with shame / Lives in death with glorious fame" (5.3.7–8), but it makes no mention of her salvation. The women in the plays for the most part are not defined in life or in death according to the religious contexts that were operative—at least according to their epitaphs—for the women of Shakespeare's family. But in the plays, as in the period, women are defined in opposition to men. The male protagonists are remembered after death for their fame (or infamy) and are promised its continuation, as was Shakespeare. The women are eulogized for their beauty and their bodies and are absorbed into nature; Ophelia is only the most extreme example of this motif.

The contrast with the women in Stratford reveals how much more the women in the plays are confined by prescriptions than are those in Stratford; in the plays women's family roles, sexual purity, and ultimate submission to men are imperative. The women who are the least confined and have the most power are represented apart from sexual roles. They achieve freedom when they have, at least temporarily, a space and a source of nurture outside the marriage paradigm, when their bonds to family, especially to fathers and husbands, are severed (when they are fatherless maids or widows), and when they act in conjunction with other women, supporting or being supported by them—that is, when they are masterless women. Such women may have been created out of memories of the sorts of women Shakespeare had been surrounded by when he was growing up. Under these conditions female characters have a greater than usual freedom to talk, to influence others, to act, and to express their sexuality; they do so in ways traditionally associated with deviant or marginal women—through male disguises, shrewishness, sexual aggressiveness, and madness.

Margaret, in *Richard III,* whose husband and children are dead, is "neither mother, wife, nor England's queen" (1.3.208), but her curses have the power to terrify, to prophecy, and to console other displaced women. Rosalind, in *As You Like It,* is enabled by her father's exile, her friendship with Celia, and her male disguise to manipulate her lover and others. Ophelia, in *Hamlet,* is a docile daughter, who by her father's death and Hamlet's and Laertes's absence is freed for the madness that allows her to express her passions and influence others. Helena, in *All's Well That Ends Well,* an orphan and the ward of a woman, cures her king and arranges her marriage and its consummation. Cleopatra, existing outside the marriage paradigm, dies into nature and for love, but she does so in order to achieve transcendent expression of her desires and to triumph over Caesar. Paulina, in *The Winter's Tale,* whose husband is dead and who has been divested of her children, preserves Hermione and engineers Leontes's repentance. At the climax of this catalogue is Volumnia, in *Coriolanus,* a widow and a mother, who embodies the rigid militaristic values Shakespeare most satirizes in men and the emotional power he most fears in women. All of these women are deviant; all are seen, or see themselves, as witches, shrews, madwomen, wayward wives, or whores. They are not merely cautionary or satiric stereotypes (Jardine 1983, chap. 3), but also anxiety-charged figures and sympathetic portrayals. Always their power is contained at the end of the play—by marriage, by madness, or by death.

The play in which women's power is not contained and in which their status is most similar to that of the Stratford women that emerges from the documentary records is also the only Shakespeare play set in contemporary England, Shakespeare's one attempt at citizen comedy. The play's title, *The Merry Wives of Windsor,* telegraphs the double anomaly. The play seems to hit home in a number of ways. The protagonists are married women whose sexuality and power are at issue; but male constructions of the women's sexuality are challenged, and the wives' considerable power is not eroded. The play is set in Windsor, a thriving bourgeois town like Stratford, and the detailed local reference, which gives the setting dramatic substance, is reminiscent of the Stratford records—petty rivalry and litigation, class conflict and mobility, lineage and coats of arms, marriage and dowries. The play is unique in a third way too: it signals its fictional status and place in the Shakespeare canon by its inclusion of characters from another Shakespeare play—characters both the same as and different from what they are in the Henry plays—as if to register their transition from history to comedy.

Furthermore, the title page of the 1602 Quarto claims that the play had been acted before the queen, and it comes down to us accompanied by a perhaps apocryphal but nonetheless telling story about the circumstances of its genesis. The queen, Nicolas Rowe relates in his 1709 biography, wished Shakespeare to "shew" Falstaff "in Love," and John Dennis claims in his 1709 dedication to *The Comical Gallant* that "this Comedy was written at her Command, and by her direction, and she was so eager to see it Acted, that she commanded it to be finished in fourteen days; and was afterwards, as Tradition tells us, very well pleas'd at the Representation" (quoted in Oliver 1978, xliv–xlv). "Tradition," then, records or invents gender and social relations of the play's production that are unique in the canon and that resonate with the play's self-consciousness about female power, social class, and genre. The play brings into focus precisely those areas in which there are discontinuities between the drama and the Stratford milieu, juxtaposing London and Windsor, aristocrats and the middle class, male fantasies of women and women's stability and constancy, Falstaff the witty rebel, expelled from the King's presence and from the court in *2 Henry IV,* and Falstaff the smug courtier, expelled from Windsor and comedy in *The Merry Wives of Windsor.*

The Merry Wives is unique among the comedies in having as protagonists married women whose marriages, motherhood, and sexuality are the center of the play. In Windsor (as in Stratford) the women defend themselves wittily, successfully, and to applause against those who would exploit or misrepresent their sexuality—against Falstaff's predatory seduction attempts, Ford's fantasies of cuckoldry, and Caius's and Slender's designs on Anne Page. Like the Stratford women, they conceive of the law as a means of self-defense: "Why, I'll exhibit a bill in the parliament for the putting down of men" (2.1.28–30) is Mistress Page's reaction to Falstaff's propositioning letter. But they need no help from Parliament. Mistress Quickly, exaggerating for the sake of duping Falstaff, affirms Mistress Page's strong-willed independence: "Do what she will, say what she will, take all, pay all, go to bed when she list, rise when she list, all is as she will" (2.2.117–20). In fact the women—the wives, Mistress Quickly, and Anne Page—control all the action of the play, but not as queens, not in male disguise, and not temporarily as a matter of holiday release. The older women's schemes are thwarted only by the daughter, who has the last word about her marriage, a triple reversal in a world where men supposedly had authority over women, parents over children, and the old over the young. In order to get their way, the women mock, manipulate, and deceive their husbands as well as Falstaff and are neither condemned, punished, nor constrained. At the conclusion of the play Ford has to beg his wife's pardon, which he receives, and Falstaff admits he has been "made an ass" (5.5.119). The final couplet of the play affirms Mistress Ford's sexuality: "Sir John, / To Master [Brooke] you yet shall hold your word, / For he to-night shall lie with Mistress Ford."

As the women defend themselves, likewise Windsor defends itself, or is defended by Shakespeare, against the incursions of outsiders from court who would disrupt it or exploit its sexual or financial resources. Falstaff himself compares his attempt at illegitimate sexual and economic exploitation to colonial exploitation: "She is a region in Guiana, all gold and bounty. I will be cheaters to them both, and they shall be exchequers to me. They shall be my East and West Indies, and I will trade to them both" (1.3.69–72). His efforts are thwarted, while the suit of Fenton, an equally impoverished aristocrat, is legitimated by sexual compatibility and love and by his renunciation of Anne "as a property" to love her for "the very riches of thyself" (3.4.10, 17). Falstaff is mocked out of Windsor, and Fenton is incorporated into it, while Windsor remains unchanged.

The class, economic, and sexual motives that impinge on the potential marriage of Anne Page are characteristic of those that influenced marriages during the period when marriage was the surest route to class or economic improvement. The achieved marriage of Fenton and Anne is characteristic of those in Shakespearean comedy in allowing sexual and romantic compatibility to override class difference (though not without the parents registering these differences). Its rightness—its combination of sexual aptness and financial usefulness—is emphasized by its antitheses, the two parody marriages of the unsuccessful suitors. Slender, though a secure and well-off Windsor insider, does not love Anne and needs confirmation of his manhood (which is perhaps why Mr. Page supports his suit); he ironically fails to achieve this when he finds himself married to a "great lubberly boy" (5.5.184). Caius, though a doctor, is a Frenchman with an accent, who still seems something of an outsider and seeks through marriage full legitimacy among the Windsor bourgeoisie; he finds himself married into the wrong gender *and* the wrong class to "oon garsoon, a boy; oon pesant, by gar" (5.5.205–6). But for him, it seems, another avenue of advancement may be found at court, where he will go for "*la grande affaire*" (1.4.52).

The play, however, delivers a mixed message about the court.

Falstaff debases its values and misuses its resources, as when, for example, he quotes a line from a song from *Astrophil and Stella,* "Have I caught thee, my heavenly jewel?" (3.3.43), to seduce Mistress Ford. But the laudatory references to the accoutrements of the Garter installation at Windsor castle idealize the court's values. This play, in which anxieties about women are in abeyance, in which Windsor townspeople are more vital and secure than the aristocrats, and in which incursions into court by Windsor citizens are more benign than those by courtiers into Windsor, perhaps projects Shakespeare's ambivalence about his relations with Stratford and London and his awareness of the distance between them. Shakespeare, once an insider in Stratford who had to get out, becomes an outsider in London who is still in the process of getting in. To do so he has to curry favor from women, from patrons, from audiences, and from Elizabeth. This seeking for favor is also a form of exploitation. If the "effect of verisimilitude" (Maclean 1982, 504) of the Sonnets bears some relation to the truth, Shakespeare's assimilation into London demanded a complex mixture of social, sexual, artistic, and financial self-assertion and self-debasement. If Falstaff in *1 Henry IV* represents Shakespeare the artist's chameleon-like power and mobility, perhaps the Falstaff of *The Merry Wives of Windsor*—dumped into the river with the dirty laundry for his pretensions to aristocratic glamour, dressed as a woman and beaten for his pretense of potency, and pinched by fairies for his exploitation of love and lust—parodies the humiliating price Shakespeare might have to pay for his artistic, economic, social, and sexual success and represents the potential for humiliating failure always implicit in that success.

Male Bonding
and the Myth of Women's Deception
in Shakespeare's Plays

Shirley Nelson Garner

The problem of trust recurs in Shakespeare's works, from his earliest to his latest. Nowhere does he present it more prominently or explicitly than in his plays that deal with the actual or supposed infidelity of women: *Much Ado About Nothing, Troilus and Cressida, Othello, Cymbeline* and *The Winter's Tale.* In only one of these plays, *Troilus and Cressida,* is the woman unfaithful. In the others she is innocent—appallingly virtuous, in fact. Nevertheless, her husband or lover, believing her guilty, may revile her, abuse her physically or psychologically, plot her death, or even murder her. Like a recurrent dream, this repeated drama follows certain patterns, which, I believe, define and satisfy male psychic needs—Shakespeare's, his male characters', or those of both.

The pattern in the four plays has a number of similar features. First, the husband's or fiancé's suspicion and jealousy are aroused very quickly by the merest suggestion, the slightest evidence, or—in the case of Leontes—no suggestion or evidence at all. Second, believing his beloved is unfaithful, the husband or fiancé expresses his pain only through anger. Third, he immediately envisions himself as a member of a community of cuckolds; he schemes to entrap his beloved, to take vengeance on her, or to do both. Fourth, he does not confront her directly until he is convinced of her infidelity; instead, he rages at her, and plots against or humiliates her. Fifth, the wife or betrothed is unquestionably innocent of infidelity; in fact, she is extraordinarily virtuous. Ironically, it is the man who begins to deceive in one form or another—to lie, plot, or spy. Sixth, the woman must die: Othello murders Desdemona; Hero and Hermione faint and are supposed dead; Posthumus believes Pisanio has murdered Imogen at his request. Seventh, after the innocent woman is mortally wounded or is thought dead, the man repents his mistake and professes his love for her; in short, he kills her, then loves her afterward. Eighth, the woman forgives him.

Some critics have found unconvincing the husband's or fiancé's sudden and extreme jealousy and his propensity to suspect or to believe slander of a woman he and others have known to be uncommonly virtuous. Others have accounted for these traits by arguing that to love completely means to become vulnerable to doubt, by acknowledging the male character's particular susceptibilities, or by contending that dramatic action must be telescoped since a play unfolds in a brief period of time. Shakespeare, however, portrayed all four men as rushing to suspect their beloveds. I think we should take their sudden and irrational suspicion and jealousy as an indication of character. It suggests that at some level of their being, all four figures *need* the women who love them to betray them.

As Shakespeare repeats this drama, he makes this need clearer and starker. In *Much Ado About Nothing* and *Othello* villains awaken Claudio's and Othello's inclination to distrust. *Much Ado* provides evidence for Claudio's suspicion; it is the one play of the four in which the infidelity is "witnessed." Others besides Claudio are persuaded of Hero's guilt. Don Pedro sees and believes, and Leonato, Hero's father, believes because men he honors testify against his daughter:

> Would the two princes lie, and Claudio lie,
> Who lov'd her so, that speaking of her foulness,
> Wash'd it with tears?
>
> (4.1.152–54)

In *Othello* Iago is always there to pique Othello's jealousy and suspicion when it begins to weaken, and he knows how to play on all of Othello's vulnerabilities. The handkerchief is flimsier proof than that presented to Claudio in *Much Ado;* nevertheless, to anyone inclined to doubt, it might serve. Since Desdemona lies in saying that she has not lost it, she strengthens the grounds for Othello's suspicion.

Though there is a villain in *Cymbeline* to provoke Posthumus, his boast of Imogen's virtue when he speaks of her to Jachimo seems deliberately framed to invite challenge. (We also learn that Posthumus has previously bragged about Imogen's virtue to other men as he competed with them in a boasting match, the ultimate aim of which seems to be to solidify men's bonds with each other [1.4.54–61].) He will not hear Philario's attempts to discourage the wager and even gives Jachimo a letter of introduction to Imogen. Failing to consider that a man with half of his estate to lose might be more likely to lie than to tell the truth, Posthumus immediately credits Jachimo's evidence despite Philario's cautions that it may not be credible.

By the time Shakespeare wrote *The Winter's Tale,* he apparently wished to portray Leontes's need to be betrayed even more nakedly than Posthumus's. The play has no villain; Leontes's suspicions arise purely out of his own dark imaginings. There is no staged act of infidelity as in *Much Ado;* no sign like the handkerchief in *Othello.* None share Leontes's vision. Camillo asserts himself strongly against it:

> 'Shrew my heart,
> You never spoke what did become you less
> Than this; which to reiterate were sin
> As deep as that, though true.
>
> (1.2.281–84)

Hermione argues eloquently on her own behalf, and even the Delphic Oracle exonerates the queen.

The determination of Shakespeare's male characters to believe that women betray them further affirms their need for betrayal. When a moment comes that the men might realize that the contrary is true and the women they suspect are faithful, they insist on their falseness. After Othello at last tells Desdemona that he suspects her of committing adultery, she assures her husband that she "never lov'd Cassio / But with such general warranty of heaven" as she might love and that she did not give him the handkerchief (5.2.59–61). Responding to Othello's angry insistence that he saw his handkerchief in Cassio's hand, Desdemona asks him to call Cassio, who she knows will deny Othello's charge. At that point Othello lies: "He hath confess'd. . . . / That he hath us'd thee" (5.2.68–70).

As determined to believe in his own betrayal as Othello, Posthumus threatens Jachimo:

> If you will swear you have not done't, you lie,
> And I will kill thee if thou dost deny
> Thou'st made me cuckold.
>
> (*Cymbeline,* 2.4.144–46)

When Leontes hears that the Delphic Oracle, whose opinion he him-self has sought, finds Hermione innocent, he coldly proclaims:

> There is no truth at all i' th' oracle.
> The sessions shall proceed; this is mere falsehood.
> (*The Winter's Tale*, 3.2.140–41)

All of these male characters find it more threatening to accept the possibility of the faithfulness of their beloveds than the possibility of their unfaithfulness.

The male characters' certainty of betrayal allows them to unleash their pent-up misogyny and fear of women as they plot vengeance, revile their beloveds and women in general, and persecute and even murder or attempt to murder the innocent women who love them. Their distrust also allows them to break their bonds with those women and return either imaginatively or actually to an exclusively male community.

From the beginning Shakespeare makes the male characters' re-sponses to their beloveds' supposed unfaithfulness extremely cruel. In *Much Ado* even before Claudio has seen anything to make him distrust Hero, he plans her humiliation: "If I see any thing to-night why I should not marry her, to-morrow in the congregation, where I should wed, there will I shame her" (3.2.123–25). Beatrice defines the mean-ness of Claudio's actions: "What, bear her in hand until they come to take hands, and then with public accusation, uncover'd slander, un-mitigated rancor—"; she is too outraged to complete the sentence and can only imagine a fantastic punishment sufficient to repay his treach-ery: "O God, that I were a man! I would eat his heart in the market-place" (4.1.303–7).

Almost as soon as Othello suspects Desdemona of infidelity, he begins to imagine murdering her:

> If there be cords, or knives,
> Poison, or fire, or suffocating streams,
> I'll not endure it.
> (*Othello*, 3.3.388–90)

He later imagines chopping her "into messes" (4.1.200). He humili-ates her and abuses her physically and psychologically as he strikes her in public (4.1.240) and plays out the brothel scene (4.2.24–94) to confirm the fantasy he has come to believe. His murder of her is actually quieter than we have been led to expect.

Convinced of Imogen's supposed infidelity, Posthumus delivers his well-known diatribe against women:

> Could I find out
> The woman's part in me—for there's no motion
> That tends to vice in man, but I affirm
> It is the woman's part: be it lying, note it,
> The woman's; flattering, hers; deceiving, hers;
> Lust and rank thoughts, hers, hers; revenges, hers;
> Ambitions, covetings, change of prides, disdain,
> Nice longing, slanders, mutability,
> All faults that name, nay, that hell knows,
> Why, hers, in part or all; but rather, all.
> (*Cymbeline*, 2.5.19–28)

He then begins to plot Imogen's murder.

Suspecting Hermione, Leontes begins to denigrate women in general:

> There have been
> (Or I am much deceiv'd) cuckolds ere now,
> And many a man there is (even at this present,
> Now, while I speak this) holds his wife by th' arm,
> That little thinks she has been sluic'd in's absence,
> And his pond fish'd by his next neighbor—by
> Sir Smile, his neighbor.
> (*The Winter's Tale*, 1.2.190–96)

He accuses her of adultery suddenly and publicly when his accusations might most surprise and humiliate her. He takes her son from her, forces her to bear her child in prison, and sends her newborn daughter out to die. Finally, he forces her to stand trial in public before she has recovered from childbirth.

Their bonds with women must be frail indeed if all of these men distrust women so quickly, seem so determined to believe that they have been betrayed, and react with such extreme harshness. It is no accident that for most of them (all but Leontes) the moment of doubt occurs just before or just after their marriages. The woman's supposed fallenness allows them to reject her because there is something wrong with her. If they see her as good, they may have to consider that they simply do not love her or that they are afraid to love her. Madelon Sprengnether has observed that in Shakespeare's tragedies "the structures of male dominance . . . conceal deeper structures of fear, in which women are perceived as powerful and the heterosexual relation is seen as either mutually violent or at least deeply threatening to the *man."* She argues that throughout Shakespeare's plays "a woman's power . . . is less social or political . . . than emotional, expressed in her capacity to give or to withhold love" (Gohlke 1980b, 172–74).

Claudio, Othello, Cymbeline, and Leontes all have strong bonds with men before their marriages—or in Claudio's case, proposed marriage—and their beloveds' supposed infidelities allow them to reassert those bonds. The first we hear of Claudio is that Don Pedro has honored him for his brave deeds in battle (*Much Ado About Nothing,* 1.1.9–17) and that he is most often in the company of Benedick, an avowed woman-hater. As Benedick says, Claudio's music has always been "the drum and fife"; yet now it quite uncharacteristically becomes "the tabor and the pipe" (2.3.12–15). He allows Don Pedro to woo Hero for him and even proposes accompanying Don Pedro to Aragon immediately after his marriage (3.2.1–4). Hero's supposed betrayal would make it unnecessary for him to disrupt his bonds with men in the slightest way. In fact, her "betrayal" draws him closer to them as they conspire to catch Hero in the act of betrayal and to punish her for it. In her essay on *Much Ado* and the distrust of women, Janice Hays has suggested that "Claudio's allegiance is still invested in the sphere of male bonding and male achievement, perhaps as a defense against the anxieties occasioned by heterosexuality" (Hays 1980, 85).

In Othello's world men are even more exclusively and intensely bonded together as warriors. Desdemona is evidently the first woman Othello has ever considered marrying, for he tells Iago:

> But that I love the gentle Desdemona,
> I would not my unhoused free condition
> Put into circumscription and confine
> For the sea's worth.
> > (*Othello,* 1.2.25–28)

Almost as soon as he is married, he begins to suspect Desdemona and is cast into an intense relationship with Iago, a relationship that seems as passionate as, and more solemn than, the one he has with Desdemona (3.3.453–80).

Posthumus's public exploitation of Imogen's chastity, as I have already said, invites challenge. It reminds me of Hector's challenge to the Greeks in Shakespeare's *Troilus and Cressida,* which is spoken in terms of Hector's promise to "make it good" that he has "a lady, wiser, fairer, truer, / Than ever Greek did couple in his arms" (1.3.274–76). Just as a woman's body is metaphorically the ground over which the Greeks and Trojans fight, it becomes the means through which Posthumus and Jachimo compete with and relate to each other.

Though Leontes's suspicion of Hermione is not aroused shortly before or after their marriage, it does awaken as Hermione appears to threaten the bond between him and Polixenes. When Hermione announces that she has persuaded Polixenes to remain in Sicilia, Leontes comments, "At my request he would not" (*The Winter's Tale*, 1.2.87). His jealousy is immediately aroused by Hermione's success in persuading Polixenes when he could not. Though he plots Polixenes's death and does not ally himself with other men in his punishment of Hermione, as Claudio and Othello do in their persecution of Hero and Desdemona, he immediately imagines himself horned (1.2.119, 146) and in his cuckoldry a sharer of the fate of a large community of men. He voices what Coppélia Kahn has described as one of the most prominent motifs of cuckoldry, "the brotherhood of all married men as potential if not actual cuckolds" (1981, 124), when he laments:

> Should all despair
> That have revolted wives, the tenth of mankind
> Would hang themselves.
>
> . . . .
> Many thousand on 's
> Have the disease, and feel't not.
>   (1.2.198–200, 206–7)

Speaking these things to Mamillius, he seems to be making an effort to bond himself with the boy, as he gives his criticism of women the sound of worldly wisdom that the father traditionally passes down to the son.

Though there are marriages between women and men in all four plays, these marriages take place, on the one hand, offstage or before the present action or are, on the other, abbreviated ceremonies without celebration. The most vividly realized "marriages" are between men. In *Much Ado* the climactic moment is the broken nuptial, in which Claudio, Don Pedro, Don John, and even Leonato join to shame Hero. The wedding in the last act is low-key by comparison. Although the marriage of Othello and Desdemona is not dramatized, Othello's story of their courtship is powerfully rendered. The dramatized marriage between Othello and Iago in act 3 eclipses that earlier story as the two kneel and make sacred vows; it concludes with Othello's proclaiming Iago his lieutenant and Iago's promising Othello, "I am your own forever" (3.3.460–80).

Posthumus and Imogen are together only briefly, at the beginning and the end of *Cymbeline*. We hear nothing of their courtship or marriage, only that they are married. Their relationship is undermined because Imogen mistakes the beheaded Cloten in Posthumus's clothes for Posthumus and because Posthumus, failing to recognize Imogen in disguise, prefaces their reconciliation by striking her. The interchanges between Posthumus and Jachimo are far more charged than any moment between Imogen and Posthumus.

From the beginning of *The Winter's Tale* Shakespeare emphasizes the bond between Polixenes and Leontes. Camillo tells Archidamus that affection so "rooted" between the two kings in childhood could not "choose but branch." Their exchanges while apart had been so lavish that they had "embrac'd as it were from the ends of oppos'd winds" (1.1.21–31). Polixenes tells Hermione:

> We were as twinn'd lambs that did frisk i' th' sun,
> And bleat the one at th' other.
>
> (1.2.67–68)

In the same scene, Leontes remembers his courtship of Hermione less happily:

> Three crabbed months had sour'd themselves to death,
> Ere I could make thee open thy white hand,
> [And] clap thyself my love; then didst thou utter,
> "I am yours for ever."
>
> (1.2.102–5)

Although the reuniting of Hermione and Leontes at the end of the play surpasses everything else in wonder and Hermione embraces Leontes, she does not speak to him but addresses her daughter instead:

> Tell me, mine own,
> Where hast thou been preserv'd? where liv'd? how found
> Thy father's court? for thou shalt hear that I,
> Knowing by Paulina that the oracle
> Gave hope thou wast in being, have preserv'd
> Myself to see the issue.
>
> (5.3.123–28)

Hermione's daughter, not her husband, gave her cause to survive (McNaron, unpublished paper).

As Claudio, Othello, Posthumus, and Leontes affirm their bonds
with men and break their bonds with women who love them, they all
engage in voyeuristic and degraded fantasies in which they imagine
their beloveds in bestial sexual acts. These fantasies—usually shared
with other men—are as much a feature of the male characters' bonding with each other as of their breaking bonds with women. Claudio
and his comrades see Borachio leaving Hero's house at midnight while
Margaret, appearing to be Hero, bids him "a thousand times good
night" (*Much Ado About Nothing*, 3.3.147–48). Claudio's debased
fantasies elaborate on that scene as he publicly accuses Hero:

> You are more intemperate in your blood
> Than Venus, or those pamp'red animals
> That rage in savage sensuality.
> (4.1.59–61)

Don Pedro depicts her as "a common stale" (4.1.65). In *Othello* it is
Iago who supplies the images of Desdemona "topp'd" (3.3.396) and
of her and Cassio

> as prime as goats, as hot as monkeys,
> As salt as wolves in pride, and fools as gross
> As ignorance made drunk.
> (3.3.403–5)

Othello is so obsessed with these images that he cannot get goats and
monkeys off his mind (4.1.263), and Desdemona becomes to him the
"cunning whore of Venice" (4.2.89). After Jachimo draws for Posthumus his erotic fantasy of kissing the mole on Imogen's breast, Posthumus, in soliloquy, imagines a degraded sexual encounter between
Jachimo and Imogen:

> This yellow Jachimo, in an hour—was't not?—
> Or less?—at first? Perchance he spoke not, but
> Like a full-acorn'd boar, a German [one],
> Cried "O!" and mounted; found no opposition
> But what he look'd for should oppose and she
> Should from encounter guard.
> (*Cymbeline*, 2.5.14–19)

In *The Winter's Tale* Leontes transforms the courtesies between
Polixenes and Hermione into "paddling palms and pinching fingers"
(1.2.115), tells Camillo his wife is "a [hobby]-horse" (1.2.276), and
imagines to Mamillius the experience of cuckolds, telling him that

there is "no barricado for a belly": "It will let in and out the enemy, /
With bag and baggage" (1.2.204–6). On the surface all of these fantasies express disgust with women, which is provoked by fear and hate;
beneath it they may manifest suppressed homosexual feelings of the
men who experience and share the fantasies.

All of these plays move toward a heterosexual solution, however. In
exploring the possibilities of women's and men's loving each other,
Shakespeare suggests that a man's idealization of his beloved dooms
their relationship to failure. The woman who must be, or is, killed is
the woman on a pedestal. In *The Winter's Tale,* Shakespeare's final
treatment of this theme, Hermione's return as a statue that comes to
life symbolizes that meaning. Paulina's direction to Hermione to "descend; be stone no more" (5.3.99) mainly describes not her action but
rather a movement in Leontes, a change in the male psyche. The new
and hopeful marriages or reconciliations of Claudio, Posthumus, and
Leontes are made possible only after each of them has had to face the
possibility of his beloved's infidelity, in other words, to accept her as a
human woman, who may, like everyone else, fall.

Othello never loses the need to idealize Desdemona. In killing her,
he wants to be assured that there is "no more moving" (5.2.93); and
after she is dead and he is grieving, he views her as a pearl—an image
of the Virgin Mary, beautiful, perfect, and pure. Calling up this
image, Othello echoes Cassio, whose greeting of Desdemona when
she arrives on Cyprus suggests a "prayer to the Virgin" (Harbage
1970, 351). For Othello, Desdemona is either virgin or whore; Cassio too "idealizes women of his own social class and spends his time
with prostitutes" (Garner 1976, 243). In both Othello and Cassio,
then, Shakespeare portrays a common male psychic split (Freud
1953, 12:182–84), and a central element in Othello's tragedy is his
failure to heal that split.

As Shakespeare repeats these dramas involving the myth of women's
deception, he gives his male characters more self-awareness and suggests that if they are to give up their deeply ingrained misogyny to love
the women to whom they are engaged or married, their change will have
to be drastic. Claudio and Othello, though repentant, give no evidence
of having learned anything about themselves from their mistakes: they
learn merely that they believed absurd lies about the women who loved
them. Posthumus, on the other hand, gains a new perspective. He finally
sees the roles of women and men in marriage in more just proportion

than he did earlier. Most remarkably, he forgives his wife before he learns that she is innocent:

> You married ones,
> If each of you should take this course, how many
> Must murther wives much better than themselves
> For wrying but a little!
>
> (*Cymbeline*, 5.1.2–5)

Although he does not understand his culpability fully, seeing only his responsibility in Imogen's "murder," his forgiveness of her "adultery" is extraordinary. Further, he breaks his bond with Jachimo. He forgives him, but seems to make it clear that they will have no more dealings with each other. When Jachimo asks him to take his life, Posthumus replies:

> Kneel not to me.
> The pow'r that I have on you is to spare you;
> The malice towards you, to forgive you. Live,
> And deal with others better.
>
> (5.5.417–20)

Though Leontes does not articulate the wrong he did Hermione so clearly as Posthumus articulates the wrong he did Imogen, he presumably comes to see himself as Paulina sees him. She becomes the voice of his consciousness and his conscience. To win Hermione back and to learn to love her, Leontes must spend sixteen years in mourning, this period suggesting that he must grow up again. We may also assume that time blunts his sexual fears since Hermione returns only when she is past childbearing age.

Although the marriage in *Much Ado* and reconciliations in the later plays may seem hopeful, they remain tenuous because so much of the male characters' burden has been to express and act out fear and hate of women and to affirm the strength of male bonding, which is based partially on that fear and hate. Further, the outcomes depend on the women's forgiveness. While I do not expect formal realism from these plays, I do expect psychological credibility. The kind of forgiveness that Shakespeare requires on the woman's part is possible only for a woman who is a saint or martyr or who has a perilously divided self.

Examining the women characters in these plays, I find that Shakespeare portrays them as increasingly whole emotionally, and consequently their responses to their husband's or fiancé's accusations and

Emilia
?

abuses are more direct and full. Nevertheless, their generosity in the face of such enormous wrongs as they suffer follows from Shakespeare's "splitting," or dividing, their characters in one way or another. Marilyn Williamson has pointed out that the splitting of women characters, which she describes as a form of doubling, "allows the expression of women's anger and hostility, emotions particularly threatening to a patriarchy, while containing them psychologically and controlling them socially" (1982, 117–18). Such splitting makes forgiveness possible as well. Among Hero, Desdemona, Imogen, and Hermione, only Imogen is allowed to experience the range of human emotions and forgive her beloved. Yet she forgives Posthumus when she is in disguise, a form of splitting that differs from the other women's.

Hero is the most thinly drawn of the four, and she must surely be the most silent of Shakespeare's female figures. Her single line among the 154 lines immediately before her exit in act 2, scene 1, of *Much Ado* and her utter silence while Don Pedro, Leonato, and Claudio arrange her marriage are striking (2.1.262–361). Just as she is without speech, so she is without defenses. Far from asserting herself against her accusers, she can only call on God to defend her (4.1.77) and faint. Shakespeare splits off the angry, aggressive response that Claudio's actions might warrant and gives it to Beatrice (4.1.289–330).

More assertive than Hero, Desdemona has a voice of her own, and as long as Othello is at her side, she can stand up to her father and the Venetian senators. Alone, with Othello set against her, she is powerless. She will not hear Emilia, who, like Beatrice, speaks with anger and good sense, condemning Othello's abuse of her mistress. Desdemona can respond to Othello's increasing rage only with various forms of denial, such as insisting that she approves of his behavior or creating fantasies of escape (Garner 1976, 247–50). In the end, she is scarcely better able to defend herself than Hero.

In *Cymbeline* Shakespeare allows Imogen to have the angry voice, for she has no vocal attendant. Although she does not express her anger to Posthumus, she directs it against him as she rails at Pisanio, whom Posthumus has ordered to murder her (3.4.40ff). Shakespeare evidently sees her differently from the other women in these plays, for he portrays her as capable of assuming the disguise of a man. Just as she can incorporate anger within her character, so she can cast aside her femininity, as it is traditionally defined. Despite Imogen's wholeness of character and Posthumus's reformation, Shakespeare expresses his ambivalence about the heterosexual recoupling by leaving Imogen in disguise at the end of the play. If we consider that Imogen is a boy actor playing a woman disguised as a man, then the restored couple would appear more as a homosexual than a heterosexual one. Imogen's disguise serves the same function that the splitting of a character does in the other plays: she becomes either more or less than woman.

In *The Winter's Tale* Shakespeare returns to the pattern of portraying women that he followed in *Much Ado* and *Othello*. The outrage at Leontes that Hermione might be expected to feel is split off and given to Paulina. Remaining wholly feminine, Hermione does not express rage. At the same time, she is firm in her dignity and argues her own case eloquently and without fear. Powerful in her own defense, she does not merely plead her innocence but is sufficiently in command of her reason to understand and make evident the impossibility of clearing herself against Leontes's charge. She argues rightly that since Leontes accuses her, there is no way she can prove her innocence, her "integrity, / Being counted falsehood" (3.2.26–27).

Behind the women's forgiveness in these plays is the working out of a male fantasy. Quite simply put, the fantasy is that a woman will always forgive a man no matter how terribly he wrongs her. Shakespeare's resolution is always a variation on the story of patient Griselda. When that resolution strains credulity, many read it as illustrating Christian forgiveness, an example to which we might all aspire. This is particularly true of *The Winter's Tale*. Such a reading—or a mythic reading, which Shakespeare invites as well—is probably the happiest construction we can give to the play. Otherwise, how are we to respond when we see a woman embrace a man who is responsible for the death of her son, has tried to kill her daughter, and has deprived her of her motherhood as well as her mature womanhood?

Even if we are comfortable with a reading that makes the psychological credibility of such an ending irrelevant, we must still see the demands of a male fantasy in control when we consider how different forgiveness is for women and men in Shakespeare. When Posthumus forgives Jachimo, there is no expectation that the two of them can make things up. Posthumus tells him to "deal with *others* better" (5.5.419; emphasis mine). Like Hermione, Prospero is often seen as a model of forgiveness; indeed, *The Tempest* focuses on his decision to forgive Antonio rather than to exact vengeance. Yet Prospero has no reconciliation with Antonio. The play does not suggest that Prospero will ever trust or love his brother again, and yet there is no blot on the quality of his forgiveness. His generosity is more in the realm of ordinary human possibility than the magnanimity demanded of Hero, Desdemona, Imogen, and Hermione.

Thinking about the whole of Shakespeare's work, I recall numerous lines that suggest how deeply charged the general issue of trust was for him as artist. The poet tells the young man in Sonnet 93:

> How like Eve's apple doth thy beauty grow,
> If thy sweet virtue answer not thy show!

As Duncan confronts his betrayal by Macdonwald, on whom, the king says, he "built / An absolute trust," he laments that "there's no art / To find the mind's construction in the face" (*Macbeth*, 1.4.11–14). We hear Lady Macbeth advise Macbeth, "Look like th' innocent flower, / But be the serpent under't" (1.5.65–66). Lear faces his mistaken sense of self: "They are not men o' their words: they told me I was every thing. 'Tis a lie, I am not ague-proof" (*King Lear*, 4.6.104–5). Shakespeare portrays again and again the risk of human relationship and the vulnerability of his characters to deception or betrayal. The hard truth that engages him is that trust must be an act of faith. You cannot know the heart of another.

Presumably both women and men suffer from this vulnerability. Yet as a male writer, Shakespeare, as we might expect, treated this theme mainly from the point of view of his male characters. They seem to feel women's betrayal more strongly than men's. Women's deceptiveness is often at the core of tragedy, and Shakespeare's tragic heroes go mad or nearly so in the face of it. The felt betrayal of a mother and of daughters accounts largely for the dramatic intensity of *Hamlet* and *King Lear*. When Antony thinks that Cleopatra has deserted him for Caesar, he is consumed with rage. The single time in his dramatic career that Shakespeare depicts a sexually unfaithful woman as a central figure, in *Troilus and Cressida*, the play is bleak and despairing. It is as though Cressida's spoiling ruins everything around her. The world of *Troilus and Cressida* becomes as rotten as the one Hamlet imagines.

That Shakespeare insistently replayed the same story in *Much Ado About Nothing*, *Othello*, *Cymbeline*, and *The Winter's Tale*, that he treated it in different genres—tragedy, comedy, and romance—and that it held his interest from the beginning to the end of his career all confirm how important it must have been to him as a dramatist. It has occurred to me that these plays offer a counterfantasy to the Sonnets. While the poet of the Sonnets unhappily suffers the betrayals of his mistress and the young friend to whom he is attracted, in the plays as men join with each other against a woman, a different alliance forms. I have wondered whether Shakespeare needed to repeat in reverse the experience of the Sonnets in order to come to terms with it.

Whatever the psychological insistence that provoked Shakespeare to repeat the story of these plays, they record how deeply threatening for their central male figures is the prospect of union with a woman. We may locate that fear, as Coppélia Kahn does, in the establishment of masculine identity, in a man's need to separate himself from his mother and the feminine, his dread of engulfment by her as he tries to establish his manhood (1981, 1–17). We may find another source for it, as Peter Erickson has argued, in patriarchal politics, which makes necessary male control of women and the feminine—that is, the emotional and nurturing—side of the masculine self (1985a, 1–9). This exorbitant need for control brings into play for Shakespeare's male figures a heightened fear of losing that control when they love a woman. However Shakespeare may have understood the causes of male fear of heterosexual union, the plays make clear that he recognized it and saw it as significant enough to depict, as a story worth telling.

Shakespeare presents the idea of the deceptive or unfaithful woman as so terrible in the imagination of his male characters that the heterosexual bond becomes particularly precarious. Men's vulnerability makes them cling to their male friends, hesitant to bond with women, and restive once they enter into a close or intimate relationship with a woman. As Shakespeare retells this story, the male lover's suspicion of his beloved comes more and more completely out of his diseased imagination, unsupported by circumstance or a villain's intervention. The movement of the plays suggests that Shakespeare came to understand that the fear he wanted to portray resided in the individual male psyche. It was internal; he did not have to provoke it from without. By the time he wrote *The Winter's Tale,* his plays had moved relentlessly toward a world where men *need* women to betray them. That need would seem to arise from their excessive vulnerability in their relationships with women and their greater security in bonds with men.

more fear,
more idealization

By the time he wrote *Cymbeline* and *The Winter's Tale,* Shakespeare seemed to want to make it more explicit that male characters who were subject to heterosexual dread also tended to idealize women. Only by idealizing a woman, by seeing her as unlike others of her sex, could a man risk union with her. This tendency to overestimate women seems to make Shakespeare's male characters more vulnerable to disillusionment, quicker to doubt, more subject to disappointment.

Shakes,
person as
connection

To an extent Shakespeare stands apart from the story that he tells. The male fear that he depicts is probably something that he knew, or else he could not have portrayed it so powerfully. At the same time, as dramatist he sees this fear for what it is, and he is not caught up in it as are the characters in his plays. He is not free as playwright, however, from a tendency to idealize women. Since he makes the outcomes of the plays depend on women's goodness and on their extraordinary capacity for forgiveness, he reveals as artist a cast of mind that resembles that of his male characters and puts too great a burden on the women he portrays.

The changes in Shakespeare's treatment of this theme occur as a consequence of his artistic and personal development. In his later career he was able to understand men's psychic needs more clearly, to portray women characters as more whole, and to imagine love between women and men as more rich and complex than he was able to imagine earlier. At the same time, he always retained a sense of the fragility of bonds between women and men as well as of the strength of men's bonds with each other, which he saw as founded largely on the exclusion of women and on homosexual attraction. No matter in what dramatic form he wrote, he expressed his deep ambivalence about the possibilities of heterosexual love. When he presents love between a woman and a man as compelling and joyful, as he does in *Othello,* the play becomes a tragedy. When the play is a comedy or a romance and works toward a hopeful ending, that ending is undercut. As I have suggested, so much of the burden of these plays is the revelation of the male characters' deeply hostile feelings toward women that it is hard to imagine the men undergoing the radical change that a harmonious marriage would require. The final scene of *Cymbeline,* in which the reunited couple appears to be two men, Imogen remaining in disguise, is emblematic of Shakespeare's lasting ambivalence.

Bed Tricks:
On Marriage as the End of Comedy in *All's Well That Ends Well* and *Measure for Measure*

Janet Adelman

In the midst of Hamlet's attack on deceptive female sexuality, he cries out to Ophelia, "I say we will have no moe marriage" (3.1.147). *Hamlet* begins with the disrupted marriage of Hamlet's mother and father; by the end of the play both the potential marriage of Hamlet and Ophelia and the actual marriage of Claudius and Gertrude have been destroyed. This disruption of marriage is enacted again in the tragedies that follow immediately after *Hamlet;* the author of *Troilus and Cressida* and *Othello* seems to proclaim with Hamlet, "we will have no moe marriage." But the comedies written during this period— *All's Well That Ends Well* and *Measure for Measure*—end conventionally in marriage; in them Shakespeare was, I think, experimenting to discover by what means he might make marriage possible again.

Marriage rests on the legitimization of sexual desire within society; insofar as sexuality is felt to be illicit, marriage itself will be equivocal at best. As Hamlet proclaims the abolition of marriage, he repeatedly orders Ophelia to a nunnery (3.1.120–49). Here the double sense of nunnery as religious institution and bawdyhouse explicates perfectly the sexual alternatives left when marriage is abolished; or rather, it explicates the sexual alternatives—absolute chastity or absolute sexual degradation—that make the middle ground of marriage impossible. These are the sexual alternatives for the male protagonists of both problem comedies, where the middle is absent and sexual desire is felt only for the illicit. Bertram and Angelo are both presented as psychological virgins about to undergo their first sexual experience. In the course of their plays, we find that both can desire only when they imagine their sexuality as an illegitimate contamination of a pure woman, the conversion in effect of one kind of nun into the other. Both plays exploit this fantasy of contamination. The drama of the last scene in each play depends heavily on the sexual shaming of the supposedly violated virgins. The public naming of Diana as a "common gamester to the camp" (*All's Well That Ends Well,* 5.3.188); Lucio's comment that Mariana, who is "neither maid, widow, nor wife," may be a punk (*Measure for Measure,* 5.1.179–80) and his extended joke about who has handled, or could handle, Isabella privately (5.1.72–77); even Escalus's claim that he will "go darkly to work" with Isabella, a claim that Lucio promptly and predictably sexualizes (5.1.278–80)—all assume the instantaneous transformation of the virgin into the whore, the transformation implicit in Hamlet's double use of "nunnery." Though the contamination is apparently undone in these scenes insofar as the continuing status of Diana and Isabella as virgins is eventually revealed, these revelations do not undo the deeper fantasies of sexual contamination on which the plots rest; at the end, as at the beginning, male sexual desire is understood as desire for the illicit, desire to contaminate.

Since the impediment to the conventional festive ending in marriage in both comedies is thus the construction of male sexual desire itself, the ending turns on the attempt to legitimize sexual desire in marriage—an attempt epitomized in both plays by the bed trick, in which the illicit desires of men are coercively directed back toward their socially sanctioned mates. (See Neely 1985, Kirsch 1981, and Wheeler 1981 for very similar accounts of the problem and the solution in both plays; of these, Neely and Kirsch tend to be more sanguine than I am about the effectiveness of the cure.) In the bed tricks in both plays the act imagined to have been deeply illicit is magically revealed as having been licit all along—but only at the expense of the male protagonists' sexual autonomy. Through a kind of homeopathic cure both Bertram and Angelo are allowed to enact fantasies of the sexual soiling of a virgin and are appropriately shamed for these fantasies, only to find out that their sexual acts have in fact been legitimate and that the soiling has taken place only in fantasy. Bertram and Angelo are thus saved from their own imaginations; presented with legitimate sexuality as a fait accompli, they can—or so we might hope—go on to accept the possibility that they have been tricked into: the possibility of sexuality within marriage. But given the status of the bed tricks as tricks and the characters' failure to provide much evidence that they have been transformed by them, our hope seems frail indeed and the marriages at the end of both plays remain equivocal. Moreover, because they so clearly betray the desires of the male protagonists, the bed tricks in both plays tend to become, not a vehicle for the working out of sexual impediments, but a forced and conspicuous metaphor for what needs working out.

Comparison with Shakespeare's source for *All's Well*—there is no bed trick in the sources for *Measure for Measure*—can help us to gauge the tonality of the bed trick in both plays. In *The Palace of Pleasure,* William Painter's translation of Boccaccio's *Decameron* (day 3, story 9), the bed trick is a rather well-mannered and genial affair, repeated often and with affection. We are specifically told that the count (equivalent to Bertram) "at his uprising in the morning . . . used many courteous and amiable words and gave divers fair and precious jewels" (Bullough 1958, 2:395). In both *All's Well* and *Measure for Measure* the bed tricks are portrayed as one-night stands that the male protagonists have no desire to repeat—and not only, I think, for reasons of dramatic economy and credibility. Both Bertram and Angelo lose desire for their virgins as soon as they have ravished them; for both, apparently, the imagined act of spoiling virginity is the only source of sexual desire. In both plays the prohibition against speaking (*AWW,* 4.2.58; *MM,* 3.1.247) and the male recoil from the object of desire utterly transform the encounter reported in Painter, so that it becomes the epitome not only of the dark waywardness of desire but also of its depersonalization, the interchangeability of the bodies with which lust plays (*AWW,* 4.4.24–25). The potentially curative affectionate mutuality of the source is utterly absent: these bed tricks demonstrate the extent to which sexuality is a matter of deception on the one side and hit-and-run contamination on the other. They do not bode well as cures.

Insofar as the bed tricks represent sexuality in these plays, it is portrayed as deeply incompatible with the continuing relationship of marriage; the very trick that imports sexuality back into marriage reveals the incompatibility. In "Upon Some Verses of Virgil," an essay that some have found a source both for *Othello* and for *All's Well,* Montaigne registers a similar sense of incompatibility. (See Cavell 1979, 474, for *Othello* and Kirsch 1981, 122–27, for *All's Well;* I am particularly indebted to Kirsch's account.) Montaigne says, "Nor is it other then a kinde of incest, in this reverent alliance and sacred bond, to employ the effects and extravagant humor of an amorous licentious-ness" (1928, 72). Here Montaigne seems to me to come very close to the psychological core of the "problem" that I find definitive of the problem comedies. When Montaigne registers his sense of the incompatibility between the sexual and the sacred by calling that incompatibility incest, he associates the soiling potentiality of sexuality with the prohibitions surrounding the male child's first fantasies of soiling a sacred space; insofar as marriage is felt as sacred, sexuality within it will replay those ancient fantasies and their attendant anxieties. Angelo's anguished self-questioning upon the discovery of his own desire reiterates powerfully the core of Montaigne's concern: "Having waste ground enough, / Shall we desire to raze the sanctuary / And pitch our evils there?" (*MM*, 2.2.169–71). For the male sexual imagination represented in both Bertram and Angelo, sexuality within marriage is, I think, an ultimately incestuous pollution of a sanctuary; they can desire only when they can imagine themselves safely enacting this pollution outside the familial context of marriage. In both plays, however, the very fact of sexuality binds one incestuously to family, so that all sexuality is ultimately felt as incestuous. I want to look at this incestuous potential within both plays and then to suggest the ways in which they finally seem to me to undercut the accommodations to sexuality apparently achieved by their bed tricks.

The recoil from a sexuality felt as the soiling of a sacred space is split in two in *All's Well* and analyzed in two separate movements. Bertram's flight from, and slander of, Diana analyze his recoil from the woman felt as whore once his own sexuality has soiled her; even at the end of the play the deep shaming that Diana undergoes makes her the repository for his sense of taint. But the flight from Diana curiously echoes Bertram's earlier flight from Helena. This initial flight analyzes his aversion toward sexual union with a woman who is terrifying to him partly insofar as she is identified with a maternal figure and thus with the incestuous potential of sexuality. In the end, I shall argue, the splitting of the sexual object into the legitimate but abhorred Helena and the illegitimate but desired Diana will be undone as Helena and Diana begin to fuse; their fusion will serve the deepest of the play's sexual paradoxes. But before the end Diana seems the solution to the problem created by Helena: the problem of sexuality within a familial context.

Bertram's initial flight from Helena is phrased in terms that suggest a flight from this familial context. Here, too, Shakespeare's management of his source emphasizes issues central to the play: the figure of the Countess and the crucial association of her with Helena are his additions to Boccaccio/Painter. *All's Well* begins with the image of a son separating from his mother, seeking a new father (1.1.5–7) and new possibilities for manhood elsewhere. The formation of a new sexual relationship in marriage is ideally the emblem of this separation from the family of origin and hence of independent manhood. But marriage with Helena cannot serve this function, both because of the association of her with Bertram's mother—an association so close that Bertram's only words to her before their enforced marriage are a parenthesis within his farewell to his mother ("Be comfortable to my mother, your mistress, / And make much of her" [1.1.77–78])—and because she becomes the choice of his surrogate father. Marriage to her would thus be a sign of his bondage to the older generation rather than of his growing independence. In Richard Wheeler's brilliant account of the play—an account to which this discussion is much indebted—Bertram's flight from Helena and his attraction to a woman decidedly outside the family structure become intelligible as attempts to escape the dominion of the infantile family (Wheeler 1981, especially 40–45; see also Kirsch 1981, 141, and Neely 1985, 70–71).

Bertram's exchange with the king suggests the extent to which marriage with Helena threatens to obliterate necessary distinctions between father and son, mother and wife:

> KING: Thou know'st she has rais'd me from my sickly bed.
> BERTRAM: But follows it, my lord, to bring me down
>   Must answer for your raising? I know her well;
>   She had her breeding at my father's charge—
>   A poor physician's daughter my wife! Disdain
>   Rather corrupt me ever!
>
>   (2.3.111–16)

Bred by his father, Helena is virtually his sister. Moreover, she becomes in the king's words virtually a surrogate mother. Lafew's reference to himself as a pander ("I am Cressid's uncle, / That dare leave two together"[2.1.97–98]) and the earlier sexualization of "araise" (2.1.76) combine to make the sexualization of the king's "she has raised me from my sickly bed" almost inevitable here (see Wheeler 1981, 75–76, and Kirsch 1981, 135). Bertram imagines himself sexually brought down by the woman who has raised up his surrogate father (see Neely 1985, 70). Beneath his social snobbery, I think we can hear a hint of the ruin threatened should Bertram become sexually allied with his surrogate father's imagined sexual partner. The escape from the parents' choice thus becomes in part an escape from the incestuous potential involved in marriage to a woman who is allied to his mother not only by their loving association but also by her position as fantasied sexual partner of his surrogate father. Bertram's response to the king suggests his terror at losing the social and familial distinctions that guarantee identity, distinctions protected by the incest taboo. His terror is unlikely to be assuaged when the king answers him by denying the distinction between Helena's blood and his: "Strange is it that our bloods, / Of color, weight, and heat, pour'd all together, / Would quite confound distinction" (2.3.118–20). Bertram's fear is, I think, exactly that the mingling of bloods (see *The Winter's Tale*, 1.2.109) in his sexual union with Helena would confound distinction.

Bertram faces an impossible dilemma: he must leave his family to become a man, and yet he can take his full place as a man in this society only insofar as he can be reconciled with his mother and the king, hence with the woman they have chosen for him. Moreover, the play insists on the full impossibility of the task facing Bertram by emphasizing at once the distance between him and his father and the social expectation that he will turn out to be like his father. From the first, Bertram's manhood is the subject of anxious speculation on the part of his mother and the king, speculation expressed in the desire that he be like his father in moral parts as well as in shape (1.1.61–62; 1.2.21–22). For them—hence for the ruling society of the play—manhood is defined as living up to one's father, in effect becoming him. Bertram himself unwittingly plays into this definition: he will accept the validity of the marriage only when Helena can show him "a child begotten of thy body that I am father to" (3.2.58–59). This stipulation in effect makes his own achievement of paternity the condition of his resumption of adult status in France: he can become a man only by becoming his father, and he becomes his father only by assuming his role *as father*—by becoming a father himself. But if paternity is imagined as becoming one's own father, then one's sexual partner again takes on the resonance of one's mother. The social world of the play and his own fantasy of himself as father finally allow Bertram his place as a man only insofar as he can form a sexual alliance with the woman he and the play identify with his mother. The route toward manhood takes Bertram simultaneously away from the mother and toward her; hence the incestuous double bind in which Bertram finds himself.

Given Bertram's association of Helena both with his mother and with his surrogate father's sexuality, we can begin to make sense of both the impossible conditions Bertram sets for Helena: the act by which Helena simultaneously makes Bertram a father and gets his father's ring is, I think, a fantasized replication of the act of parental intercourse by which Bertram himself was bred. Hence the complex logic governing the exchange of rings in the dark: Bertram's father's ring is given unawares to Helena, the mother's choice, and the ring taken from Helena turns out to have been the father king's. Even here, when poor Bertram thinks that he has escaped his family, the exchange of rings is in effect between father and mother; in the last scene the ring play turns out to have been a symbolic sexual exchange between surrogate parental figures. (On the sexualization of the rings see Adams 1961, 268–69.) In attempting to define his manhood by locating it elsewhere, Bertram thus finds himself returned to his mother's choice; flee as he might, there is no escaping Helena. Indeed, in its portrayal of Helena the play seems to me to embody a deep ambivalence of response toward the mother who simultaneously looks after us and threatens our independence. Astonishing both for her willfulness and her self-abnegation, simultaneously far below Bertram's sphere and far above it, apparently all-powerful in her weakness, present even when Bertram thinks most that he has escaped her, triumphantly proclaiming her maternity at the end, Helena becomes the epitome of the invisible maternal power that binds the child, especially the male child, who here discovers that she is always the woman in his bed.

Insofar as *All's Well* splits the sexually desired woman from the maternally taboo one, the project it sets for itself in reinstituting marriage is to legitimize desire, to import it back into the sacred family bonds. The bed trick is, as I have suggested, an attempt at such importation. But the bed trick as Shakespeare presents it here fails to detoxify or legitimize sexuality; instead it tends to make even legitimate sexuality illicit in fantasy, a "wicked meaning in a lawful deed" (3.7.45–47). Despite Shakespeare's apparent attempt to rescue sexuality here, he seems incapable in this play of imagining any sexual consummation—legitimate or illegitimate—that is not mutually defiling. Musing on the bed trick that technically legitimizes sexuality, Helena makes this sense of mutual defilement nearly explicit:

> But, O, strange men,
> That can such sweet use make of what they hate,
> When saucy trusting of the cozen'd thoughts
> Defiles the pitchy night.
>
> (4.4.21–24)

It's very hard to say just what is defiling what here. The sexual interchange itself is replaced in Helena's words by a defiling interchange between "saucy trusting" and "pitchy night," in which "saucy trusting" seems to stand in for Bertram's part and "pitchy night" for Helena's. We might imagine that the defilement here is the consequence of Bertram's belief that he is committing an illicit act; but in fact Helena suggests that the very trusting to deception that legitimizes the sexual act is the agent of defilement. The defilement thus seems to be the consequence of the act itself, not of its status as legitimate or illegitimate. Moreover, in her odd condensation of night, the bed, and her own apparently defiled body, Helena seems to assume the mutual defilement attendant on this act. In the interchange, Bertram/trust defiles Helena/night. But the night itself is "pitchy"; and as Shakespeare's frequent use reminds us, pitch defiles (see, for example, *Much Ado About Nothing*, 3.3.57, *Love's Labor's Lost*, 4.3.3, and *1 Henry IV*, 2.4.413). Bertram thus defiles that which is already defiled and that which defiles him in turn; that is, in the process of trying to sort out legitimacy and defilement, the play here reveals its sense of the marriage bed as both defiled and defiling. The bed trick thus works against itself by locating the toxic ingredient in sexuality and then replicating rather than removing its toxicity.

It is, moreover, revealing that both the sexual act and the bed tend to disappear in Helena's account, the one replaced by the mental process of trusting to deception, the other by the pitchy night. The sexual act at the center of *All's Well* is absent; its place in our imagination is taken by the process of working out the deception. One consequence of this exchange is the suggestion that mistrust and deception are at the very root of the sexual act, as though the man is always tricked, defiled, and shamed there, as though to engage in sexual union is always to put oneself into the manipulative power of women. At the same time, the disappearance of the sexual act in Helena's musing on the bed trick points toward the larger disappearance of the sexual act enabled by the bed trick. Ultimately, that is, the bed trick in *All's Well* seems to me as much a part of a deep fantasy of escape from sexuality as it is an attempt to bring the married couple together; as its consequences are unraveled in the last scene, it allows for a renewed fantasy of the flight from sexuality even while it seems to be a means of enabling and legitimizing sexual union.

Just before Helena appears in the last scene, Diana says, "He knows himself my bed he hath defil'd, / And at that time he got his wife with child" (5.3.300–301). In effect she separates the mental from the physical components of the sexual act, Bertram's intentions from his actual deed, ascribing the shame and soil to herself and the pregnancy to Helena. This split in part explains the insistence on Diana's shame in the last scene; her words here identify her role as substitute strumpet, the figure onto whom Bertram and the play can displace the sense of sexuality as defilement, thus protecting Helena from taint. The structure of the last scene is calculated to replicate the magical legitimization of sexuality in the bed trick insofar as it substitutes the pure Helena for the shamed Diana in our imaginations; we are put through the process of imagining a defiling sexual contact with Diana and then released from that image by the magical reappearance of Helena. (Hence, I think, the lengthy insistence on the mutual shame of Diana and Bertram, which is not strictly necessary for the plot.) But in the process of repudiating the taint attaching to sexuality, the last scene enables a fantasy repudiating sexuality itself. As Diana begins the process of repudiating her shame, the sexual act is done and then undone in our imaginations as the ring—emblematic of the sexual encounter—is given ("this was it I gave him, being a-bed" [5.3.228]) and ungiven ("I never gave it him" [5.3.276]). The business of the ring makes this portion of the last scene into a ritual of doing and undoing, from which the soiled Diana emerges purified, not a "strumpet" but a "maid" (5.3.290–93). Diana's last words—the ri........ which the appearance of Helena is the solution—again hint at this ritual of doing and undoing: in substituting the pregnant wife for the defiled bed— "he knows himself my bed he hath defil'd, / And at that time he got his wife with child"—Diana comes close to making the bed itself disappear, as though the act of impregnating did not take place in that bed at all. Her words suggest the almost magical quality of the act by which Bertram impregnates Helena: defiling one woman, he impregnates another. The pregnancy is thus presented as the result of Bertram's copulation with Diana, as though the child were Helena's by a magical transference through which Diana gets the taint and Helena gets the child.

Diana's riddle reinterprets the bed trick in effect as an act split into a defiling contact and a miraculous conception. As the defiled bed disappears, the sexual act itself seems to vanish, to become as imaginary as Bertram's knowledge of defilement. The stress throughout the scene has been on the undoing of the sexual act rather than on conception. In the logic of fantasy here, I think that the sexual act has not happened at all, not with Diana and not with Helena. The prestidigitation expressed in Diana's riddle brings the promised birth of Helena's child as close to a virgin birth as the facts of the case will allow. The sense of miracle that greets Helena's return is not wholly a consequence of her apparent return from the dead; it also derives partly from the apparently miraculous conception that Diana's riddle points toward. At the end Helena can thus assume her new status as wife and mother without giving up her status as miraculous virgin; she can simultaneously cure through her sexuality and remain absolutely pure. This simultaneity should seem familiar to us: it in fact rules the presentation of Helena's cure of the king, where her miraculous power depends equally on her status as heavenly maid and on the sexuality that could "araise King Pippen" (2.1.76). (See Neely's fine discussion of Helena's various roles, 1985, especially 65–70.) The play asks us nearly from the beginning to see Helena both as a miraculous virgin and as a deeply sexual woman seeking her will: thus the early dialogue with Parolles, in which we see her meditating both on how to defend her virginity and on how to lose it to her liking (1.1.110–51). Helena's two roles are ultimately the reflection of the impossible desire for a woman who can have the powers simultaneously of Venus and of Diana—who can in effect be both Venus and Diana, both generative sexual partner and sacred virgin. (Adams [1961, 262–64] finds the desire possible insofar as procreation legitimizes sexuality.) This is the fantasy articulated in Helena's re-creation of the Countess's youth, when "your Dian / Was both herself and Love" (1.3.212–13). The role of the character Diana should ultimately be understood in this context. As Helena chooses Bertram at court, she imagines herself shifting allegiance from Diana to Venus (2.3.74–76). The emergence of the character Diana shortly after Helena renounces her allegiance to the goddess Diana suggests the complexity of the role that Diana plays: if Bertram can vest his sense of sexuality as soiling in her, Helena can also vest her virginity in her. Both as the repository of soil and as the preserver of virginity, she functions as a split-off portion of Helena herself: hence, I think, the ease with which her status as both maid and no maid transfers to Helena in the end. Both in the bed trick and in the larger psychic structures that it serves, Helena can thus become Venus and reincorporate Diana into herself.

The buried fantasy of Helena as Venus/Diana, as secular virgin mother, is the play's pyrrhic solution to the problem of legitimizing sexuality, relocating it within a sacred familial context. The solution is pyrrhic insofar as it legitimizes sexuality partly by wishing it away; it enables the creation of familial bonds without the fully imagined experience of sexuality. But this is exactly what Bertram has told us he wants. The impossible condition that Helena must meet stipulates that she can be his wife only when she can prove herself a virgin mother, that is, prove that she is with child by him without his participation in the sexual act. This condition suggests that she can be safely his only when she can remove sexuality from the establishment of the family and hence sanctify and purify the family itself. The slippery riddle of the bed trick satisfies this condition both for Bertram and for the audience: he knows he has not had sexual relations with Helena; and we have watched the sexual act be defined out of existence in the last scene. Here sexuality can be allowed back into the family only through a fantasy that enables its denial: the potentially incestuous contact with Helena is muted not by denying her association with his mother but by denying the sexual nature of the contact. The fantasy of Helena as virgin mother thus allows Bertram to return to his mother and surrogate father; he can now accept his mother's choice and achieve paternity safely, in effect becoming his father without having had to be husband to his wife/mother.

In the multiple fantasies of *All's Well* the marriage can be consummated only insofar as Bertram can imagine himself as defiling a virgin or insofar as the act itself is nearly defined out of existence, so that it becomes a fact without act as it becomes a sin without sin, a "wicked meaning in a lawful deed, / And lawful meaning in a lawful act, / Where both not sin and yet a sinful fact" (3.7.45–47). Despite the overt attempt to make sexuality curative, suspicion of sexuality remains the dominant emotional fact of the play. Even here, where

Shakespeare attempts Pandarus-like to bring two together, we are left with a sense of failure about the sexual act itself and with a final queasiness about the getting of children.

It is no accident that the unborn child of *All's Well,* who epitomizes the attempt to bring sexual desire back into the bonds of the family, reappears at the start of *Measure for Measure* as the product of an illicit union, the sign of sin that condemns its parents by proclaiming their sexuality publicly. The transformation of the pregnant Helena into the pregnant Juliet is diagnostic of the relation between the two plays: the sexual queasiness that lies behind Bertram's flight from both Helena and Diana is given much fuller expression in *Measure for Measure,* with the consequence that the getting of children is the problem, not the purported solution. Here the bed trick cures nothing: it is technically necessary to the plot but carries no emotional weight because no curative power is vested in sexuality. The sexuality presented queasily as a forced cure in *All's Well* has here become a death sentence, whether by Angelo's restitution of the law or by the disease that seems its inevitable attendant. In this play's curious literalization of the Elizabethan pun on "die" that identifies death and orgasm, sexuality is the original sin that brings death into this world (see Skura's brilliant discussion of the pun and the association of sexual intercourse and death in *Measure for Measure,* 1981, especially 260–66). Here Claudio, Angelo, and Lucio are all condemned to die for their participation in sexuality; and they are saved, not by the machinations of a curatively sexual woman, but by those of a sternly asexual man.

The very distinction between licit and illicit sexuality on which *All's Well* seems to depend has broken down here, at least until Mariana appears halfway through the play; as this world is initially presented to us, all sexuality is illicit. After we have met Mariana, the play works hard to reinforce the distinction that has been obliterated, in effect to clear a space for legitimate sexuality. Hence the Duke's assurance that the sexual union of Angelo and Mariana is legal and no sin, despite its resemblance to the sin of Claudio and Juliet. But the very insistence of his assurance—an assurance that he feels compelled to give although Mariana shows no signs of needing it—should remind us that this apparently crucial distinction would be apt to disappear, and not just

in the minds of modern audiences, were it not insisted on. The degree
to which modern scholars differ in assigning degrees of legitimacy to
the two relationships suggests the flimsiness of the distinction (see, for
example, Ranald 1979, 77–79, and Nagarajan 1963, 116–18; Nuttall
wisely dissolves the distinction [1975, 52–53]). When the Duke condemns the means by which Pompey supports himself, for example,
legality or illegality does not seem to be the chief issue:

> say to thyself,
> From their abominable and beastly touches
> I drink, I eat, [array] myself and live.
> Canst thou believe thy living is a life,
> So stinkingly dependent?
> (3.2.23–27)

Richard Wheeler has pointed out that the hatred of the body here is
very close to the hatred the Duke expresses in his advice to Claudio
(1981, 122); this hatred is prior to, and independent of, the degree of
legality of either of their actions. For both men "all th' accommodations that thou bear'st / Are nurs'd by baseness" (3.1.14–15). The
Duke's question to Pompey—"Can thou believe thy living is a life, / So
stinkingly dependent"—reiterates his question to Claudio, "What's
yet in this / That bears the name of life?" (3.1.38–39). For all life is
nursed by baseness, stinkingly dependent on the fact of our conception. No wonder the baby Juliet carries is not a hope for the future but
"the sin you carry" (2.3.19), the emblem of a life so stinkingly dependent; no wonder the bed trick in *Measure for Measure* is written, as it
were, from the point of view of Diana, designed to preserve virginity,
not to consummate sexual union.

The identification of the baby as "the sin you carry" confounds the
act with the product of the act; like the Duke's speech to Pompey, it
reveals a fundamental discomfort with the facts of human conception.
I have argued that Bertram's return to Helena in *All's Well* is empow-
ered partly by the fantasy that she is a secular virgin mother who
enables the formation of family without sexual bonds. The desire to
escape from sexuality expressed covertly in this fantasy is much more
overtly the subject of *Measure for Measure,* where the Duke, Angelo,
and Isabella all proclaim their exemption from ordinary sexual processes and where the attempt to establish a nonsexual family of spiritual fathers, brothers, and sisters is transparent in the plot. But this

desire—permitted in fantasy in *All's Well*—is punished in *Measure for Measure*. Angelo and Isabella are brought face to face with their own sexuality and in effect made to acknowledge their place in the human family; the extremity of their self-exposure—both to themselves and to us as witnesses—seems in fact their punishment for the fantasies they embody. *All's Well* urges Bertram toward sexuality within the family and ultimately allows for a fantasy of escape from that sexuality; *Measure for Measure* enables the fantasy of escape from sexuality into a nonsexual family and then punishes the bearers of that fantasy.

The fantasy of escape from sexuality is most violently expressed and punished in the person of Angelo; the explosive rigidities of his sexual imagination are at the center of the play. These rigidities are embodied in the very geography of the city (see Berry 1976/77, 147–48): the battle within him between fierce repression of sexual desire and equally fierce outbursts of degrading and degraded desire is given a local habitation and a name in the geography that separates nunnery and brothel. The play begins with the order to raze the brothels (the spatial equivalent of beheading Claudio), but the central action imagined in it is instead the razing of the nunnery, the violation of sacred space in the person of Isabella. And this violation is the spur to Angelo's desire: "Having waste ground enough, / Shall we desire to raze the sanctuary / And pitch our evils there?" (2.2.169–71). The "strumpet, / With all her double vigor, art and nature" (2.2.182–83) could not tempt him because for him desire is necessarily the ravishing of a saint—a ravishing that collapses the distinction between brothel and nunnery as it transforms the sanctuary itself into a brothel/privy polluted by the evil of his own bodily wastes. The attempt to escape from sexuality by isolating the sanctuary from the brothel thus ends by bringing the two violently together. The violence of this conjunction is, I think, the consequence of the violence with which Angelo's imagination had initially split nunnery and brothel apart; it allows for no middle ground, no moated grange, no place for legitimate sexuality within marriage. This violence is translated into Angelo's violence toward the person of Isabella (see Wheeler 1981, 100). His words to her—"Be that you are, / That is a woman; if you be more, you're none" (2.4.134–35)—suggest a punitive need on his part to prove all women the same, all equally subject to soil, and so to undo the psychic geography of brothel and nunnery that governs him so rigidly. For if she agrees to his demand, she demonstrates in effect that there was never a sanctuary, that the place he imagined polluting was already polluted. The terms of Angelo's desire—his fantasy of polluting the sanctuary—thus virtually dictate the creation of Isabella as a nun to be violated.

Measure for Measure implies that Angelo will be fully human only when he can accept his own bodily condition. The fantasy of a life without human sexual ties is from the first vested in Angelo; the play sets out to test the claim that Angelo does not have an ordinary human body with ordinary human needs, that his "blood / Is very snow-broth" (1.4.57–58), his urine "congeal'd ice" (3.2.110–11). The figure of Angelo is the locus classicus in Shakespeare for the fantasy of escape from the consequences of original sin, escape from the act of parental sexuality by which one was engendered. Near the center of the play Lucio specifically associates Angelo's apparent exemption from human passion with an exemption from "this downright way of creation":

> LUCIO: They say this Angelo was not made by man and woman after
> this downright way of creation. Is it true, think you?
>
> DUKE: How should he be made then?
>
> LUCIO: Some report a sea-maid spawn'd him; some, that he was begot
> between two stock-fishes.
>
> (3.2.104–9)

In Lucio's fantasy, Angelo's life is not nursed by baseness, not stinkingly dependent; the Duke's unusual willingness to participate in Lucio's joke, even to entertain for a moment the possibility of an alternative means of creation, marks the centrality of this fantasy in the creation of Angelo.

The violent extremity with which Angelo is portrayed, as well as the violence of the shame to which he is reduced, is evidence of his status as scapegoat—evidence, that is, of Shakespeare's vindictiveness toward the bearer of this impossible fantasy. For the play sets out to demonstrate ruthlessly the obverse of the fantasy expressed here: insofar as Angelo proves himself sexual, he demonstrates that he has inherited the sin of his origins; he becomes in effect the sin his mother carried. This conjunction dictates the terms in which Angelo expresses his awareness of his own violent sexuality: "In my heart the strong and swelling evil / Of my conception" (2.4.6–7). Through his pun on "conception" his desire to raze the sanctuary becomes linked with his pressing acknowledgement of the downright way he was conceived: in feeling sexual desire for the first time, he feels the damning presence of the act of parental sexuality that conceived him. The pun moreover suggests that his sexuality feels to him like the reduplication of maternal as well as paternal sexuality. "Strong and swelling" initially seems to carry the weight of his new-felt phallic potency. But the pun on "conception" reinterprets this phrase, making it into an implicit reference to pregnancy, as though he feels himself identified with his mother, female and soiled, pregnant with his own sexuality (see Sundelson 1983, 71–72, on Angelo's fear of becoming female). The sanctuary razed is thus associated with the maternal body; Angelo's sexual conception reiterates the soiling of that body by reduplicating its pregnancy in himself.

For Angelo sexuality is the inherited sin of conception; the curative attempt of the play is thus to reconcile Angelo literally to the necessities of original sin. Hence the logic by which Angelo is brought to face his own sexuality in a garden—a garden, moreover, anatomically linked with the female genitalia (see Desai 1977, 490; Berry 1976/77, 151). In his reliving of the fall, he imaginatively reenters the female body, the origin from which he had seemed to claim exemption; he is thus brought to face the sin of origin. The death sentence that is the consequence of this fall is the outward sign of Angelo's subjection to mortality and the appropriate punishment for his original sin.

As Angelo articulates his sexual conception, he places it in apposition to the figure of the strong and distant father whom that conception betrays:

> Heaven hath my empty words,
> Whilst my invention, hearing not my tongue,
> Anchors on Isabel; heaven in my mouth,
> As if I did but only chew his name,
> And in my heart the strong and swelling evil
> Of my conception.
>
> (2.4.2–7)

This apposition suggests another of the splits that rule Angelo: the spiritual father is here removed from the female realm of sexuality, the heart in which the swelling conceptions take place. This father is realized for Angelo in the figure of the Duke; hence the ease with which he identifies his unseen observation with that of "pow'r divine" (5.1.369). The Duke is in effect the distant heavenly father who returns to judge;

like all mankind, Angelo is rescued from the consequences of his original sin only by the mercy of that father. But that mercy is dependent on
the key figure of Mariana, who alone of the play's characters can experience desire without a sense of contamination (see Neely's fine discussion, 1985, 96–98). Mariana's hope that Angelo's confrontation with
his own sexuality will have cured him—her wonderfully wistful "Best
men are moulded out of faults" (5.1.439)—is at the heart of the play's
curative attempt. The play on *fault/foutre* throughout (see, for example,
2.1.40 and 2.2.138) should enable us to hear the fullness of the hope
expressed here: not only that Angelo may be improved by the confrontation with his specifically sexual faults, not only that he will be able to
tolerate his own sexuality as the legacy of the *fault/foutre* that molded
him, but that the sin of origin is the common ground of human goodness. (See Hyman's view that life can come only out of shame and vice,
1975, especially 12.) "Best men are moulded out of faults," Mariana
finally implies, because in the downright way of creation, that is the
only way men are molded at all.

Despite the play's drive toward cure, the hope embodied in Mariana
is frail. She herself is introduced into the plot only when the bed trick
needs her; she never becomes a fully realized figure. Moreover, the bed
trick itself remains imaginatively unrealized for the audience and of
dubious value for Angelo himself. Even after Angelo finds that he has
bedded his virtual wife, even after their marriage ceremony is performed, he is so filled with self-loathing and shame that he craves
"death more willingly than mercy" (5.1.476), a condition from which
the mere fact that Claudio is alive seems unlikely to rescue him. Nothing in the end of the play has the imaginative force of Angelo's confrontation with Isabella; that confrontation, rather than the hope vested in
Mariana, is likely to remain definitive of sexuality for Angelo and,
through him, for the audience.

I have suggested that the vision of sexuality expressed through Angelo virtually creates Isabella as a sanctuary to be violated. But we
respond to Isabella not simply as an icon in a male fantasy about
sexuality but also as a vividly and independently alive character with
fantasies of her own. In fact the encounter of Angelo and Isabella is so
explosive in part because the fantasies each embodies mesh so well.
Isabella's initial flight to the nunnery and her desire for more restrictions there tell us that she, like Angelo, wishes to be exempt from
ordinary human sexuality and from the ordinary bonds so engendered.

When Angelo asks her to embrace female frailty by "putting on the destin'd livery" (2.4.138), he allows us to understand that this is precisely the livery Isabella had hoped to escape by putting on the livery of the nun. In effect the religious community frees her both from sexuality and from the bonds of the sexual family, working to establish a new family for her, remaking the original family relationships in a spiritual family in which *sister, brother, father* are free from the taint of sexuality. The play tests her commitment to her two kinds of sisterhood (see, for example, 2.2.19–21 and 2.4.18) and ultimately stresses the primacy of the natural, rather than the religious, bond. But at the same time it provides her with a spiritual and purified father in the form of the Duke and resolves the crisis of sexuality only in his presence. In the figure of Isabella the play thus simultaneously tests and enables the fantasy of the asexual family.

Like Angelo, Isabella seems to understand her own frailty by reference to the act of parental conception. She responds to Angelo's assertion that women are frail with a hysteria that voices an underground fantasy in which hereditary participation in the downright way of creation binds women to their fate as sexual beings:

> ANGELO: Nay, women are frail too.
> ISABELLA: Ay, as the glasses where they view themselves,
> Which are as easy broke as they make forms.
> Women? Help heaven! men their creation mar
> In profiting by them. Nay, call us ten times frail.
> (2.4.124–28)

Her conventional comment on women's vanity merges with her condemnation of the fragility of women in their ordinary reproductive role: both mirrors and women "make forms"; both are frail. Women are broken, she implies, in the process of making forms. This acknowledgment of women's role in making forms seems to call up its opposite, a brief fantasy of an all-male and presumably nonsexual creation; the extent to which Isabella entertains this male fantasy can be gauged by the fact that she goes on to imagine this all-male creation as spoiled by concourse with women. This is the fantasy that Posthumus will articulate more clearly when he asks, "Is there no way for men to be, but women / Must be half-workers?" (*Cymbeline*, 2.5.1–2); as Isabella articulates it, the fantasy becomes one more version of the Fall, the spoiling of male creation by women. And in imagining this creation, she conspicuously marks the passage from *them* to *us*, acknowledging herself as one of the polluting women. The pronoun sequence suggests that her implicit meditation on the downright way of creation has brought home to her her own involvement in female frailty, the inescapability of the female sexuality that is an inheritance from mother to daughter. *All's Well That Ends Well* twice invokes such an inheritance ("To speak on the part of virginity is to accuse your mothers" [1.1.136–37]; "now you should be as your mother was / When your sweet self was got" [4.2.9–10]). Isabella's assumption of frailty seems to work by the same logic. The very facts of conception threaten to bind her to her nature as a sexual being; Isabella's participation in sexuality is an extension of her mother's frailty—the frailty that she manifested in conceiving her.

If we follow Isabella through this fantasy, we can begin to understand more clearly the passionate terms in which she responds to Claudio's pleas that she save his life by agreeing to Angelo's proposition:

> Wilt thou be made a man out of my vice?
> Is't not a kind of incest, to take life
> From thine own sister's shame? What should I think?
> (3.1.137–39)

Why incest? I think we first understand her response as invoking the brother-sister incest that figured in *All's Well*. Insofar as Isabella is identified with Juliet, both by her reference to their childhood interchanging of names (1.4.45–48) and by Angelo's explicit attempt to persuade her to do what Juliet has done ("such sweet uncleanness / As she that he hath stain'd" [2.4.54–55]), even the union of Claudio and Juliet may carry incestuous overtones. Moreover, the play persistently promotes the identification of Angelo himself with Claudio insofar as it asks Angelo to find a like guiltiness in himself (see 2.1.8–16 and 2.2.64–66, 136–41). It is in fact in response to Isabella's invocation of this identification that Angelo first feels desire, a desire signaled by his abruptly telling Isabella to leave (2.2.66) or attempting to leave himself (2.2.143). (Many have commented on the dynamics of this encounter. See, for example, Charney; Rosenberg 1972, 54–57; and Levin 1982, 262–63.) If Angelo is in fantasy identified with Claudio, then sexual commerce between Angelo and Isabella would again evoke the threat of brother-sister incest. Nonetheless, Isabella's language suggests that the primary act of incest imagined here is not between brother and sister. Both "Wilt thou be made a man out of my vice?" with its pun on *vice* (see Wheeler 1981, 111) and "to take life / From thine own sister's shame" imagine Claudio born from Isabella, born from the shame or vice that is her sexuality. Purchasing Claudio's life at the price of sexual commerce with Angelo would make her into Claudio's mother in the act of engendering him (Wheeler 1981, 111; see also Reid 1970, 279). By replicating this act, the monstrous bargain with Angelo would not only insist that Isabella is the inheritor of her mother's frailty; it would also force Isabella to take her mother's place in a fantasied act of incest with her father, from which her brother Claudio would be made a man.

This fantasy may dictate Isabella's violent dissociation of her father from the act of engendering Claudio; immediately after she has called the act incestuous, she adds:

> What should I think?
> Heaven shield my mother play'd my father fair!
> For such a warped slip of wilderness
> Ne'er issu'd from his blood.
>   (3.1.139–42)

Her poignant "What should I think?" suggests the extent to which the saving idea of her mother's infidelity serves a defensive function, removing her father from the act she imagines herself replicating. The removal of the father from sexuality here seems to me central to an understanding of the Duke's relation to Isabella and hence of his place in the play. Like Angelo, Isabella invokes a spiritual father removed from sexuality precisely at the moment that sexuality becomes most troublesome; and again like Angelo, that father eventually is embodied in the person of the Duke. We can follow this process of embodiment more clearly if we follow the fantasy that mediates the Duke's first appearance to Isabella as spiritual father in act 3, scene 1. In act 2, scene 4, Isabella steels herself against Angelo's proposal in part by imagining her brother's "mind of honor" that would gladly prefer his own death to his sister's pollution (2.4.179–83). When he in fact speaks with the voice that she imagines there, he is fully his father's son, speaking with his father's voice: "There spake my brother; there my father's grave / Did utter forth a voice" (3.1.85–86). Insofar as her brother's willingness to die protects her from sexuality, he is her father's son and speaks with his voice. But as soon as his desire for life threatens her exemption from sexuality, he becomes radically his mother's child, the product of her sexual betrayal of his father (see Wheeler 1981, 114). He can be the voice of his father only insofar as he protects Isabella from sexuality. When that protection fails, he ceases to be his father's son: he "ne'er issu'd from his blood." This act of dissociation frees her father from sexuality just as the protection of Claudio as father-brother fails her—and the Duke appears to her magically as a nonsexual father protector within ten lines. Indeed, when Claudio had proclaimed his willingness to die, he had in fact been speaking with the voice of this father: it is of course the Duke who has just taught him his (temporary) willingness to die. The Duke as friar is, I am suggesting, the embodiment of the fantasied asexual father who will protect Isabella from her own sexuality: it is striking that Isabella calls him "good father" (3.1.238, 269) only after he offers her a way to save Claudio while maintaining her exemption from sexuality, thus enabling her to avoid the destined livery.

The appearance of the Duke-friar as a protective brother-father thus answers Isabella's need for a safe asexual family: hence the shock and dismay with which many audiences respond to his proposal of marriage. The Duke who has protected Isabella from sexuality now invites, or perhaps coerces, her participation in it; given both the ease with which the distinction between legitimate and illegitimate sexuality breaks down in this play and the suddenness with which the sainted Duke, like the sainted Angelo, announces his desire, his proposal threatens disturbingly to reiterate Angelo's. (Many others note this kinship; see, for example, Levin 1982, 259–60, and Berry 1976/77, 153.) His proposal thus focuses all the ambivalence about sexuality in the play: is it an attempt to escape from the rigidity of nunnery and brothel by carving out an area of legitimate sexuality, or is it one more attempt to invade the sanctuary?

The Duke's marriage proposal follows from the attempt in the bed trick to legitimize sexuality and hence to work toward the expected comic conclusion of marriage. But the concluding marriages suggest that the attempt fails: for Angelo and Lucio, and perhaps for Claudio, marriage is not a matter of comic festivity but a punishment for a sexual sin. (In the context of these marriages it makes sense to ask what sin in Isabella the Duke proposes to punish by marriage.) Distrust of sexuality remains so great that we are not allowed to see the reunion on stage of the one potentially happy couple, Claudio and

Juliet. Even after sexual soil has been shifted from Isabella to Mariana and then removed from her by the revelation of her virtual marriage to Angelo, a sense of sexual disease persists. Our uneasiness with the final marriage proposal reiterates our uneasiness with the Duke's role throughout: though he directs both Isabella's and Angelo's accommodation to sexuality (see Kirsch's excellent discussion, 1981, 80–89), his own relation to sexuality is deeply problematic. (Uneasiness with the Duke, especially with his sexuality, is now a critical commonplace. See, for example, Levin 1982 and Paris 1981 throughout; Berry 1976/ 77, 152–59; Rosenberg 1972, 61–71; and Sundelson 1983, 98–100.) In the person of the Duke the play pulls in two directions at once: even while Shakespeare apparently uses him to reconcile the others to their own human nature, he reincarnates a fantasy of escape from that nature, becoming fully an "ungenitur'd agent" (3.2.174) just as Angelo is made to give up that status. Even at the beginning he disdains "the dribbling dart of love" (1.3.2) with an intensity that nearly rivals Angelo's, but he is spared the testing that Angelo must undergo. In his brilliant discussion of *Measure for Measure* Richard Wheeler suggests persuasively that Shakespeare preserves Vincentio as an ideal figure by displacing "conflict away from [him] and into the world around him"; "Shakespeare . . . uses Angelo as a scapegoat who suffers in his person the consequences of a conflict Vincentio is thereby spared" (Wheeler 1981, 133, 138). The Duke tells Angelo, "Be thou at full ourself" (1.1.43); and while Angelo enacts the conflicts of the Duke's sexual self, the Duke escapes into the role of friar, the unproblematically "ghostly father" (4.3.48, 5.1.126). In effect, the Duke splits into two figures, the sexual Angelo and the asexual friar. But this split replicates the very split in Angelo—between sexuality and absolute purity, the brothel and the sanctuary—that the play seems designed to cure (see Wheeler 1981, 139). Insofar as the cure rests on the invisible and all-seeing presence of the Duke as asexual ghostly father, the cure replicates the disease. (See Skura 1981, 252–54, for another account of the way in which the cure replicates the disease.)

The Duke's attempt to undo Angelo's psychic structure through the bed trick is only marginally successful because that psychic structure is too deeply embedded in the emotional geography of the play, as in the Duke himself. The rigidity of the psychic structure that would like to exclude sexuality altogether (or at least place it safely beyond bounds, outside the city walls) is reflected not only in the characters of Angelo,

Isabella, and the Duke but also in the rigidity and fixity of all the play's physical locations. Brothel and nunnery, prison, moated grange, Angelo's garden—all are felt as distinct places rigidly separated from each other. The Duke promises to embody cure insofar as he crosses boundaries, moving from monastery to prison and moated grange, apparently psychically in control of nunnery, brothel, and the garden in which they meet in fantasy through the bed trick. In the final open street scene the play attempts through the person of the Duke to bring all these locales—each of them representative of a particular psychic space—together and out into the open. But instead of enabling genuine transformations in these places or genuine communication between them, the Duke seems only to transgress their boundaries, enforcing entrance rather than allowing change. Despite his efforts, these psychic places remain separate: married or unmarried, Lucio will remain an inhabitant of the brothel, Isabella of the nunnery, and Angelo of the fallen garden that his sexual fantasy has created. For the play has throughout made its meaning through its radical division into separate places, a division that cannot be canceled by ducal (or authorial) fiat any more than the bed trick can cancel the violence of the sexual splittings that haunt Angelo's imagination—violence that has split even the Duke himself. Our imaginations remain possessed not by Mariana and the promise of marriage that she holds forth but by the triad of Angelo, Isabella, and the Duke: Angelo as the image of sexuality conceived both as corrupting and as inescapable; Isabella as the image of the ferocity of the desire to escape from sexuality so conceived; and the Duke as the image of the asexual ghostly father who alone can protect his children from sexuality. Even at the end the play remains dichotomized into a region of sexual soil, below family, and a region of purity, above it. The Duke's proposal to Isabella suggests Shakespeare's desire to end this dichotomy; our shock—and Isabella's silence—suggest his incapacity to do so.

If we take the bed tricks of *All's Well* and *Measure for Measure* as diagnostic of the two plays, then the shift in their management can point to the ways in which *Measure for Measure* is an undoing of *All's Well*. (Both Neely 1985, 92–95, and Wheeler 1981, 12–13, 116, compare these bed tricks in terms very similar to mine.) In *All's Well* marriage is a cure, even if an enforced cure; in *Measure for Measure* it is a punishment. Despite its final muted fantasy of Helena as virgin mother, *All's Well* had seemed to promise that legitimate sexuality could be redemptive; in *Measure for Measure* the relationship between legitimate and illegitimate sexuality itself becomes vexed and all sexuality seems corrupting. Characteristically, then, the bed trick in *All's Well* functions dramatically to enforce marriage, while the bed trick in *Measure for Measure* functions to protect virginity. The direction of these differences is summarized in the shift in the agent through whom the bed tricks are realized. The bed trick in *All's Well* is under the management of Helena, a powerfully sexual woman. But exactly this management seems to be the central image that calls forth male fears in the play—fears of being drained or spent (see, for example, 2.3.281 and 3.2.41–42), ultimately fears of being absorbed into a female figure imagined as larger and more powerful than oneself, fears that Lavatch localizes in his "That man should be at woman's command, and yet no hurt done!" (1.3.92–93). *Measure for Measure* responds to the fears released in *All's Well* by redoing the bed trick so that it is under the management of a powerful and asexual man, in whose hands the women are merely cooperative pawns (see Riefer's discussion of the diminution of Isabella's power, 1984). That is, the play takes power back from the hands of the women and consolidates it in the Duke; and it allows him special power insofar as it represents him as a ghostly father, divorced from the bonds of natural family. In effect, then, *Measure for Measure* redoes the sexual act under the aegis of the protectively asexual father rather than of the sexually intrusive mother; in the end it is the pure father rather than the sexual mother who proves to have been everywhere unseen. That the doing and undoing in this pair of plays so closely anticipates that of *The Winter's Tale* and *The Tempest* suggests the centrality of these issues in Shakespeare's imagination.

The Personal Shakespeare: Three Clues

William Kerrigan

The absence of personality is a bad omen for most human pursuits, and literary criticism is particularly in need of personality. For criticism is always in some respect evaluative. Although it is possible to be high-minded about our judgments, confining them to ideas, configurations, and loose conglomerates such as "patriarchy" and "monarchy," the various modes of evaluation from wonder and gratitude to suspicion and indictment usually aim at the personality of the author. So I want to know what I can of Shakespeare's. To what else am I so indebted, and with what else, here and there, am I so exasperated? An author-function? I have three clues and a strong hunch about where in Shakespeare's work these traces of personality combine in a triumph both artistic and psychological. None of the three is arcane or inferentially remote, and the first is very well known indeed.

The impressive characters in Shakespeare, beginning with Richard, Duke of Gloucester, are often plotters, schemers, disguisers, stage managers, role players—actors, in a word, acting having been, of course, the author's first profession. Illeism, self-reference in the third person, is a recurrent feature of their rhetoric. The traditional doctrine of the king's two bodies seems almost to have been made for Shakespeare. In the full context of his work the self-dramatizing monarch becomes an emblem for character itself, which has at least two sides: one public and vocational, and a second "behind the scenes," which is presumed to deploy the outward personality in a self-interested way, whether self-interest be virtue, loyalty, honor, success, or something else. Character can be thought of as the most intimate seat of ideology, as an assembly of emotions, the producer of a first-person statement, the residue of individual experience, a locus of choice. But the two-sided character we find in Shakespeare's drama, though it may appear in all of these guises, is fundamentally a structure of ambition. The source of greatness, villainy, and even humor in his plays lies in the fact that character's interior side wants in some fashion to rule. Sovereignty is ambition's everyday form. "Shall we have a play extempore?" says the merry fat man who will seize the role of king (*1 Henry IV*, 2.4.279–80), reminding us of all those fools, clowns, servants, low-life walk-ons, and peripheral aristocrats who play at being, as Carew said of Donne, monarchs of wit. Character is an act of ambition. Kingship, the supreme ambition, is itself a role enacted. The question of how people are represented in Shakespeare leads us to the theatrical reality, the supple metaphor, of acting—the aspect of his work sometimes referred to as metatheater. "How many ages hence," Cassius declares (*Julius Caesar*, 3.1.111–13), breaking the solid reality of history into an open series of future reenactments, "Shall this our lofty scene be acted o'er, / In states unborn, and accents yet unknown!"

To my knowledge, the most arresting modern statement about this reflexive vision of the ubiquity of theater occurs in Borges's little parable "Everything and Nothing" (1964, 248–49). This is not exactly an orthodox treatment of Shakespeare's fascination with playing a part, for Borges conflates the performing selves in his dramas with another standard item of bardolatry (negative capability) to posit in the author an enabling personal defect. The Borgesian Shakespeare creates others with such prodigious fertility because, "like the Egyptian Proteus" (249), he himself is no one; behind his face and his words lies "only a bit of coldness" (248). Compelled always by the absence of fixed or given self to assume roles, Shakespeare confesses here and there in his drama to the chill of hollow impersonality: "The fundamental identity of existing, dreaming and acting inspired famous passages of his" (249).

Probably Borges was thinking of Pico della Mirandola's revision of Genesis in the *Oration on the Dignity of Man,* which has often been cited by intellectual historians as the creation myth required by a new and drastic Renaissance selfhood. The works of the first five days having filled all the slots on the chain of being, man alone in God's creation cannot be the instantiation of a predetermined essence: like the Shakespeare of Borges, like the cloud in *Antony and Cleopatra,* man is the "nothing" able to become "everything," free to fashion his own identity. This "self-transforming nature" was symbolized, Pico declares, in a passage Borges echoes, "by Proteus in the mysteries" (Cassirer, Kristeller, and Randall 1956, 225). "It may be," Borges has written elsewhere in *Labyrinths,* "that universal history is the history of the different intonations given a handful of metaphors" (1964, 192). What seemed to Pico the immense generosity of the creator, who made protean man a self-defining creature in his own image, Borges presents—and he suggests that Shakespeare presents—in another intonation as a fearful lack of center. The Piconian assumption that man and God share a predicate by virtue of their lack of original circumscription also returns with a difference in Borges's parable, which ends with a dialogue between Shakespeare and his author. The dramatist prays "to be one and myself" (249). The deity replies: "Neither am I anyone; I have dreamt the world as you dreamt your work, my Shakespeare, and among the forms in my dream are you, who like myself are many and no one." Just as Shakespeare placed confessions of his inexistence in corners of his work, so Shakespeare himself, we are left to infer, is the corner of God's art wherein we can read the nature of our creator. Shakespeare is deity's signature.

No doubt this is, in one sense, a particularly spaced-out contribution to the already dubious cryptogrammic tradition in Shakespeare studies. Many critics would wish to place at the core of this author a theatricality more festive than a "bit of coldness." But the parable does alert us to the epochal reach of Shakespearean self-enactment: as an intricate exploration of Burckhardtian subjectivity, of the self as a work of art, his drama has a distinctly Renaissance personality. Better still, it implies that Shakespeare possessed an expansive personality in Hegelian terms. He spanned periods, and we can find traces in his work of both the Renaissance notion of willed magnificence and the more modern sort of self-dramatization conveyed by that central "bit of coldness." Borges's phrase answers to those moments, such as the midnight terror of Richard III, when character becomes unglued, desire elusive, and the self deploying a self can no longer tell who's who. Although the parable rests on themes congenial to Borges—for instance, his repeated fascination with self-knowledge as self-destruction through infinite regress and with the coincidence of death and revelation—as a contribution to Shakespeare studies it rightly suggests that play in this drama is not in its deepest implications mere disguise or role playing, both of which assume a fixed selfhood deliberately hidden behind a pretense, but being itself. Many of Shakespeare's characters, if not so extremely as Hamlet, come to know *seems* as they consider how to be and not to be. Personality is impersonation, so Shakespeare had an extraordinary affinity with actors. He viewed situations, and created some of his memorable characters, through the schema of his own vocation—acting, his master metaphor for life.

My second clue is as evident and pervasive as the first, though it has not been tagged so clearly in the critical literature. When Lysander assures Hermia that "The course of true love never did run smooth; / But either it was different in blood— / . . . Or else misgraffed in respect of years— / . . . Or else it stood upon the choice of friends—" and so on through a long catalogue of ill-fitted pairs (*A Midsummer Night's Dream*, 1.1.134–49), we know that he is remembering, however anachronistically for an ancient Athenian, a storehouse of European tales and histories. Misgrafted love facing obstructions: what could be more traditional? Yet, as with the topos of the king's two bodies, Shakespeare welcomed this tradition wholeheartedly, so much so that when we think of Shakespeare against the backdrop of Western literature, one of the first things it would be just to say about him is that he is the supreme artist of the improbable love match, concerned over and over again with the attraction between antagonists, foreigners, disparates—people on either side of a difference, border, or firing line. Concerns of such constancy might as well be termed obsessions.

In his epyllia Shakespeare wrote of a goddess's passion for a mortal and a murderous prince's for a chaste wife. He celebrated in a riddling lyric the phoenix and the turtle who "Saw division grow together" until they "fled / In a mutual flame." The aging poet lover of the Sonnets becomes the unlikely thrall of a young man, "the master-mistress of my passion" (Sonnet 20), and then, lunatic as well as poet and lover, the debased slave of a dark lady. In his drama we encounter a long parade of improbable couplings, such as, for openers, the hilariously discordant love of Titania for Bottom and Richard's miraculous wooing of Lady Anne ("And yet to win her! All the world to nothing!"). There are four major versions at least of love between the representatives of great rivals—Romeo and Juliet, Pyramus and Thisbe, Troilus and Cressida, and that couple from opposite worlds, Antony and Cleopatra. Christian and Jew make a match; Angelo, the stoniest heart in town, falls for the woman of flintiest virtue; princes embrace tavern louts and skeletal jesters; manly Lady Macbeth must put up with a womanly husband, and even someone like Goneril has to deal with the disparity of an Albany. Who will Miranda love? Who else but the son of a man who has wronged her father. Hamlet, before he has seen the ghost, thinks that his mother has inexplicably shifted her affection from "So excellent a king,

that was to this / Hyperion to a satyr" (*Hamlet*, 1.2.139–40). An especially rare twosome inhabits the most domestic of the tragedies, which
might be viewed as a stunning redistribution of the basic dramatic
elements of the Sonnets. The deceiving faithlessness of the lady is only
apparent and has been shifted to the male friend; the aging poet is now
an old dark general who has courted an innocent white maiden so
improbably that magic seems to her father and other Venetians the
likeliest explanation, and Othello himself will disbelieve in her incredi-
ble love when confronted with the failed magic of his handkerchief.

Incongruous attraction in Shakespeare is sometimes reciprocal, sometimes not, but it almost always threatens to become self-destructive. The
many books on reason and Elizabethan moral hierarchy in our author
are not so much wrong as they are partial and unresponsive. They fail to
register the theatrical dignity given in Shakespeare to the second part of
the soul. His plots deliberately ignite combustible love. He served the
passions of *thymos*—the Homeric term for a warrior's high spirits that
Plato later appended to the middle echelon of the soul—with his most
lavish poetry. Think how rarely the schoolroom abstractions appear;
not even Macbeth says anything remotely like the "Evil be thou my
good" of Milton's Satan. Shakespeare was interested in certain topics
from the philosophical tradition (Kermode [1971, 186–99] mentions
time in this context, and to that we must add justice), but the invariable
in his work is risky passion, preeminently love.

When it came to love, Shakespeare had a left-wing imagination. He
was a *hetero*sexual, a lover of otherness. Across the conflicts of the
world, across its separatenesses and insularities, he placed love matches.
His imaginative preference for radical exogamy suggests in its social
dimension an appetite for comic solutions to the conflicts of the world
and puts us in mind of some of the ways marriage has been discussed in
modern anthropology: "Marriage is primarily of importance as a knot
in the network of kinship links that bind . . . a society together. It is the
formally recognized means of recruiting new members to a line of de-
scent, and it creates alliances between such lines" (Mair 1977, 19).
Psychologically Shakespeare's appetite for dramatizing strange attrac-
tions may betray oedipal discomfort. That would be the likely case were
we dealing with someone who habitually indulged, rather than habitually imagined, such passions. Heterogeneous love choice disguises the
role of parents in the shaping of one's love life, while still drawing
pleasure and a feeling of heroic courage from the violation of taboo.

My second clue sorts with the first. Ordinary lovers, drawn to people not unlike themselves, tend to experience love as motivated by lovable qualities in the object. Their attraction seems right, necessary, and fated, and thus compelled they let the rituals take over. But the characteristic Shakespearean pair is forced by their heterogeneity into acting. Since their love is to some extent outlawed, they cannot slip into the comforts of ritual courtship. They have chosen unconventional roles for themselves, and must improvise unwritten scripts for the conduct of their love—much as Shakespeare did, perhaps, by leaving his wife in Stratford.

It seems to me that one of the secrets of Shakespearean drama lies in its connoisseur's appreciation for intricate fates. Have you heard what dire things befell the Danish prince? Can you imagine what King Harry was like as a boy? Do you know how the weird Venetian duke finally got married? Much as gossip does, the plays undertake to satisfy a taste for bizarre events, and gossip, too, thrives on surprising pairs. I venture that Shakespeare, told of a choice English or Italian example, would not have responded as many people do ("Really? *Her?* What does he think he's doing?" or "What does she see in *him?*"), but, viewing the couple from all possible angles, would have proceeded to calculate the genre: comic? tragicomic? romantic? This was the kind of story that ignited his imagination—love fired across the borders of difference.

My third clue concerns one of Shakespeare's intimate and peculiarly troubled visions of that border. In those moments of furious distress sometimes gathered under the heading of "sex nausea" or "sex disgust," Shakespeare opens places in the male mind no other English Renaissance poet reveals to us, perhaps because they had no such locations to show.

Recently Gordon Braden and I have been studying (for an article on Milton's Eve) Renaissance poems indicting orgasm. The Elizabethan prototypes were Donne's "Farewell to Love" and Jonson's translation of the Pseudo-Petronius's *Foeda est in coitus et brevis voluptas,* which begins "Doing a filthy pleasure is, and short." Both lyrics led a vigorous afterlife in the seventeenth century, when the attack on orgasm or, as it was called, "fruition" became a libertine topos. Suckling, King, Cowley, Rochester, and others contributed to this peculiar genre, often recommending, as Jonson does, infinite foreplay in place of consummation. These poems speak of depression and depletion, a mourning for lost sexual desire that follows in the wake of orgasm. They pinpoint flaws in the design of male sexuality, as if rediscovering at the level of nature the old moral and theological critiques of sexual passion. Emptiness and privation live at the heart of it. One poet compared the spurts of orgasm to open-veined suicide in a lukewarm bath (Bullen 1895, 15), and Henry King noted the inevitable degradation of the woman in postcoital male hearts:

> Thus foul and dark our female starres appear,
> If fall'n or loosned once from vertues Sphear.
> Glow-worms shine onely look't on, and let ly,
> But handled crawl into deformity:
> So beauty is no longer fair and bright,
> Then whil'st unstained by the appetite.
> (Bullen 1895, 70)

Notice that male appetite does the staining. This is characteristic of the antifruition poems: they are disciplinary exercises aimed, more or less winkingly, at the flawed implementation of male desire.

Shakespeare's Sonnet 129 belongs to this genre:

> Th' expense of spirit in a waste of shame
> Is lust in action, and till action, lust
> Is perjur'd, murd'rous, bloody, and full of blame,
> Strange, extreme, rude, cruel, not to trust,
> Enjoy'd no sooner but despised straight,
> Past reason hunted, and no sooner had,
> Past reason hated as a swallowed bait
> On purpose laid to make the taker mad:
> [Mad] in pursuit and in possession so,
> Had, having, and in quest to have, extreme,
> A bliss in proof, and prov'd, [a] very woe,
> Before, a joy propos'd, behind, a dream.
>   All this the world well knows, yet none knows well
>   To shun the heaven that leads men to this hell.

But this antifruition lyric is unique in two ways. First, Shakespeare states that no man knows how to shun the heaven that leads to this hell, whereas other poets in the tradition suppose that they *do* know—simply abstain ("If all faile," as Donne says, " 'Tis but applying worme-seed to the Taile") or infinitize foreplay. The horror in the Shakespeare sonnet derives from the combination of revulsion with ineradicable attraction. Its speaker is trapped in a cycle of conflict. Second, Shakespeare uniquely among the Renaissance males who wrote poems against fruition abhors the vagina. In the final line "this hell" may refer to the state of postcoital disillusionment, but the earlier suggestion that someone manipulates the animal appetite of male lust ("a swallowed bait / On purpose laid to make the taker mad") makes the site of damnation, "this hell," the female genitals; the trope reappears more coarsely still in Sonnet 144. The other antifruition lyrics have a playful, rakish air. Grim and tormented, Shakespeare fires the final word of the sonnet with its full charge of terror. We have to turn to a prose source like Burton's vituperation on women to find anything comparable to Shakespeare's sense of being snared in hell by a demon's poisoned food, and even there the rhetoric of disgust— stench, disease, foulness—is not fierce enough to seek out serious theological articulation. Renaissance literature offers us numerous occasions to reflect on woman as foreigner, stranger, and category crosser, the bane of male sanity. Shakespeare, entwining genital fixation with a theological melodrama of fallenness and damnation, intensifies these everyday Renaissance themes. The transition from Sonnet 146, where a choice is posed between salvation and lustful indulgence, to Sonnet 147, where the poet squanders Christian immortality right before our eyes, knowing full well that "desire is death," is among the most breathtaking in the history of the sonnet sequence. At such moments the author's interest in heterogeneous lovers seems virtually allegorical: man and woman are in and of themselves separate creatures from rival parties, and every love must be thrown across gulfs of animosity, disillusionment, and despair.

As we know, Shakespeare returned to sex horror in several of the great tragedies. John Dover Wilson (1932, 48–49; see also Jones 1949, 118–19) assumed that Shakespeare had fallen into a depression that lay upon his work like a motionless cloud. The truth, I think, is more dynamic than that. The tragedies suggest that Shakespeare was constrained to express this intolerably dire nexus of image and conviction so that he could escape it. Every time the sex disgust appears, large aspects of the play are working to defuse or neutralize its intensity.

Hamlet feels that his flesh has been sullied by his mother's inconstant womb. Her vagina serves as his root metaphor for the rank "unweeded garden" of this fallen world. It taints his mind. Woman cracks apart along the classic Freudian line—virgins safe in their nunnery, prostitutes wallowing in their nunnery. Hamlet repeats for his mother the advice he earlier offered Ophelia, abstinence being the mature equivalent of preserved virginity:

QUEEN: O Hamlet, thou hast cleft my heart in twain.
HAMLET: O, throw away the worser part of it,
         And live the purer with the other half.
                              (*Hamlet*, 3.4.156–58)

But a number of things about Hamlet, including his vision of fleshly corruption, emerge transformed or reborn from the graveyard scene. There the body sullied at birth is imaginatively cleansed of genital association, as Hamlet learns with palpable relish the commonplace lesson—new to him, it almost seems—that all men die, that they and all their contentions, however great, return to dust. This new earthiness appears to still his anxieties about the afterlife and put him in contact with a heavenly father: there is a special providence in the *fall* of a sparrow; it hits the ground, as Hamlet has in the graveyard. Matter is simply matter, no longer charged with *mater*. But of course Mother Earth has a womb. When Gertrude speaks in the graveyard, she expressly compares Ophelia's "bride-bed" with her grave, and a moment later Hamlet and Laertes are grappling in that hole for right ownership of the rhetoric of mourning. Rash Hamlet has now completed the great movement of the play set in motion by Claudius in the opening scenes. The fraternal rivalry between Claudius and old Hamlet must be handed down into the next generation, replacing the cross-generational conflict between Claudius and Hamlet with a lateral conflict between symbolic brothers, and in this sense renewing the primal eldest curse. Childless, virginal, uncontaminated Ophelia is now the woman at issue. The fight between Laertes and Hamlet will be resumed in the final scene, where the rough-hewn ends of vengeance and untainted mind can at last be fit together.

Othello's tormented imagination arrives by stages at the Shakespearean entanglement of unclean female genitals and theological damnation. He would, in the nascence of his jealousy, "rather be a toad / And live upon the vapor of a dungeon / Than keep a corner in the thing I love / For others' uses" (*Othello*, 3.3.270–73); here his disgust arises primarily from the debased condition of the cuckolded husband. One act later the self-image of the toad has migrated to the "corner in the thing I love" and been assigned to Desdemona's lovers:

> The fountain from the which my current runs
> Or else dries up—to be discarded thence!
> Or keep it as a cistern for foul toads
> To knot and gender in!
>   (4.2.59–62)

The image of adultery is now the unbearable disgust. Patience, looking upon this, will become a man of action: "Turn thy complexion there, / Patience, thou young and rose-lipp'd cherubim— / Ay, here look grim as hell" (4.2.62–64). Like a demonic Saint Peter, Desdemona keeps "the gate of Hell" (4.2.92). In the grip of figures such as these, Othello stalks into the bedroom ready to play a god full of twisted wrath.

If we assume that Shakespeare was struggling against a dark and terrible rage against woman's sexuality, the personal strategy of *Othello* looks like simplicity itself. The jealousy of his hero allows the author to indulge this wrath, even to the point of righteous murder, while all the time Desdemona's innocence waits in the wings to indict the self-destructive folly and irrationality of this fury. It is suggestive that Shakespeare appears wholly uninterested in the questions a moral philosopher would want to ask: What if Othello were right about Desdemona? Would the murder then be justified or honorable? He rather focuses on the ironic disparity between Othello's diseased conviction and Desdemona's emphatic innocence—and on Iago, the creator of this disparity. This play is Shakespeare's least disguised expression of the conflicted emotions that intersect in sex disgust, and he works out the angered sexuality of Desdemona's murder in minute detail, from the figurative marriage between Othello and misogynous Iago to its consummation on the bridal sheets.

The words hurled against female lust in *King Lear* (4.6.110–30) are famously unmotivated by the plot of the play. While this speech, and others compatible with it, may bear in a thematic way upon Gloucester's plight, Lear himself has not been wronged by the sexuality of his daughters, and if there is a "sulphurous pit" responsible for his agony, the womb of his queen would seem to be the most logical choice. No study of the closely woven imagery of the play will dispel the impression that Shakespeare set Lear railing with the artistic task of denouncing everything "base" and ineluctably produced the female centaur, human above but hellish at the base.

After Freud, we readily understand this notorious speech in act 4 as an exposure of the sexual undercurrent in Lear's initial disavowal of Cordelia. His sex disgust renders explicit the jealousy implied earlier when Lear assumed that his refusal of a dowry would drive away Cordelia's suitors: "For you, great King, / I would not from your Love make such a stray / To match you where I hate" (1.1.208–9). Lear's anger over female lust, like his rant in general, serves to defend him against the obvious truth that he has wronged Cordelia. In this sense his sexual rage is a substitute for self-accusation, and when he regains Cordelia, the personal savior who lifts him at his awakening from a hell of guilty punishment, Lear's rage is dissolved. It is the same movement we encounter in *Hamlet:* sex disgust can be managed when shifted to the next generation, except that here the shift is from the sexual partner, the second woman in the life of a man (says Freud), to the daughter—a notch further down, as it were, than Hamlet's transition from Gertrude to Ophelia.

King Lear in this respect foreshadows the romances. In *The Tempest* Miranda and Prospero have actually enjoyed on their island a long sojourn reminiscent of Lear's hopeful anticipation of imprisonment. We can measure the oedipal stakes for a father of the bride in Prospero's testiness, his attack on Ferdinand's impiety toward Alonso, his imposition on the suitor of the very same punishment meted out to the sexually ambitious Caliban, and the implied equation between his loss of Miranda ("a third of mine own life") and his mortality ("Every third thought shall be my Grave"); the third woman in the life of a man figures death because his Oedipus complex is repeated at her marriage, and again the beloved, though this time in her final form, must be sacrificed to another. The father's only sane defense is symbolically to reverse the situation and, exacting the deference due a father-in-law, install himself in Ferdinand's superego (Kerrigan 1984, 5–15). Hence, for example, Prospero's cranky insistence on premarital chastity. As we consider the final arrangements made for sexual rage in Shakespeare's drama, we should note that the relative peace achieved through daughters is not entirely sacrificial. I suspect that fatherliness held positive relief for Shakespeare. For as is not the case with the mother and the beloved, a man must never touch—need never touch— the vagina of the third woman in his life.

These, then, are my three clues: a deep attunement to acting, a fascination with improbable couples, and an uneasy vulnerability to a peculiarly sexual or genital form of misogyny.

It seems to me that these clues converge most tellingly in the last of the great tragedies, which I take to be *Antony and Cleopatra*. This is a transitional work, its pathos inseparable from a plea to escape tragedy. Both the protagonists yearn at their death for another world where love can be given a second chance—yearn to be, as it were, in another genre. But before Shakespeare tries his art on the new rules of romance, he makes one last effort to recombine characteristic elements of his drama and resolve in a tragic format his anger over female sexuality. It is indicative of the centrality of sex disgust in Shakespeare's tragic imagination that when a positive female sexuality—a woman who has known more than one man—does at last appear in his theater, she is not marginal but at stage center, dispensing a word-hoard of opulent myths and metaphors. Is it still necessary to say that the play belongs to her? The last act surely does. After three acts ricochet back and forth between the geographical and metaphysical polarities of Rome and Egypt, *Antony and Cleopatra* divides into two one-act minitragedies, *Antony* and *Cleopatra*.

This Cleopatra is unmistakably Shakespeare's, her character formed of heightened examples of our three clues to his personality. Thus she is a consummate actress, the supreme player of the player that is herself, and as Madelon Sprengnether reminds us in this collection, she urges herself to suicide with the thought of watching her greatness defiled by a squeaking boy. She is the most exotic woman in the canon, and the disparateness of this improbable couple is marked more intricately than any other through theme and symbol. Finally, in no other play, not even in Hamlet, is the vagina symbolized so variously and with such tactile force. We sense it in the mud of the Nile, in the sails of her ship, in her perfumes, and in the "Egyptian dish" serving that world-famous food. The queen's ear, as it is crammed with tidings, undergoes a genital metamorphosis. Her very wrinkles ("Think on me, / That am with Phoebus' amorous pinches black / And wrinkled deep in time") are vaginal, and in the end even her mind, able to assess the "odds" and measure the "soldier's pole," delineates her man in its generous cleft.

This tragedy undoes the knot of sex disgust. There is no theology to complicate sexual love, but only a lesser thing, stoicism: we are back before Christian Europe, in Rome rather than Italy. There is no shift to a younger generation, for Cleopatra is all the women in the life of man: a mother in the regal gravity with which she dons symbolism, a lover in her erotic arts and the ferocity of her life-and-death possessiveness, a daughter in her silly ruses and tempter tantrums. She unifies the virgin and the whore ("the holy priests / Do bless her when she is riggish"). The most revealing comment of all comes from Enobarbus, who caps his account of Cydnus by assuring the gossip-hungry Romans that for the lover of Cleopatra there is no sexual disillusionment, no depression or depletion, and every time is as the first time:

> Age cannot wither her, nor custom stale
> Her infinite variety: other women cloy
> The appetites they feed, but she makes hungry
> Where most she satisfies.
>
> (2.2.234–37)

Perhaps we have grown so familiar with this speech that we fail to register the fact—the arresting Shakespearean fact—that it exalts Cleopatra by exempting her from the sexual disillusionment caused by "other women." Her highest praise is that she does not occasion sex disgust.

But a derivative of sex disgust does indeed appear in the play, and it becomes increasingly central to the logic of its plot, until at act 5 it stands forth as the major cause of the action. Antony and Cleopatra are ringed about by the vulgar disdain and official disapproval of stoic Rome. In this subdued form—public, martial, pragmatic, and intellectualized—sex disgust thrives in the recurrent judgment that Cleopatra is a whore and Antony a doting, emasculated thrall. The struggle between the mythological greatness of the lovers and this sharp debasement proceeds simultaneously with the "real" struggle for the world. Finally, the world lost, only the battle over the judgment of the lovers remains to be decided.

When Cleopatra holds the stage alone, the question before her is whether or not to defeat this judgment. If, turning her ship yet once more, she negotiates with Caesar and is led through Rome in one of those dusty equestrian processions that balance off the erotic water pageants of Egypt, then the lovers are utterly defeated, and Rome triumphs as an idea—a bearer of true assessment—as well as a military force. Her first gesture is to conjure that colossal Antony whom no living man could equal—an imaginative ideal not unlike Hamlet's deification of his dead father.

Indeed, Cleopatra and Hamlet are the two Shakespearean characters who undergo the severest version of what I have elsewhere called "the death test," the idea that one cannot really tell how one person feels about another until that other person is dead or presumed to be dead (Kerrigan 1984, 12). That Cleopatra understands the death test we know from the false report sent to Antony, which made his suicide into an assertion of love as well as a stoic liberation from intolerable fortune. Hamlet can pass the test of his filial loyalty only by *not* committing suicide, whereas Cleopatra can win her victory only by committing suicide. Her suicide is equivalent to the worth of their love, her fidelity to their love, and the legend that worth and that fidelity will inspire. She must, and does, make a second voyage to Cydnus, reaffirming their initial passion.

By temperament I suspect attempts in art or in criticism to romanticize suicide, heroism's dead end. But it is impossible to believe that Shakespeare was entirely immune to a tendency of this sort. Suicide is arguably the most theatrical form of death and unquestionably the quietus consistent with Renaissance selfhood. Right to the end the self *als Kunstwerk,* as a work of art, will deploy itself as its own created object.

For Cleopatra, once again, suicide is the only role left that can confirm the value of her love and defeat the Roman version of sex disgust. The watery woman of "infinite variety" must become "marble constant" and take as her center, her fixed and final role, Antony's worthy queen. When she draws herself toward this triumphant fixity by anticipating the sight of "some squeaking Cleopatra" boying her greatness "i' th' posture of a whore," the effect, I think, is to create in the theater a sublime instance of marble constancy. The role proclaims its autonomy. The fact that a boy *is* squeaking her greatness even as she disdains this impersonation does not puncture the theatrical illusion but separates the role unfolding before us from all theatrical contingencies: nothing can break into the insistence of the part itself. Companies of actors will come and go with varying success; what remains is the play, Shakespeare's personal contribution to any given performance. As Cleopatra dismisses future impersonations of herself, the ultimate constancy of her self-enactment becomes identical to Shakespeare's constant art.

The suicide that vanquishes Roman debasement is the most moving, most beautifully and surprisingly symbolic in the entire canon. The clown arrives, his witticisms bearing one last time the everyday misogyny of Shakespearean drama—women as liars, women in league with the devil. We forget them completely when Cleopatra in her final seconds reveals a nobility elastic enough to equate her death with something so crass, so street-wise—yes, so Italian!—as "a lover's pinch, / Which hurts, and is desired." Cleopatra, dressed for her final act, deals death to Iras with a kiss. Once again jealousy prompts her: she must get to Antony first. Then, in a masterful arrangement of primal symbols, the asp at her breast becomes a nursing baby. A nursing baby: that form in the chain of its symbols in which the phallus can be given back its semen and restored to life, the precise opposite of the hells of privation and depletion that weigh upon male sexuality in the antifruition poems of the Renaissance.

Antony-like for once, Octavius Caesar himself seems to get caught in the strong toils of this definitive assertion. The point has been proved: he will bury Cleopatra next to Antony, consenting at last to their union. He realizes that his own glorious story, the founding of the Roman Empire, must now share history's attention with a tragedy of authentic love.

> and their story is
> No less in pity than his glory which
> Brought them to be lamented.
> (5.2.361–63)

The glory of the Empire produced an awful lot of prose but also, to be sure, the *Aeneid* and its many imitations. Shakespeare's play is the greatest version ever of the other story, the story of its "pity."

Critics sometimes wonder whether our emotional indulgence in these suicidal lovers ought to be checked by Roman realism or Christian faith. The world for love? For the second part of the soul? Life in exchange for affirmed love—the unpardonable sin of suicide?

These are worthy questions, but if we approach the play from the personality of its author, we will not be long concerned with them. What is Roman politics from that viewpoint, and what, after Rome's victory, is life? Derivatives of sex disgust. A kiss rates all that might be won or lost in this drama because Shakespeare, the person that was Shakespeare, writes out of, and about, a specifically erotic ambition in *Antony and Cleopatra*—an urge to defeat the accusations of misogynous rage. There is a lot to care about in the world. If this seems a paltry and private aim, we must bear in mind that Shakespeare's was a lucky personality in Hegelian terms, which is one reason why he still enables us to make sense of ourselves.

As he allied his dramatic art with the mythological greatness of his lovers, Shakespeare struck against the designs of history. The glorious story of Octavius helped to underwrite the absolutist monarchies of Renaissance Europe; the vain potentates of Burckhardt's Italy, striving to be recognized in their imperial magnificence, created a style of dire self-fashioning that can be observed throughout the political history of the Renaissance. Yet the epoch's taste for self-enactment was also expressed in art, and especially in the national theaters, where it led to transformed visions of self-consciousness, clearer exposures of the roots of desire, and new assessments of the sacrifices exacted by honor and ambition. Broadly speaking, the author of *Antony and Cleopatra* set the art of the Renaissance against its power. His Antony is an Aeneas who stays in Africa with Dido. His Dido is a woman whose final constancy questions at its historical source the "glory" of a masculine ambition that, revived many centuries later, inspired the politics of the Renaissance. Whereas the self-enactment of his Octavius has a "bit of coldness" at its heart, his Cleopatra is driven by love to make an art of herself. Taken expansively, the "pity" accorded his lovers is a wish, a pitiful wish in a powerless play, that the Renaissance might not have been as it was. Finally Shakespeare wrote a tragedy in which acting and improbable love triumph over sexual disillusionment, which turned out to be the same thing as staging a counterepic that absorbs and subordinates the imperial drives of his age.

The Boy Actor and Femininity
in *Antony and Cleopatra*

Madelon Sprengnether

> Saucy lictors
> Will catch at us like strumpets, and scald rhymers
> Ballad's out a' tune. The quick comedians
> Extemporally will stage us, and present
> Our Alexandrian revels: Antony
> Shall be brought drunken forth, and I shall see
> Some squeaking Cleopatra boy my greatness
> I' th' posture of a whore.
>> (*Antony and Cleopatra*, 5.2.214–21)

In this moment of extraordinary theatrical bravado, Shakespeare reminds us that the spectacle of femininity created by Cleopatra is an
illusion due to an aspect of the Elizabethan stage that most modern
audiences would prefer either to ignore or to forget—the representation of women by boy actors. Several contemporary critics have discussed Shakespeare's use of this convention, though most have written
to dismiss the significance of an underlying maleness in Shakespeare's
portrayals of women. Jan Kott, for instance, discusses the layers of
transvestism in the disguises of Rosalind and Viola in terms of Shakespeare's concern with the illusory nature of reality (1966, 219). Juliet
Dusinberre contends, somewhat differently, that Shakespeare's use of
the boy actor freed him from stereotypical portrayals of femininity,
permitting him a deeper examination of the nature of women (1975,
270; see also Hayles 1980 and Kuhn 1977).

Both Leah Marcus (1986) and Catherine Belsey (1985) maintain
that the layering of identity Shakespeare achieves through his use of
the boy actor serves to complicate (or to disrupt) the portrayal of a
unified sexual identity in the comedies. I am more interested, however,
in Peter Erickson's argument that the convention of the boy actor
allows the exploration of traditionally feminine behavior by men while

sustaining the fantasy of an all-male community (1982, 80). Prior to Lisa Jardine's study (1983), only Leslie Fiedler had seriously considered the issue of homoerotic appeal (1972, 27). Jardine contends, on the basis of her reading of the antitheatrical tracts, that the spectacle of boys dressed as women on stage was meant to be sexually enticing and that the plays call attention to this fact (1983, 29). Jardine is correct, I think, in asserting the representational nature of Shakespeare's portrayals of femininity and in stressing the significance of the antitheatrical tracts. I believe, however, that homoerotic appeal is only one aspect of the effects Shakespeare achieves through his use of the boy actor.

The boy actor is fundamental not only to Shakespeare's stage but also to his equivocal representations of femininity, allowing him to portray women as both "other" and "not other." The effects of such equivocation account in part for the wide divergence of opinion among critics concerning Shakespeare's attitudes toward women. By relating the implications of Cleopatra's allusion to her underlying masculinity to some of the other meanings of femininity in *Antony and Cleopatra,* I expect to illuminate the subject of gender conflict in Shakespeare's plays as well as to indicate the scope of his feminism. I also hope to show how it is possible to read Shakespeare's portrayals of femininity as both subversive and conservative and thus to interpret his own attitudes (inferred from his plays) as both pro and anti woman.

I

The boy actor, by blurring the sex role distinctions represented by clothes, functions as a destabilizing element in the hierarchical ordering of gender (Dusinberre 1975, 231; Jardine 1983, 156). In any clearly defined hierarchical system, I believe, subversive or counter pressures will emerge. Within the patriarchally ordered development of Western Christianity, for instance, one finds the medieval cult of the Virgin and the heretical phenomenon of courtly love, both of which threaten a purely masculine consolidation of power. The Renaissance rediscovery of classical antiquity, with its wealth of mythic challenges to gender hierarchy, enriched the possibilities for such representations in Elizabethan literature (Davies 1986). Spenser's *Faerie Queene,* which acts as a vast commentary on the conflicts inherent in any gender hierarchy, exploits every tactic available to an Elizabethan writer to destabilize patriarchal structures, while managing on a heroic scale to hold radically opposing forces in tension. For Shakespeare, who profited from the same rich classical and Christian heritage as Spenser, the boy actor provides yet another opportunity for staging the issue of gender, for posing and ultimately equivocating about this question.

To understand Shakespeare's particular self-conscious use of the boy actor, it is helpful to consider some contemporary responses to the convention of cross-dressing on the Elizabethan stage. The antitheatrical tracts, while clearly hostile to this practice, pose significant objections. As Jardine notes, these objections focus with particular intensity on the issues of effeminacy and homosexuality (1983, 17). They also point to the subversion of male dominance. Each of these concerns, although treated differently by Shakespeare (with ambivalence rather than condemnation), is relevant to his plays.

Citing the injunctions in Deuteronomy against men and women exchanging clothing, John Rainoldes goes on to discuss the danger of kissing beautiful boys:

> When *Critobulus* kissed the sonne of *Alcibiades,* a beautiful boy, *Socrates* saide he had done amisse and very dangerously: because, as certaine spiders, *if they doe but touch men onely with their mouth, they put them to wonderfull paine and make them madde: so beautifull boyes by kissing doe sting and powre secretly in a kind of poyson, the poyson of incontinencie.*
>
> (1599, 18)

In another passage Rainoldes is even more explicit in his condemnation of homosexuality, which he sees figured on stage in the romantic relations portrayed by male actors:

> Those monsters of nature, which *burning in their lust one toward an other, men with men worke filthines,* are as infamous, as *Sodome:* not the doers onelie, but the sufferers also.
>
> (44)

Phillip Stubbes, though less direct in his allusion to homosexuality, nevertheless raises the same objection:

> For proofe whereof, but marke the flocking and running to Theaters & curtens, daylie and hourely, night and daye, tyme and tyde to see Playes and Enterludes, where such wanton gestures, such bawdie speaches: such laughing and fleering: such kissing and bussing: such clipping and culling: Such winckinge and glancinge of wanton eyes, and the like is

used, as is wonderfull to behold. Than these goodly pageants being done, every mate sorts to his mate, every one bringes another homeward of their way verye freendly, and in their secret conclaves (covertly) they play the Sodomits, or worse.

(1583, Sig. L8ʳ–L8ᵛ)

For Stubbes clothing also acts as a sign of sexual differentiation:

It is written in the 22. of Deuteronomie, that what man so ever weareth womans apparel is accursed, and what woman weareth mans apparel is accursed also. . . . Our Apparell was given us as a signe distinctive to discern betwixt sex and sex, & therfore one to weare the Apparel of another sex, is to participate with the same, and to adulterate the veritie of his own kinde. Wherefore these Women may not improperly be called Hermaphroditi, that is, Monsters of bothe kindes, half women, half men.

(Sig. [F5ᵛ])

Clothing represents not only sexual difference but also the hierarchy of gender relations. When the usual order is subverted on stage, Stubbes argues, it fosters other kinds of subversion among the audience:

The Women also there have dublets & jerkins as men have heer, buttoned up the brest, and made with wings, welts and pinions on the shoulder points, as mans apparel is, for all the world, & though this be a kinde of attire appropriate onely to man, yet they blush not to wear it, and if they could as wel chaunge their sex, & put on the kinde of man, as they can weare apparel assigned onely to man, I think they would as verely become men indeed as now they degenerat from godly sober women, in wearing this wanton lewd kinde of attire, proper onely to man.

(Sig. [F5ʳ–F5ᵛ])

Finally, Stubbes associates the practice of cross-dressing with the power of women over men:

I never read nor heard of any people except drunken with Cyrces cups, or poysoned with the exorcisms of Medea that famous and renoumed Sorceresse, that ever woulde weare such kinde of attire as is not onely stinking before the face of God, offensive to man, but also painteth out to the whole world, the venereous inclination of their corrupt conversation.

(Sig. [F5ᵛ–F6ʳ])

The *Histrio-Mastix* of William Prynne repeats with added emphasis the preoccupations of Rainoldes and Stubbes. For Prynne the associations among effeminacy, homosexuality, and female dominance are clear. Thus cross-dressing not only excites men "to selfe-pollution, (a

sinne for which Onan was destroyed:) and to that unnaturall Sod-
omiticall sinne of uncleanesse, to which the reprobate Gentiles were
given over" (1633, 208); it also transforms them into women:

> And must not our owne experience beare witnesse of the unvirillity of
> Play-acting? May *we not daily see our Players metamorphosed into*
> *women on the Stage, not only by putting on the female robes, but*
> *likewise the effeminate gestures, speeches, pace, behaviour, attire, deli-*
> *cacy, passions, manners, arts and wiles of the female sex, yea, of the*
> *most petulant, unchaste, insinuating Strumpets, that either Italy or the*
> *world affords?*
>
> (171)

Prynne adds another consideration of interest to the action of *Antony*
and Cleopatra, where the central female figure clothes herself in the
habit of Isis:

> Fourthly, a mans clothing himselfe in Maides attire, is not onely an
> imitation of effeminate idolatrous *Priests and Pagans, who arrayed*
> *themselves in womans apparell when they sacrificed to their Idols, and*
> *their Venus, and celebrated Playes unto them;* which as *Lyra, Aquinas,*
> *and Alensis well observe,* was one *chiefe reason, why this Text of Deu-*
> *teronomy prohibits, mens putting on of womens apparell, as an abomi-*
> *nation to the Lord:* but a manifest approbation and revivale of this their
> idolatrous practice. Therefore it must certainly *be abominable,* and
> within the very scope and letter of this inviolable Scripture, even in this
> regard.
>
> (207)

The antitheatrical tracts are useful because they are so explicit.
They indicate the kinds of reaction a member of Shakespeare's audience might have in witnessing boys dressed as women and playing
female roles. Although the responses of such an audience were un-
doubtedly less extreme than those of the Puritans, their associations
may well have been similar. As Jonas Barish points out, the antitheatrical prejudice, as represented by anxiety in the face of "dance, music,
gorgeous attire, luxurious diet, cosmetics, feminine seductiveness, feminine sexuality, transvestism, etc.," emerges in every age and exists to
varying degrees in all of us—not excluding Shakespeare himself (1981,
115). The playwright's ambivalence toward the stage, according to
Barish, reveals itself in his conflicting portrayals of duplicity, or the
capacity to "play a part," an aspect of human behavior that is closely
allied with the feminine. The antitheatrical prejudice stems from "an
ethical emphasis in which the key terms are those of order, stability,

constancy, and integrity, as against a more existentialist emphasis that prizes growth, process, exploration, flexibility, variety and versatility of response" (117). On the one hand Desdemona; on the other, Cleopatra. What the Puritans condemn, Shakespeare takes as matter for dramatic exploration.

The boy actor portrays simultaneously the condition of difference and no difference. In terms of Shakespeare's plays this means that the boy actor represents, on the one hand, a loss of masculinity and male dominance and, on the other, the possibility of a single-sex (homosocial or homosexual) society. It seems to suit Shakespeare to stage and restage this issue rather than to push it toward some form of resolution. Equivocation on the question of gender in his plays permits a destabilization of hierarchical relations between the sexes without ultimately disturbing the structure of the whole. While the representation of sexual difference by male actors appears to undermine the image of masculine authority (as argued by the antitheatrical tracts), it also permits a wholly male definition of femininity—a condition in which sexual difference appears not to exist. In this light one can see how critics have understood Shakespeare's attitudes toward women in such widely divergent terms.

II

In a series of essays on Shakespeare's tragedies I have described some of the ways in which he portrays woman as "other," representing sexual difference as alien and threatening (Gohlke 1980a, 1980b, 1982, and Sprengnether 1986; see also Adelman 1980, Garner 1981, Kahn 1981, and Wheeler 1981). The Shakespearean hero (whether comic or tragic) typically resists heterosexual union out of fear of betrayal—real or imagined. He regards the woman who is the object of his attention with varying degrees of anxiety and mistrust, subjecting her to verbal and sometimes physical abuse. Painting and prostitution become the emblematic expression, for him, of her radical untrustworthiness or unreadability. The power of woman as "other" derives, moreover, as much from her maternal role as from her romantic one. In her emotional control over him, the hero may regard her as a witch.

I can also see a significant way in which woman is "not other" in these plays. The hero consistently associates emotional vulnerability with femininity, so that he himself is capable of playing "the woman's part." Although he resists such an acknowledgment, fearing the annihilation of his masculine identity, he finally incorporates it into his awareness. In this sense femininity becomes a masculine attribute.

In his ambivalence toward his feeling self, however, the hero portrays both sides of the question of femininity. The woman in himself is simultaneously alien, intrusive, or "other" and an aspect of his maleness, hence "not other." In this regard his position is analogous to that of the boy actor in female dress, whose ambiguous appearance represents the spectacle of a man turned into a woman or a woman who is really a man.

In general, the tragedies emphasize the otherness of femininity both in the hero's relationships with controlling women and in his attempts to exorcise or repress the femininity he feels within. This stance also characterizes much of the action in *Antony and Cleopatra*, yet the play as a whole occupies a unique position in relation to the question of femininity. Poised between the worlds of tragedy and romance, suspended, as it were, between genres, *Antony and Cleopatra* itself strives to suspend the issue of gender, to refuse the categories of masculine and feminine, as it strives to reject other categories of binary opposition.

III

> That time? O times!
> I laugh'd him out of patience; and that night
> I laugh'd him into patience; and next morn,
> Ere the ninth hour, I drunk him to his bed;
> Then put my tires and mantles on him, whilst
> I wore his sword Philippan.
>   (*Antony and Cleopatra*, 2.5.18–23)

This moment of revelry, with Cleopatra's evocation of playful cross-dressing, sums up many of the gender concerns of the play. For Antony, love confounds both gender identity and gender roles, causing him first to flee Egypt and Cleopatra, then to condemn himself for loss of manly honor, and finally to commit an act of erotic violence against himself in an attempt both to redeem his manhood and to lose it by sealing his fate with Cleopatra's in death. Most of the play stresses the otherness of woman in the problematic character of Cleopatra and in her effects on Antony. The allusion to cross-dressing, however, an oblique reminder that Cleopatra herself is a boy in woman's clothing, looks forward to the end of the play, where once again we are asked to consider this single-sex convention of the Elizabethan stage.

My point is not that Shakespeare destroys the illusion of femininity as "other" but rather that he chooses to equivocate on this issue in a way that suspends the conventional gender hierarchy without finally dislodging it. Shakespeare's portrayal of Cleopatra, moreover, suggests that the otherness of woman can most easily be accepted or tolerated (without violence, revulsion, or condemnation) when it is simultaneously perceived as "not other."

Antony's relationship to Cleopatra and to femininity in general is not unlike that of other Shakespearean tragic heroes, and to that extent he repeats their patterns of ambivalence. Though suspicious, like Macbeth and Coriolanus, of succumbing to feminine impulses, he more nearly resembles Romeo and Othello in the specific manner of his undoing. In his moments of worst anxiety concerning feminine betrayal, moreover, he lashes out, like Hamlet and Lear, against the woman who most compels his love. His involvement with Cleopatra seems to threaten a fatal submission to femininity, from without as well as from within.

In the beginning of the play Antony voices fears of confinement and control ("These strong Egyptian fetters I must break, / Or lose myself in dotage" [1.2.116–17]). Later, he refers more explicitly to Cleopatra's effect on him as emasculation:

> You did know
> How much you were my conqueror, and that
> My sword, made weak by my affection, would
> Obey it on all cause.
>
> (3.11.65–68)

Antony is not the only one to observe that Cleopatra has robbed him of his sword. Early in the play Caesar, ever a harsh critic of emotional excess, refers to Antony as "not more manlike / Than Cleopatra; nor the queen of Ptolomy / More womanly than he" (1.4.5–7). Later Enobarbus, objecting to Cleopatra's participation in battle, claims that "Photinus an eunuch" and Cleopatra's maids manage the war (3.7.14–15). So prevalent is this perception that it is shared by common soldiers: "So our leader's [led], / And we are women's men" (3.7.69–70).

Antony, in his emotional vulnerability to Cleopatra, regards himself and is regarded by others as dangerously effeminate, a condition which in turn causes him to be subject to a woman. It is not surprising that he blames his flight from battle on Cleopatra's "full supremacy" over his spirit (3.11.59). Earlier Cleopatra, as she proposes to play billiards with Mardian, makes a revealing comparison: "As well a woman with an eunuch play'd / As with a woman" (2.5.5–6). While the double entendre suggests the inadequacy of women with one another as sex partners, the underlying identification of women with eunuchs has equally disturbing implications for the men in the play. To be a "woman's man," whether led by a woman or dressed in woman's clothing, is to be a eunuch. Enobarbus, summarizing much of the play's preoccupation with the hero's susceptibility to feminine emotions and to feminine control, states simply, "Transform us not to women" (4.2.36). In the light of statements such as these, Antony's moment of playful transvestism seems almost as sinister in effect as the dire warnings of the antitheatrical tracts would have us believe.

The mythic background of the play generally supports the kind of role reversal dramatized in the main action. There is even a suggestion of the revival of ancient goddess worship in the references to Cleopatra's kinship to Isis. Mars disarmed by Venus, Hercules subject to Omphale, the body of Osiris recovered by Isis—the play evokes all of these images (Adelman 1973), reinforcing the characters' concern with female dominance and the corresponding loss of masculinity. Eros appears both intrusive and subversive of masculine identity, the dissolution of boundaries between the lovers imaged in Antony's death both a violation and a consummation of his selfhood.

Through act 4 the action of the play emphasizes the otherness of femininity in the enigmatic presence of Cleopatra and in the feminization of the hero by love. There is another side to this story, though, suggested by Enobarbus's descriptions of Cleopatra early in the play and more fully developed in act 5. While Antony, giving vent to his feelings of betrayal, condemns Cleopatra in her capacity for dissimulation, calling her a witch and a whore, her artfulness at other times elicits praise and admiration. Enobarbus defends her against Antony's abrupt dismissal ("She is cunning past man's thought" [1.2.145]) with the claim that "she makes a show'r of rain as well as Jove" (1.2.150–51). It is not simply the power of Cleopatra's sexual attraction to which Enobarbus pays tribute here but also her art. In his description of her meeting with Antony he once again extols the work of fancy over nature (2.2.197–201). Overshadowed in the middle of the play

by questions concerning her motivation and fidelity, this aspect of
Cleopatra's charm reemerges in act 5 with a new significance. Here the
consideration of lies links the questions of sexual fidelity and imaginative truth.

The play's concern with the relationship between art and nature
takes a powerful and sudden turn in Cleopatra's "dream" of Antony,
where she provides her lover with mythic stature (5.2.79–92). In the
face of Dollabella's skepticism about the reality of such a figure, Cleopatra erupts:

> You lie up to the hearing of the gods!
> But if there be, nor ever were one such,
> It's past the size of dreaming. Nature wants stuff
> To vie strange forms with fancy; yet t'imagine
> An Antony were nature's piece 'gainst fancy,
> Condemning shadows quite.
>
> (5.2.95–100)

According to Cleopatra, it is the literal-minded Dollabella who lies,
while her dream achieves the status of nature—a transcendent nature,
to be sure (Adelman 1973). This kind of defense of the imaginative
truth of art has important implications for the portrayal of Cleopatra
as someone whose appearance is artfully constructed and whose motives, particularly concerning her sexual fidelity, tend to be opaque.
These concerns are rhetorically intertwined, in a typically Shakespearean fashion, through puns.

It is the characteristic of puns to suspend meaning by suggesting
alternative, often conflicting, avenues of interpretation. They offer a
principle of undecidability. Shakespeare fully exploits this principle in
the exchanges between Cleopatra and the clown concerning lies and
sexual fidelity, where he suspends the question of "honesty" in matters
of sex as in matters of art. This suspension of meaning concerning
issues of appearance and reality finally involves the representation of
gender when Shakespeare explicitly reminds us that Cleopatra is not
an actress (manipulating her appearance for the sake of her effect on
Antony) but an actor—a boy in woman's clothing. But by refusing to
decide the issue of Cleopatra's "honesty"—the truth of her appearance
as lover and as artist—Shakespeare also refuses to decide her gender.
The illusion of femininity she creates (the product of theatrical cross-
dressing) may thus be seen as either truthful or deceptive. In this

manner Shakespeare comes as close as he can, rhetorically, to a suspension of the question of gender.

When asked by Cleopatra whether any have died from the "worm," the clown replies ambiguously:

> Very many, men and women too. I heard of one of them no longer than yesterday, a very honest woman—but something given to lie, as a woman should not do but in the way of honesty—how she died of the biting of it, what pain she felt. Truly, she makes a very good report o' th' worm; but he that will believe all that they say, shall never be sav'd by half that they do.
>
> (5.2.250–58)

The clown's equivocations about the effect of the serpent's bite— whether it be mortal or "immortal"—seem appropriate to the other equivocations concerning death in the play—whether it be a form of gratification or of loss, a dissolution of self or a violent intrusion into it. The equivocation concerning "honesty" is even more significant. This passage defends lies in the service of truth, as it defends sexuality in the service of honor, fidelity, or chastity. Yet the linking of connotations of untruth and unchastity in the word *lie,* so prevalent in Shakespeare's darkest images of female sexuality, cannot be ignored. The clown himself embellishes this theme:

> I know that a woman is a dish for the gods, if the devil dress her not. But truly, these same whoreson devils do the gods great harm in their women; for in every ten that they make, the devils mar five.
>
> (5.2.273–77)

His rhetoric, in its most positive interpretation, justifies Cleopatra's imaginative vision, her artful manipulation of appearances, and her sexuality. In its least favorable light it reminds us of her capacity for deceit or betrayal, her ability to lure Antony into the "heart of loss." As someone who lies, her medium, like that of Prospero or Shakespeare himself, is illusion—and, of course, acting.

Here Shakespeare's treatment of femininity directly concerns his own art. By suspending the questions of Cleopatra's fidelity and of the truthfulness of her appearance—the most troubling aspects of her "otherness"—Shakespeare permits another development to emerge, one that associates theater with femininity without the anxiety that usually attends femininity in the tragedies. Shakespeare's sudden reminder of the illusion of femininity, in his reference to the boy actor, assists this movement.

By alluding to the fact that Cleopatra is male—"not other"—in the midst of his most remarkable evocation of female otherness, Shakespeare accomplishes several things. Most obviously, it seems to me, he diminishes Cleopatra's threat. Her power, no longer defined as unequivocally female, acquires a new set of meanings. It can, in particular, be appropriated by men, who often regard art as uncomfortably female and hence suspect (Barish 1981). The uncoupling of the threat of emasculation from the exercise of feminine powers of illusion permits Shakespeare an ease and range of imaginative expression in the end of the play unusual even for him. It also, paradoxically, allows him to represent female sexuality with less rigidity and greater tolerance than he seems capable of in other plays. Through the figure of the boy actor Shakespeare equivocates on the subject of gender, as he equivocates on the issues of truth and fidelity. By suspending these questions, he not only magnifies his own art but also succeeds in creating a representation of femininity more satisfying in its complexity than his portraits of more virtuous or more villainous women.

Shakespeare's portrayal of Cleopatra is, I believe, unique in its suspension of the question of infidelity, the most threatening aspect of female otherness for his tragic heroes. While the comedies finesse this question in large part by featuring virgins, the romances accommodate themselves to this troubling dimension of femininity by splitting the sexual woman into two figures: the virgin (most often a daughter) and the sexually experienced woman (a wife or mother). Both figures undergo rituals of purification, the daughter through a trial of her chastity and the wife or mother through expulsion, symbolic death, or simply prolonged suffering. Shakespeare's capacity to "imagine a Cleopatra" neither virginal nor cleansed of her sexuality owes much, I believe, to his momentary—and rhetorical—suspension of the question of gender.

IV

The boy actor becomes for Shakespeare the locus of conflicting attitudes, the best resolution of which, in the figure of Cleopatra, appears to be no resolution at all, a refusal to fix the issue of either gender or gender hierarchy. In postmodern terms such a refusal resembles the strategy attributed to Nietzsche by Derrida in his study of woman as truth (1978). According to Derrida, Nietzsche's "woman" neither affirms nor denies the truth of castration, thus rendering the question of sexual difference undecidable. Shakespeare's final portrait of Cleopatra accomplishes something similar. More often, however, the oscillating image of the boy actor as female and male, "other" and "not other," serves to represent the apparent subversion of gender hierarchy within the context of a male-ordered society.

It is easy to understand how the subversive elements in the figure of the boy actor have led critics to assert Shakespeare's latent feminism, not only in his sympathy for the plight of women, but also in his creation of strong female characters. Critics seeking representations of active femininity in the classic texts of Western literature have been quick to praise Shakespeare for his spunky heroines, particularly those in comedy (Cook 1980; Dash 1981). Those who affirm Shakespeare's feminist sympathies also generally take the position that he created characters who are real and believable as women. They tend to dismiss the convention of the boy actor as irrelevant to the question of femininity or, like Dusinberre (1975), to assert that the convention freed Shakespeare from feminine stereotypes. Carol Neely describes this mode of feminist criticism as "compensatory" because of its corrective function in relation to criticism that minimizes the importance of Shakespeare's women characters (1981, 6).

However useful it is in establishing the complexity of these characters, "compensatory" criticism requires a special kind of selective attention—a willed indifference to Shakespeare's carefully staged reminders that his women are really men. In my own view it is more fruitful to consider the extent of Shakespeare's ambivalence on the subject of gender than to argue for or against his heroines. I take Shakespeare's self-conscious use of the boy actor as virtually the emblem of this ambivalence.

Through the figure of the boy actor Shakespeare stages the projection of a female otherness (both threatening and subversive) and its neutralization or reappropriation into the structure of masculinity or masculine power. The capacity of the boy actor to represent woman as "other" and "not other" allows Shakespeare to examine femininity both as an aspect of sexual difference and as an undeveloped potential within men. These explorations take different forms in different genres.

In comedy the absence of the most threatening female "other," the sexually mature woman, combined with playful allusions to cross-dressing, produces heroines whose power supports the institution of marriage and the maintenance of a stable patriarchal order (Erickson 1982; Garner 1981). The tragedies, on the whole, enact the hero's resistance to femininity, as manifest in his responses to women whom he regards as powerful. His story tends to climax in his acknowledgment of the femininity within, though such an awareness takes an enormous toll, destroying himself along with the female "other." Thus while the tragedies on the whole support the values associated with femininity, the apparent price of the hero's appropriation of femininity is death. The romances, which attempt to recast the histories of the tragic heroes with less drastic consequences, do so in part by subjecting the female "other" to rituals of trial and purification while taking care to consolidate lines of patriarchal authority. The power of the female "other" appears most destructive when freed from patriarchal control and its playful ground in transvestite masculinity.

Yet Shakespeare's drama, concerned throughout his career with the issues of art and illusion, appearance and reality, revolves around the question of femininity, just as it revolves around the boy actor. The Puritans condemned the spectacle of men dressed as women, whether as men subject to women or simply as womanish men. Shakespeare exploited this condition as a means of examining his ambivalence on the issue of woman as "other" and his interest in the figure of the feminine (or androgynous) man. In plays where the projection of female otherness is most effective the action is often most violent, a condition that places Shakespeare in the mainstream of patriarchal attitudes toward women. In his fascination with the possibility of male androgyny, on the other hand, he appears to be less conventional.

Because Shakespeare was capable of creating characters who revile and abuse women as well as ones who embrace values they define as feminine, critics are understandably divided on the question of his attitudes toward women. This issue, I believe, is inseparable from that of his stage practice, itself a product of patriarchal compromise. The point is not that Shakespeare could not imagine femininity as powerful or even as a desirable masculine attribute but rather that these attitudes find expression within a convention that sustains the structure of gender relations it appears to call into question. Shakespeare, despite his genius in other matters, does not transcend the limits of this convention.

The function of the boy actor for the Elizabethan stage was fundamentally conservative, in perhaps the same way that the medieval cult of the Virgin and the development of courtly love did as much to uphold the patriarchal order of religion and society as to disrupt it (Warner 1983; Kristeva 1986). Patriarchal structures may in fact require such movements, within constraints, to validate their own authority. I suspect that the position of Shakespeare within the canon of English literature and his almost universal veneration have something to do with his function in this regard. Shakespeare's plays satisfy the radical impulse to subvert established structures of authority, along with a certain masculine need to incorporate aspects of femininity, yet they do not propose any serious alternative to the patriarchal understanding of woman as "other." If we wish to find a clue for such an alternative in Shakespeare, however, I would suggest that the portrayal of Cleopatra, in its temporary suspension of the question of gender and the creative ambiguity that entails, offers the richest vein of possibility.

The Tempest: Shakespeare's Ideal Solution

Bernard J. Paris

I

As J. B. Priestley has observed, "until his final years" Shakespeare "was a deeply divided man, like nearly all great writers. There were profound opposites in his nature, and it is the relation between these opposites . . . that gives energy and life to his work" (1963, 82). Critics have tended to define these opposites in terms of masculine and feminine traits. In *The Personality of Shakespeare* Harold Grier McCurdy concludes that Shakespeare "was predominantly masculine, aggressive," but that his "masculine aims have a way of running counter to the feminine components in him, which incline toward idealistic love and domestic virtues" (1953, 159). In *Psychoanalysis and Shakespeare* Norman Holland presents a similar picture. As these critics see it, the division in Shakespeare is between an aggressive, vindictive, power-hungry masculine side, which generates "images of . . . violent action" (Holland 1966, 142), and a gentle, submissive, idealistic feminine side, which dislikes cruelty and is given to loving-kindness and Christian charity. Shakespeare is afraid of his feminine side and employs "aggressive masculinity . . . as a defense against it" (Holland 1966, 141–42); he can express tenderness and charity only when his aggressive needs have been satisfied.

This view is in conflict with the traditional picture of a "gentle Shakespeare" (Jonson) who is "civil," "upright," and "honest" (Chettle) and "of an open and free nature" (Jonson). In the heyday of what Samuel Schoenbaum calls "subjective biography" most critics held the charitable side of Shakespeare's personality to be uppermost (see Dowden 1910). Brandes felt that Shakespeare's strong reaction to evil was partly the result of his idealism (1899, 420), and Bradley observed that it is "most especially in his rendering of . . . the effects of *disillusionment* in open natures that we seem to feel Shakespeare's personality" (1963, 325).

In what is perhaps the most sophisticated attempt to relate Shakespeare's works to "the evolving temperament of [the] author," Richard Wheeler finds "a division in Shakespeare's imagination" between masculine and feminine modes of forming an identity and of relating to the world. The masculine mode involves "the assertion of self-willed . . . autonomy over destructive female power or over compliant feminine goodness," while the feminine mode seeks a "trusting investment of self in an other" and "turns on the mutual dependence of male and female" (1981, 221). Wheeler's understanding of the opposites in Shakespeare derives from the theories of Margaret Mahler, which posit an initial state of oneness or symbiosis with the mother, followed by a process of separation and individuation that is essential to the establishment of an autonomous identity. This process is subject to a variety of disturbances that produce powerful needs for a renewal of merger or for the assertion of independence. Both the movement toward merger and the movement toward autonomy have destructive potentialities: "The longing for merger threatens to destroy precariously achieved autonomy; the longing for complete autonomy threatens to isolate the self from its base of trust in actual and internalized relations to others" (206). Wheeler does not find one side of Shakespeare's personality to be dominant. Rather, he sees a continual "interaction of conflicting needs for trust and autonomy" (207) both within individual plays and in the corpus as a whole.

Like many other critics, I, too, see Shakespeare as "a deeply divided man" whose works reflect his inner conflicts. My understanding of the opposites in Shakespeare derives from the theories of Karen Horney (1950), which posit that people respond to a threatening environment by developing both interpersonal and intrapsychic strategies of defense. In our interpersonal strategies we move toward people and adopt a self-effacing or compliant solution; we move against people and adopt an aggressive or expansive solution; or we move away from people and become resigned or detached. There are three subtypes of the expansive solution: narcissistic, perfectionistic, and arrogant-vindictive. Each solution carries with it certain needs, values, and character traits. Each involves also a conception of human nature, a view of the world order, and a bargain with fate in which the behaviors prescribed by that solution are supposed to be rewarded. In the course of development individuals come to make all three of these moves compulsively, and since these involve incompatible character structures and value systems, they are torn by inner conflicts. In order to gain some sense of wholeness, they emphasize one move more than the others, but the subordinate trends continue to exist.

While interpersonal difficulties are creating the movements toward, against, and away from people, as well as the conflict between these moves, concomitant intrapsychic problems are producing their own strategies of defense. To compensate for feelings of self-hate, worthlessness, and inadequacy, individuals create an idealized image of themselves and embark on a search for glory. The creation of the idealized image produces a whole structure of defensive strategies, which Horney calls the "pride system." Individuals take intense pride in the attributes of their idealized self and on the basis of these attributes make "neurotic claims" on others. They impose stringent demands and taboos on themselves, which Horney calls "the tyranny of the should." The function of the shoulds is "to make oneself over into one's idealized self." Since the idealized image is for the most part a glorification of the self-effacing, expansive, and detached solutions, the individuals' shoulds are determined largely by the character traits and values associated with their predominant defense. Their subordinate trends are also represented in the idealized image, however; and, as a result, they are often caught in a "crossfire of conflicting shoulds" as they try to obey contradictory inner dictates.

Shakespeare seems to have intuitively understood and dramatically portrayed the kinds of phenomena Horney has analyzed. The major tragedies, for example, depict characters who are in a state of psychological crisis as a result of the breakdown of their strategies of defense. Hamlet, Iago, Othello, and Lear all have bargains with fate that are undermined when the world fails to honor their claims, while Macbeth violates his own bargain by failing to live up to his shoulds (Paris 1977, 1980, 1982, 1984b). Hamlet's bargain is that of the self-effacing solution, Iago's is arrogant-vindictive, and Lear's is narcissistic. Othello makes both a narcissistic and a perfectionistic bargain, while Macbeth tries to form a new, arrogant-vindictive bargain after he has violated his perfectionistic one. Shakespeare displayed an intuitive understanding of all of these strategies and of the conflicts between them. He seems to have been particularly fascinated by the conflict between the arrogant-vindictive and the self-effacing solutions, which Horney calls the "basic conflict," and this fascination tells us something about his own psyche.

I do not propose Horney's theory as all-encompassing, but I do find that it illuminates a great deal in Shakespeare. Those who are not as comfortable with it as I am can translate the insights it yields into their own terminology, as I do with the insights of others. Indeed, it seems to me that the critics whom I have been citing have described Shakespeare's personality in terms that are quite compatible with a Horneyan approach. The vengeful, aggressive, power-hungry side of Shakespeare corresponds to what I would describe as his arrogant-vindictive trends, while the forgiving, submissive, idealistic side corresponds to his compliant tendencies. McCurdy and Holland depict a Shakespeare who is predominantly aggressive but who has powerful, though submerged, self-effacing trends, while Brandes and Bradley describe a man who believes in the world-picture of the self-effacing solution and whose aggressive tendencies emerge as a result of his disenchantment. What Wheeler describes as the trust/merger pattern in many ways parallels Horney's account of the self-effacing solution, in which the individual counts on other people for love and protection and tends to merge with them in relationships of morbid dependency. The autonomy/isolation pattern seems to involve both the movement away from other people and the movement against them. Since Horney's theory is predominantly synchronic, not much work has been done tracing the early origins of the defensive moves she describes (see, however, Feiring 1983). It is possible that Horney and Mahler can be integrated by seeing the Horneyan strategies as originating in the vicissitudes of the separation/individuation process. Fear of separation generates the movement toward other people, whereas fear of reengulfment generates longings for power and independence.

From a Horneyan point of view there is more than one conflict in Shakespeare. There are conflicts between perfectionistic and compliant and perfectionistic and arrogant-vindictive trends (Paris 1981, 1982), as well as impulses toward detachment. His major conflict, however, is between his arrogant-vindictive and his self-effacing tendencies. Horney does not identify these tendencies as masculine or feminine, since she does not believe that they are biologically linked to either sex; but she notes that Western culture has tended to reinforce aggressive behavior in males and compliant behavior in females and to frown on compliant men and aggressive women. Because such linkages occur both culturally and in Shakespeare's works, it makes a certain amount of sense to speak of Shakespeare's conflict as occurring between the masculine and feminine components of his nature. I prefer the Horneyan terminology, however, which does not presuppose distinctively masculine and feminine psychologies.

Whereas some critics see Shakespeare as predominantly aggressive, I favor the traditional view of him as predominantly generous, open, and idealistic. As I see it, he is less concerned with establishing his masculinity than with finding ways to release his aggression without violating his need to be virtuous. McCurdy and I have opposite readings of *The Tempest*. He sees it as embodying Shakespeare's "ideal solution" because Prospero's demonstration of power permits him to "admit . . . Christian charity" (1953, 162), whereas I see it as embodying Shakespeare's ideal solution because Prospero's magical powers permit him to satisfy his sadistic and vindictive impulses without sacrificing his moral nobility. I think that Shakespeare fears his aggressive side more than his submissive or charitable impulses, though he has mixed feelings about both.

II

The Tempest is one of only two Shakespearean plays whose plot, as far as we know, is entirely the author's invention. It is, more than any other play, a fantasy of Shakespeare's. What, we must ask, is it a fantasy of? What psychological needs are being met, what wishes fulfilled? One way of approaching this question is to look at the unrealistic elements in the play, particularly Prospero's magic. The function of magic is to do the impossible, to grant wishes that are denied to us in reality. What is Prospero's magic doing for him? And for Shakespeare? Why is it there? What impossible dream does it allow to come true?

Before he is overthrown, Prospero is a predominantly detached person, in Horneyan terms. The detached person craves serenity, dislikes responsibility, and is averse to the struggle for power. His "two outstanding neurotic claims," says Horney, "are that life should be . . . effortless and that he should not be bothered" (1950, 264). Prospero turns his responsibilities as duke over to his brother, rejects the pursuit of "worldly ends" (1.2.89), and retires into his library, which is "dukedom large enough!" (1.2.110). He immerses himself in a world of books, seeking glory not through the exercise of his office, which involves him in troublesome relations with other people, but through the pursuit of knowledge. As a result of his studies he becomes "the prime duke, being so reputed / In dignity, and for the liberal arts / Without a parallel" (1.2.72–74). He is not without ambition and a hunger for power, but he satisfies these expansive needs in a detached way. His study of magic is highly congruent with his personality. The detached person has an aversion to effort and places the greatest value on freedom from constraint. Magic is a means of achieving one's ends without effort and of transcending the limitations of the human condition. It is a way of enforcing the neurotic claim that mind is the supreme reality and that the material world is subject to its dictates; indeed, it symbolizes that claim. Through his withdrawal into the study of magic Prospero is pursuing a dream of glory far more grandiose than any available to him as Duke of Milan. It is no wonder that he prizes his volumes above his dukedom (1.2.167–68). He becomes "transported / And rapt in secret studies" and grows a "stranger" to his state (1.2.76–77).

Reality intrudes on Prospero in the form of Antonio's plot, which leads to his expulsion from the dukedom. Although many critics have blamed Prospero for his neglect of his duties, Prospero does not seem to blame himself or to see himself as being responsible in any way for his fate. He interprets his withdrawal as a commendable unworldliness and presents his behavior toward his brother in a way that is flattering to himself:

> and my trust,
> Like a good parent, did beget of him
> A falsehood in its contrary as great
> As my trust was, which had indeed no limit,
> A confidence sans bound.
>
> (1.2.93–97)

There are strong self-effacing tendencies in Prospero that lead him to think too well of his fellows and to bestow on them a trust they do not deserve. Overtrustfulness has disastrous consequences in the history plays and tragedies but it has no permanent ill effects in the comedies and romances. Prospero glorifies his excessive confidence in his brother and places the blame for what happens entirely on Antonio's "evil nature" (1.2.93). He seems to have no sense of how his own foolish behavior has contributed to his fate.

Antonio's betrayal marks the failure of Prospero's self-effacing bargain; his goodness to his brother, which he had expected to be repaid with gratitude and devotion, is used by Antonio to usurp the dukedom. This trauma is similar to those that precipitate psychological crises in the protagonists of the tragedies, crises from which none of them recover (Paris 1980). Prospero's case is different because of his magic. Like the protagonists of the tragedies, Prospero is enraged with those by whom he has been injured and craves a revenge that will assuage his anger and repair his idealized image. Unlike the characters in the realistic plays, however, he has a means of restoring his pride without being terribly destructive to himself and to others. He spends the next twelve years dreaming of his revenge and perfecting his magic in preparation for his vindictive triumph. *The Tempest* is the story of his day of reckoning.

Propsero has numerous objectives on this day, all of which he achieves through his magic. He wants to punish his enemies, to make a good match for his daughter, to get back what he has lost, to prove through his display of power that he was right to have immersed himself in his studies, and to demonstrate that he is the great man that he has felt himself to be, far superior to those who have humiliated him. The most important function of his magic, however, is that it enables him to resolve his psychological conflicts. Once he has been wronged, Prospero is caught between contradictory impulses. He is full of rage, which he has a powerful need to express, but he feels that revenge is ignoble and that he will be as bad as his enemies if he allows himself to descend to their level. What Prospero needs is what Hamlet could not find and what Shakespeare is trying to imagine: a way of taking revenge and remaining innocent (Paris 1977). This is a problem that only his magic can solve. *The Tempest* is above all a fantasy of innocent revenge. The revenge is Prospero's, but the fantasy is Shakespeare's, whose conflicting needs resemble those of his protagonist.

The storm with which the play opens is an expression of Prospero's rage. It instills terror in his enemies and satisfies his need to make them suffer profoundly for what they have done to him. If the vindictive side of Prospero is embodied in the storm, his self-effacing side is embodied in Miranda, who is full of pity for the suffering of the "poor souls" who seem to have "perish'd" (1.2.9). Since Miranda is the product of Prospero's tutelage, she represents his ideal values, at least for a woman; and it is important to recognize that she is extremely self-effacing. When Prospero begins to tell the story of their past, she says that her "heart bleeds / To think o' th' teen that I have turn'd you to" (1.2.63–64); and when he describes their expulsion, she exclaims, "Alack, what trouble / Was I then to you!" (1.2.152–53). She wants to carry Ferdinand's logs for him, feels unworthy of his love, and swears to be his servant if he will not marry her (3.1). Like her father before his fall, she has an idealistic view of human nature. The "brave vessel" that has sunk "had no doubt some noble creature in her" (1.2.6–7), and she exclaims, when she first sees the assembled company, "How beauteous mankind is! O brave new world / That has such people in't!" (5.1.183–84). Prospero is no longer so idealistic, but he has retained many of his self-effacing values and has inculcated them in Miranda. He approves of her response to "the wrack, which touch'd / The very virtue of compassion in thee" (1.2.26–27) and assures her that "there's no harm done" (1.2.15). Through his "art" he has "so safely ordered" the storm that there is "not so much perdition as an hair / Betid to any creature in the vessel / Which thou heard'st cry" (1.2.28–32). Miranda says that if she had "been any god of power" (1.2.10) she would never have permitted the wreck to happen; but neither does Prospero. Through his magic the wreck both happens and does not happen. His magic permits him to satisfy his vindictive needs without violating the side of himself that is expressed by Miranda (Kahn 1981, 223). To further alleviate his discomfort with his sadistic behavior and with Miranda's implied reproaches, Prospero maintains that he has "done nothing but in care" of her (1.2.16) and justifies his actions by telling the story of Antonio's perfidy.

Prospero's delight in the discomfiture of his enemies is revealed most vividly in his response to Ariel's account of his frightening behavior during the tempest. He asks Ariel if he has "perform'd to point the tempest" that he, Prospero, has commanded, and when Ariel replies that he has, Prospero reacts with enthusiastic approval and obvious sadistic pleasure: "My brave spirit! / Who was so firm, so constant, that this coil / Would not infect his reason" (1.2.206–8). His response inspires Ariel to elaborate:

> Not a soul
> But felt a fever of the mad and play'd
> Some tricks of desperation. All but mariners
> Plung'd in the foaming brine and quit the vessel,
> Then all afire with me. The King's son Ferdinand,

> With hair up-staring (then like reeds, not hair),
> Was the first man that leapt; cried "Hell is empty,
> And all the devils are here!"
>
> (1.2.208–15)

Once again Prospero expresses his approval: "Why, that's my spirit!" (1.2.215). Since Ariel has carried out his orders "to every article" (1.2.195), we must assume that the madness and desperation Ariel describes are precisely what Prospero intended. He is pleased not only by the terror of his enemies but also by that of Ferdinand, his future son-in-law. He is rather indiscriminate in his punishments, as he is later in his forgiveness.

Prospero can enjoy the terror of his victims because he has not injured them physically: "But are they, Ariel, safe?" (1.2.217). Not only are they safe, but their garments are "fresher than before" (1.2.219). In the history plays and the tragedies revengers incur guilt and bring destruction on themselves by doing physical violence to their enemies. Prospero is a cunning and sadistic revenger, who employs his magic to inflict terrible psychological violence on his enemies while he shields them from physical injury and thereby preserves his innocence. To his thinking, as long as no one is physically injured, "there's no harm done" (1.2.15). Prospero finds harmless such things as having everyone, including the good Gonzalo, fear imminent destruction, having them run mad with terror at Ariel's apparitions, and having Ferdinand and Alonso believe each other dead.

Prospero's cruelty toward his enemies may not appear to say much about his character because it seems justified by their outrageous treatment of him. He is prone to react with aggression, however, whenever he can find a justification, however slight, for doing so. (I am taking what Harry Berger, Jr. [1970], calls "the hard-nosed," as opposed to the "sentimental," view of Prospero; other hard-nosed critics include Abenheimer 1946, Dobree 1952, Leech 1958, and Auden 1962.) He says he will put Ferdinand in chains and force him to drink sea water and to eat mussels, withered roots, and acorn husks (1.2.462–65), and he makes him remove thousands of logs "lest too light winning" of Miranda "make the prize light" (1.2.452–53). This seems a weak excuse for his sadistic behavior. He even threatens Miranda when she beseeches him to have pity on Ferdinand: "Silence! One word more / Shall make me chide thee, if not hate thee" (1.2.476–77).

The pattern frequently is that Prospero is benevolent until he feels that his kindness has been betrayed or unappreciated, and then he becomes extremely vindictive. He feels betrayed by Antonio, of course, and unappreciated by Ariel when that spirit presses for liberty. He justifies his enslavement of Ariel by reminding him that it was his "art" that freed the spirit from Sycorax's spell, and he threatens him with torments similar to those Sycorax had inflicted if he continues to complain. Prospero's threats seem to me an overreaction. He will peg Ariel in the entrails of an oak merely for murmuring. He makes enormous claims on the basis of his kindness, and if others do not honor these claims by displaying loyalty, gratitude, and obedience, he becomes enraged. If he is ready to punish Ariel and to hate Miranda for very slight offenses, think of the vindictiveness he must feel toward Antonio. Ariel is self-effacing and knows how to make peace with Prospero. He thanks him for having freed him and promises to "be correspondent to command / And do [his] spriting gently" (1.2.297–98). This allows Prospero to become benevolent once again, and he promises to discharge Ariel in two days. Ariel then says what Prospero wants to hear: "That's my noble master!" (1.2.299). This is the way in which Prospero insists on being perceived. Indeed, Prospero's anger with Ariel when he murmurs derives in part from the fact that Ariel has threatened his idealized image by making him seem unkind.

Ariel plays Prospero's game, but Caliban does not. Prospero is initially very kind to Caliban; he strokes him, gives him treats, educates him, and lodges him in his cell. Caliban at first reciprocates; he loves Prospero and shows him "all the qualities o' th' isle" (1.2.337). When Caliban seeks to violate Miranda's honor, however, Prospero turns against him, and from this point on he treats Caliban with great brutality. Here, too, Prospero overreacts. He is so enraged, I think, because Caliban has repeated Antonio's crime, accepting Prospero's favors and repaying them with treachery. Prospero discharges onto him all of the anger he feels toward the enemies back home, who, before the day of reckoning, lie beyond his power.

Prospero exhibits a major contradiction in his attitude toward Caliban. He feels that Caliban is subhuman, but he holds him morally responsible for his act and punishes him severely. If Caliban in fact is subhuman, then he is not morally responsible and should simply be kept away from Miranda, a precaution Prospero could easily effect. If he is a moral agent, then he needs to be shown the error of his ways; but Prospero's punishments are merely designed to torture him and to break his spirit. The contradiction in Prospero's attitude results from conflicting psychological needs. He needs to hold Caliban responsible because doing so allows him to act out his sadistic impulses, but he also needs to regard Caliban as subhuman because this allows him to avoid feeling guilt. If Caliban is subhuman, he is not part of Prospero's moral community, and Prospero's behavior toward him is not subject to the shoulds and taboos that are operative in his relations with his fellow human beings. Caliban provides Prospero with a splendid opportunity for justified aggression, for being vindictive without losing his nobility.

Prospero's rationalization of his treatment of Caliban works so well that the majority of critics have accepted his point of view and have felt that Caliban deserves what he gets, although some have been sympathetic toward Caliban's suffering and uneasy about Prospero's behavior (Auden 1962, 129). Prospero is constantly punishing Caliban, not just for the attempted rape, but also for the much lesser crimes of surliness, resentment, and insubordination. When Caliban is slow in responding to Prospero's summons, "Slave! Caliban! / Thou earth, thou!" (1.2.313–14), Prospero calls him again in an even nastier way: "Thou poisonous slave, got by the devil himself / Upon thy wicked dam, come forth!" (1.2.319–20). Caliban does not yield a "kind answer" (1.2.309) but enters with curses, and Prospero responds by promising horrible punishments:

> For this, be sure, to-night thou shalt have cramps,
> Side-stitches that shall pen thy breath up; urchins
> Shall, for that vast of night that they may work,
> All exercise on thee; thou shalt be pinch'd
> As thick as honeycomb, each pinch more stinging
> Than bees that made 'em.
>
> (1.2.325–30)

This is a very unequal contest since Caliban's curses are merely words, an expression of ill will, whereas Prospero has the power to inflict the torments he describes. Prospero looks for penitence, submissiveness, and gracious service from Caliban and punishes him severely for his spirit of defiance. He seems to be trying to torture Caliban into being a willing slave, like Ariel, and he is embittered by his lack of success.

Prospero and Caliban are caught in a vicious circle from which there seems no escape. The more Caliban resists what he perceives as Prospero's tyranny, the more Prospero punishes him; and the more

Prospero punishes him, the more Caliban resists. He curses Prospero even though he knows that his spirits hear him and that he may be subject to retaliation—"yet I needs must curse" (2.2.4). The need for this emotional relief must be powerful, indeed, in view of what may be in store for him:

> For every trifle are they set upon me,
> Sometime like apes that mow and chatter at me,
> And after bite me; then like hedgehogs which
> Lie tumbling in my barefoot way, and mount
> Their pricks at my footfall; sometime am I
> All wound with adders, who with cloven tongues
> Do hiss me into madness.
>
> (2.2.8–14)

It is remarkable that Caliban's spirit has not been broken as a result of such torments. And it is no wonder that Caliban seizes the opportunity he thinks is presented by Stephano and Trinculo to revolt against Prospero. "I am subject," he tells them, "to a tyrant, / A sorcerer, that by his cunning hath / Cheated me of the island" (3.2.42–44). Is this far from the truth? He claims that Prospero's spirits "all do hate him / As rootedly as I" (3.2.94–95). It is impossible to say whether or not this is true, but it might be. Even Ariel has to be threatened with terrible punishments and reminded once a month of what Prospero has done for him.

Prospero does not need to use his magic to resolve inner conflicts in his relationship with Caliban because regarding Caliban as subhuman allows him to act out his vindictive impulses without guilt or restraint. The combination of his sadistic imagination and his magic makes him an ingenious torturer. He could have used his magic more benignly if he had regarded Caliban as part of his moral community, but this would have generated conflicts and deprived him of his scapegoat. (See Berger 1970, 261, on Caliban as scapegoat.) Prospero insists, therefore, that Caliban is uneducable:

> A devil, a born devil, on whose nature
> Nurture can never stick! on whom my pains,
> Humanely taken, all, all lost, quite lost!
>
> (4.1.188–90)

His judgment is reinforced both by Miranda, who abhors Caliban in part because his vindictiveness violates her self-effacing values, and by Caliban's plot, which seems to demonstrate his innate depravity. Since there is no point in being humane to a born devil, Prospero is free to "plague" him "to roaring" (4.1.192–93).

Many critics agree that Caliban is a hopeless case, but some are impressed by his sensitivity in the speech "The isle is full of noises" and by his declaration that he will "seek for grace" (5.1.296; see Berger 1970, 255). His plot can be seen as a reaction to Prospero's abuse rather than as a sign that he is an "abhorred slave / Which any print of goodness wilt not take" (1.2.351–52). Prospero must hold on to his image of Caliban as a devil in order to hold on to his idealized image of himself. If Caliban is redeemable, then Prospero has been a monster. The exchange of curses between Prospero and Caliban indicates that they have much in common. What Prospero hates and punishes in Caliban is the forbidden part of himself. His denial of moral status to Caliban is in part a rationale for his vindictive behavior and in part a way of denying the similarities that clearly exist between them. Prospero is doing to Caliban what Caliban would do to Prospero if he had the power.

Prospero is much more careful in his treatment of his fellow humans, some of whom strike us as being considerably more depraved than Caliban. Indeed, Prospero calls Caliban a devil but feels that Antonio and Sebastian "are worse than devils" (3.3.36). Nonetheless, they are members of his moral community, and his shoulds and taboos are fully in operation in relation to them. Not only does he conceal his vindictiveness from himself (and from many of the critics) by employing his magic to punish them without doing them any "harm" but he justifies his treatment of them by seeing it as conducive to their moral growth. His object is not revenge but regeneration and reconciliation. Ariel articulates Prospero's perspective in the banquet scene. He accuses the "three men of sin" (3.3.53)—Antonio, Sebastian, and Alonso—of their crimes against "good Prospero" (3.3.70), threatens them with "ling'ring perdition" (3.3.77), and indicates that they can escape Prospero's wrath only by "heart's sorrow / And a clear life ensuing" (3.3.81–82). Even as Prospero is knitting them up in "fits" and exulting in the fact that "they are now in [his] pow'r" (3.3.90–91), he is being presented in a very noble light. He manages to take revenge in such a way that he emerges as the benefactor of his victims.

After he has tormented them so much that "the good old Lord Gonzalo" (5.1.15) is in tears at the sight and even Ariel has "a feeling / Of their afflictions" (5.1.21–22), Prospero relents, as he had intended to do all along. Although he is still furious with the evil three, claiming that "with their high wrongs [he is] struck to th' quick" (5.1.25), now his perfectionistic and self-effacing shoulds are stronger than his vindictive impulses. He releases them from his spell in part because his cruelty is making him uneasy and in part because his need for revenge has been assuaged to some extent by their suffering. He proclaims that "the rarer action is / In virtue than in vengeance" (5.1.27–28), but he says this only after he has gotten a goodly measure of vengeance. While he makes it seem that his only purpose has been to bring the men of sin to penitence, that is hardly the case. This is a play not only about renouncing revenge but also about getting it.

There has been much debate over whether Prospero's enemies do indeed repent. Prospero's forgiveness is made contingent on penitence and a clear life thereafter, but only Alonso seems to merit his pardon. Whereas Alonso displays his remorse again and again, Sebastian and Antonio show no sign of repentance or promise of reformation. They have plotted against Prospero in the past, they try to kill Alonso during the course of the play, and they seem at the play's end still to be dangerous fellows. Many critics have speculated on the likelihood of their continued criminality upon their return to Italy, and in 1797 F. G. Waldron wrote a sequel to *The Tempest* in which Antonio and Sebastian betray Prospero during the voyage home and force him to retrieve his magic.

Why, then, does Prospero forgive them? It may be that he believes they have repented, but I do not think he does. While Antonio is still under his spell, Prospero says, "I do forgive thee, / Unnatural though thou art" (5.1.78–79); and when he has returned to full consciousness, Prospero forgives him again, in an even more contemptuous way:

> For you, most wicked sir, whom to call brother
> Would even infect my mouth, I do forgive
> Thy rankest fault—all of them.
>
> (5.1.130–32)

As Bonamy Dobree (1952) has suggested, Prospero's forgiveness seems more like a form of revenge than a movement toward reconciliation. It is a vindictive forgiveness, which satisfies his need to express his scorn and bitterness while appearing to be noble. Antonio's undeservingness contributes to Prospero's sense of moral grandeur; the worse Antonio is, the more charitable Prospero is to forgive him. This is Prospero's perspective as well as that of the play's rhetoric; but from a psychological point of view Prospero's forgiveness seems compulsive, indiscriminate, and dangerous—inappropriate to the practical and moral realities of the situation but necessary if Prospero is to maintain his idealized image.

For most of the play Prospero's idealized image contains a combination of arrogant-vindictive and self-effacing traits, which are reconciled by means of his magic. He needs to see himself as a humane, benevolent, forgiving man, and also as a powerful, masterful, dangerous man who cannot be taken advantage of with impunity and who will strike back when he has been injured. The first four acts of the play show Prospero satisfying his needs for mastery and revenge, but in ways that do not violate the dictates of his self-effacing side. By the end of act 4 he has achieved his objectives. He has knit up Antonio, Sebastian, and Alonso in his spell and has thwarted the plot of Caliban, Stephano, and Trinculo, with a final display of innocent delight in the torture of the conspirators. Prospero sets his dogs (two of which are aptly named Fury and Tyrant) on them, and tells Ariel to

> charge my goblins that they grind their joints
> With dry convulsions, shorten up their sinews
> With aged cramps, and more pinch-spotted make them
> Than pard or cat o' mountain.
>
> (4.1.258–61)

"At this hour," Prospero proclaims, "lie at my mercy all mine enemies" (4.1.262–63). From this point on he becomes increasingly self-effacing. At the beginning of the next act he gives up his vengeance and determines to renounce his magic. Once he abandons his magic, he has no choice but to repress his arrogant-vindictive trends, for it was only through his magic that he was able to act them out innocently.

Prospero represses his vindictive side for a number of reasons. He has achieved as much of a revenge as his inner conflicts will allow, and he has shown his power. Now, in order to satisfy his self-effacing shoulds, he must show his mercy. He cannot stop behaving vindictively until his anger has been partially assuaged, but he cannot continue to do so once his enemies are in his power. That he is still angry is clear from the manner of his forgiveness, but the imperative to forgive is now more powerful than the need for revenge. Given his inner conflicts, Prospero is bound to feel uncomfortable about his aggressive behavior; and now that he has had his day of reckoning, his negative feelings about it become dominant. He regards revenge as ignoble, and he "abjures" his "rough magic" (5.1.50–51). His choice of words here is significant. He seems to feel ashamed of his magic (even as he celebrates his powers) and guilty for having employed it. Why else would he use the word "abjure," which means to disavow, recant, or repudiate? Whereas earlier he was able to enjoy his power, he now has a self-effacing response to it. He gives up his magic because he needs to place himself in a humble position and to show that he has not used his power for personal aggrandizement but only to set things right, to bring about moral growth and reconciliation.

With his "charms . . . o'erthrown," Prospero, in the Epilogue, adopts an extremely self-effacing posture. Since he can no longer "enchant," he can "be reliev'd" only by prayer,

> Which pierces so that it assaults
> Mercy itself and frees all faults.
> As you from crimes would pardon'd be
> Let your indulgence set me free.
> (Epi. 17–20)

Prospero sees himself here not as the avenger but as the guilty party, perhaps because of his revenge; he tries to make a self-effacing bargain in which he judges not, so that he not be judged. We can now understand more fully his motives for forgiving the "men of sin." Beneath his self-righteousness Prospero has hidden feelings of guilt and fears of retribution. By refusing to take a more severe form of revenge, to which he certainly seems entitled, he protects himself against punishment. By forgiving others, he insures his own pardon. Giving up his magic serves a similar purpose: it counteracts his feelings of pride and places him in a dependent, submissive position. Although Prospero's remarks in the Epilogue are in part a conventional appeal to the audience, he remains in character and expresses sentiments that are in keeping with his psychological development.

When we understand Prospero's psychological development, he seems different from the figure celebrated by so many critics. Those who interpret The Tempest as a story of magnanimity, forgiveness, and reconciliation are responding correctly, I think, to Shakespeare's thematic intentions, while those who take a more "hard-nosed" view of the play are responding to the psychological portrait of Prospero.

There is in this play, as in some others, a disparity between rhetoric and mimesis that generates conflicting critical responses and reflects the inner divisions of the author.

The rhetoric of the play justifies the vindictive Prospero and glorifies the self-effacing one. It confirms Prospero's idealized image of himself as a kindly, charitable man who punishes others much less than they deserve and only for their own good. The action of the play, meanwhile, shows us a Prospero who is bitter, sadistic, and hungry for revenge. The disparity between rhetoric and mimesis is a reflection of Prospero's inner conflicts and of Shakespeare's. The rhetoric rationalizes and disguises Prospero's vindictiveness and celebrates his moral nobility (see Sundelson 1980, 38–39). Its function is similar to that of Prospero's magic, which enables Prospero to have his revenge yet remain innocent in his own eyes and in the eyes of the other characters. The magic and the rhetoric together enable Shakespeare to deceive both himself and most audiences as to Prospero's true nature.

III

Harold McCurdy and I both feel that *The Tempest* is Shakespeare's "ideal solution," but we differ in defining the problem that Shakespeare is trying to solve. For McCurdy Shakespeare's problem is how to "admit the loving-kindness of Christian charity" without feeling spineless, and the solution is to accompany it with such a demonstration of power that it "appears gracious and magnanimous" rather than weak (1953, 162). McCurdy sees Shakespeare as a predominantly aggressive person who is afraid of his softer emotions and who can express them only when his toughness and mastery have been firmly established. For me Shakespeare's problem is how to give expression to the hostile, vindictive, aggressive side of his personality without violating his stronger need to be noble, loving, and innocent; the solution is to create situations that permit justified aggression and innocent revenge. I see Shakespeare as a predominantly self-effacing person who is afraid of his aggressive impulses and who can express them directly only when it seems virtuous to do so.

From *1 Henry VI* to *The Tempest* a frequent concern of Shakespeare's plays is how to cope with wrongs, how to remain good in an evil world. In the histories and the tragedies the tendency of the main characters is to respond to wrongs by taking revenge; but this response contaminates the revenger and eventually results in his own destruction. In Horneyan terms, the arrogant-vindictive solution, with its emphasis upon retaliation and vindictive triumph, does not work. But the self-effacing solution does not work in these plays either, for many innocent, well-intentioned but weak characters perish. Hamlet's problem, as I see it, is how to take revenge and remain innocent. The problem is insoluble and nearly drives him mad. In a number of the comedies and romances Shakespeare explores a different response to being wronged—namely, mercy and forgiveness. Because of the conventions of these genres, with their providential universe and miraculous conversions, wronged characters do not have to take revenge: either fate does it for them, or they forgive their enemies, who are then permanently transformed. In these plays the self-effacing solution, with its accompanying bargain, works very well, but only because the plays are unrealistic.

What I infer about Shakespeare from his plays is that he has strong vindictive impulses but even stronger taboos against those impulses, and a fear of the guilt and punishment to which he would be exposed if he acted them out. He does act them out imaginatively in the histories and tragedies, and he is purged of them through the destruction of his surrogate aggressors. He also fears his self-effacing side, however, and he shows both himself and us, through characters like Henry VI, Hamlet, Desdemona (Paris 1984b), and Timon, that people who are too good and trusting cannot cope and will be destroyed. In the tragedies he portrays the inadequacy of both solutions. In some of the comedies and in the romances he fantasizes the triumph of good people and avoids guilt either by glorifying forgiveness or by leaving revenge to the gods. In *The Tempest*, through Prospero's magic, he imagines a solution to Hamlet's problem: Prospero is at once vindictive and noble, vengeful and innocent. Although he takes his revenge through his magic, by raising a tempest and inflicting various psychological torments, he does not really "hurt" anybody; and when he has had his vindictive triumph, he renounces his magic and forgives everyone.

The Tempest offers an ideal solution to the problem of how to cope with wrongs without losing one's innocence—but only through the first four acts. The solution collapses when Prospero renounces his magic, for his magic was the only means by which he could reconcile his conflicts and keep evil under control. He does not at the end seem to have attained psychological balance or to have discovered a viable way of living in the real world.

Magic enables Prospero to attain only a temporary psychological equilibrium. It solves one set of problems, but it generates new inner conflicts, which he attempts to resolve by becoming extremely self-effacing. As we have seen, he abjures his magic because of a need to disown his pride and to assuage the feelings of guilt aroused by his exercise of power. Prospero has never been comfortable with power, which is one reason he delegated his authority to Antonio, and he seems unduly eager to relinquish it here. The problem is that though Prospero feels guilty with power, he feels helpless without it, as the Epilogue indicates. Even with all of his objectives achieved, Prospero seems weary rather than triumphant at the end. He will see the nuptials solemnized in Naples:

> And thence retire me to my Milan, where
> Every third thought shall be my grave.
> (5.1.311–12)

Since he has given up his secret studies and has no taste for governance, what, indeed, is there for Prospero? It is no wonder that he longs to withdraw into the quietude of death.

We see Prospero at the end in the grip of self-effacing and detached trends that do not promise to make him an effective ruler. Even so "sentimental" a critic as Northrop Frye observes that Prospero "appears to have been a remarkably incompetent Duke of Milan, and not to be promising much improvement after he returns" (1969b, 1370). There have been many misgivings about Prospero's forgiveness of Antonio as well as doubts about his ability to cope upon their return to Italy. The forgiveness, as we have seen, is compulsive and indiscriminate. There is no evidence of repentance on Antonio's part and no reason to think that he will meekly submit to Prospero's rule. Antonio should, at the least, be put into jail; but Prospero can neither do this nor, we suspect, keep him under control. Like the Duke in *Measure for Measure* and many other of Shakespeare's self-effacing characters, Prospero cannot exercise authority and deal effectively with the guilty. At the end of *The Tempest* Shakespeare seems back where he started in the plays about Henry VI, with a nobly Christian ruler who cannot cope with the harsh realities of life.

Like Prospero at the end of *The Tempest,* Shakespeare at the end of his career seems to have resolved his inner conflicts by repressing his aggressive impulses and becoming extremely self-effacing. In *Henry VIII* he begins at the point he had reached by the end of *The Tempest*. The desire for revenge, which had inspired such a marvelous fantasy in *The Tempest*, is no longer present. Character after character is wronged and responds in a remarkably charitable manner, asking forgiveness and blessing his or her enemies. There is no need to cope with evil; rather we must submit ourselves patiently to the divine will, which has a reason for everything. As J. B. Priestley has said, Shakespeare was "a deeply divided man," the "opposites" of whose nature gave "energy and life to his works." In *Henry VIII* the opposites are gone, and the result is a vapid moral fable in which we no longer feel the presence of a complex and fascinating personality. This play makes it clear that Shakespeare's inner conflicts had much to do with the richness and ambiguity of his art.

What Is Shakespeare?

David Willbern

During the spring of 1819 a young American writer visited Shakespeare's birthplace in Stratford-on-Avon. While in what he termed the "squalid chambers" of the actual birthroom, Washington Irving noted "a striking instance of the spontaneous and universal homage of mankind to the great poet of nature." Such veneration displayed itself on the walls of the chamber, which were covered with the handwritten names of previous visitors. A garrulous old woman showed Irving through the house, displaying various authentic relics (Shakespeare's tobacco box, his sword, his very chair), while her visitor listened with that "resolute good-humored credulity" that befits a tourist. As was the custom, he sat in Shakespeare's chair. Afterward he wandered the Stratford countryside, where he felt the spirit of the Bard pervade the spirit of the place, suffusing the landscape like a romantic muse, illuminating forests, hills, and houses in "the prism of poetry" (Irving 1983, 983–1001).

A few decades later another American author made the requisite literary pilgrimage. In the summer of 1855, having been appointed by President Franklin Pierce as the American Consul at Liverpool, fifty-year-old Nathaniel Hawthorne visited Stratford. He was surprised by the small size of Shakespeare's birthroom, and like Irving he noted that the ceiling, walls, and even windowpanes of that famous chamber were "entirely written over with names in pencil, by persons . . . of all varieties of stature." Unlike Irving, Hawthorne maintained a skeptic's stance. He refused to add *his* name to the scribblings of the multitude, and had "Shakespeare's chair" still occupied the scene, he would have been unlikely to sit in it. While in the house, he "felt no emotion whatever—not the slightest—nor any quickening of the imagination." Although he could now envisage a more solid idea of the man, he was "not quite sure that this [was] altogether desirable" (Hawthorne 1962, 129–34).

Fifty years later, at the turn of the century, two more American writers followed in the footsteps of their predecessors. They were more skeptical yet—Samuel Clemens and Henry James were both anti-Stratfordians. Clemens's contribution to the question was a volume entitled *Is Shakespeare Dead?* (1906), wherein he advanced the cause of the Baconians. Though James preferred no particular rival candidate, he spoke of "the lout from Stratford" and wrote that "the divine William is [a] fraud." Still he suffered torment at the unguessed riddle of Shakespeare's genius (Edel 1972, 145–46). So fascinated was James by this mystery that he wrote a story about it. "The Birthplace" (1903) represents his challenge to bardolatry and his idea of transcendent authorship.

The story concerns an English couple hired to look after the birthplace of "the supreme poet, the Mecca of the English-speaking race." The poet is never named. The caretaker, Morris Gedge, is charged with presenting "the Facts" established over centuries. Of greatest interest to Gedge and tourists alike is "the low, the sublime Chamber of Birth":

> It was empty as a shell of which the kernel has withered, and contained neither busts nor prints nor early copies; it contained only the Fact—*the* Fact itself.
>
> (263)

Morris Gedge takes to sitting in the birthroom alone, in the dark, and gradually begins to lose faith in the room, in the birthplace, in the birth—in short, in the Facts. His lapse of both "piety and patriotism" is encouraged by the arrival of a young American couple from New York. When the husband asserts, " 'The play's the thing.' Let the author alone," Gedge fervently agrees and adds:

> "It's all I want—to let the author alone. Practically . . . there *is* no author; that is for us to deal with. There are all the immortal people—*in* the work; but there's nobody else."
>
> "Yes," said the young man—"that's what it comes to. There should really, to clear the matter up, be no such Person."
>
> "As you say," Gedge returned, "it's what it comes to. There *is* no such Person."
>
> The evening air listened, in the warm, thick midland stillness, while the wife's little cry rang out. "But *wasn't* there—?"
>
> "There was somebody," said Gedge, against the doorpost. "But They've killed Him. And, dead as He is, They keep it up. They do it over again, They kill Him every day."
>
> (283–84)

James's story is about God, paternity, and the mystery of sexuality. It is also about Shakespeare and the developing Shakespeare mythology of the late nineteenth century. James's mysterious idea of Shakespeare so fascinated him that he reanimated it in an introduction to *The Tempest* composed for Sir Sidney Lee a few years later, in 1907. Here James writes that "the man himself, in the Plays, we directly touch, to my consciousness, positively nowhere: we are dealing too perpetually with the artist, the monster and magician of a thousand masks." Instead of a withered kernel in an empty shell, we find the author "at the centre of the storm":

> There in fact, though there only, we find that serenity; find the subject itself intact and unconscious, seated as unwinking and inscrutable as a divinity in a temple, save for that vague flicker of derision, the only response to our interpretive heat, which adds the last beauty to its face.
>
> (297–98)

What is Shakespeare? Where do we find that subject and make it visible? How do we distinguish the proper name from the authorial name, Shakespeare from "Shakespeare"? How can we make the inscrutable subject itself respond to our interpretive heat? Irving and Hawthorne observed with admiration or dismay the autographs written over every surface in Shakespeare's birthroom, as though a sacred space had been honored or violated. In "The Birthplace" James wrote over Shakespeare by erasing him from the story and then re-creating "Him" in the author's own transcendent image of idealized Author. Is Shakespeare then an inscrutable divinity, a being before whom, as Yeats maintained, "the world was almost as empty . . . as it must be in the eyes of God" (Yeats [1924] 1961, 106–7)? Is he "a ghost, a shadow now," as Joyce's Stephen Dedalus would have it, "a voice heard only in the heart of him who is the substance of his shadow, the son consubstantial with the father" (Joyce 1934, 194)? Perhaps he was "just like any other man," as Hazlitt wrote, "but that he was like all other men. . . . He was nothing in himself; but he was all that others were, or that they could become. . . . He was like the genius of humanity" (Halliday 1958, 88). This idealization is epitomized in Borges's parable: "There was no one in him; . . . there was only a bit of coldness, a dream dreamt by no one. . . . No one has ever been so many men as this man, who like the Egyptian Proteus could exhaust all the guises of reality" (Borges 1964, 248–49). In this parable Shakespeare becomes finally a secondary deity, a demiurge who dreams his world as he himself is dreamed by God.

Erased, written over, mythologized, and apotheosized, Shakespeare has become the critical *occasion for idealization*. His is the exemplary authorial space that we whitewash over and on which we inscribe our names. Twenty years ago Alfred Harbage described Shakespearean idolatry as a wish for a secular theology in an age buffeted by the loss of faith. Lately, in the tradition of Nietzsche, Barthes, and Foucault, "Shakespeare" has begun to signify the ultimate instance of the author as dead father: a corpus that speaks from an absence, the author who arrives, if at all, DOA (though perhaps reports are exaggerated). As the primal patriarchal agent of authorship he becomes a transcendental anonymity (Barthes 1977, 142–47; Foucault 1977, 113–38). Or he represents the seminal spirit of modern literature, a source without origin or rival: a Shakes*père* of the Western world (Bloom 1973, 11).

These contemporary models of transcendent patriarchal authorship are powerfully adumbrated by Shakespeare. Enter, stage left, the Ghost of King Hamlet. This spectral narrator unfolds a tale that his listener inscribes in the "book and volume" of his brain, incorporating this story as his own, making it the motive and the cue for his passion and re-action. The Ghost is first a "questionable shape," but Hamlet identifies it in his own terms: "I'll call thee Hamlet" (1.4.43–44). A similar moment opens the play: the question "Who's there?" is met with the charge "Nay, answer me. Stand and unfold yourself." Reflective self-identification is legitimate, yet it is also faulty, an identity mistook, an act of *méconnaissance*. Stage tradition holds that Shakespeare himself played the role of King Hamlet's Ghost. If so, then the principle of authorship thus displayed posits a ghostly and questionable narrator who is backed by a substantial and identifiable actor who authors his own player's speech. Shakespeare enacts an answer to the question of authorship even as he dramatizes its dilemmas. The figure of Shakespeare the actor reciting the lines of "Shakespeare" the author from within a royal suit of armor that holds both absence and presence embodies a simultaneous invention of modern *and* postmodern ideas of authorship. His figure is not in the carpet, but behind the visor or the arras.

Shakespeare wrote during a period when modern ideas of the author were being invented, or historically redesigned. As Renaissance printers invented the book, Renaissance poets invented the author.

Between the conventional anonymity of Spenser's *Calender* and the personal exhibitionism of Jonson's *Works* Shakespeare explored (behind the scenes) the aesthetic space between the "speaking fiction" (character) and the "real writer" (person)—to use Foucault's terms. During this time the cultural significance of what Foucault called "the author function" was changing (Erickson 1985b). Literary texts were becoming identified by author and owned by producer and authorizing agent; anonymity was becoming intolerable. The grounds of literary creation were being enclosed, like sixteenth-century English pastureland. Unlike his contemporaries Marlowe, Jonson, and Chapman, Shakespeare did not attempt to aggrandize himself or to construct an idealized image of himself as author. He preferred to work *within* the dramatic arena, rather than to boast of his mastery *of* it. For Shakespeare *actor* and *author* were literally synonymous: in the variable spelling of his day, "auctor." He was simultaneously player and poet, not merely in his profession, but in his concept of his art. Whereas today Shakespeare's text is the *writing,* and dramatic productions are the *reading,* in 1600 writing and reading, or inscription and representation, were unified in dramatic production at the Globe. Shakespeare's plays had an immediate, here-and-now origin and enactment, in which he participated. As poet, his plays were not separate from him since he was also their reader, actor, producer, and director. As player, his scripts were not strange to him since he wrote and revised them as he and his company performed. He embodied the perfect merger of "author's pen" and "actor's voice" (*Troilus and Cressida,* Pro. 24). He could physically animate his own text, or he could retire from it, in a gesture of absence, while maintaining an active presence in it. His is the new and privileged position of the modern "playwright" (the term did not exist before Shakespeare). In order to conceptualize the genius of Shakespearean authorship in its historical moment, we need a theory of "auctorship."

The historical invention of the modern author as secular authority for the production of individualized texts correlates with developing Renaissance concepts of personhood, or what Barthes called "the prestige of the individual" (1977, 145). Shakespeare occupies an original position in such concepts. Whereas Marlowe invented the dramatic egotist, Shakespeare invented the dramatic ego. *Hamlet* is of course the central enactment. A more limited example comes from the penultimate scene of *Richard II.* Confined to his cell, Richard prefigures the Cartesian ego attempting to imagine its existence and, implicitly, its death. Richard searches for himself in analogy (comparing the prison to the world, or his time to a clock) and in drama (in one person he plays many people). Identity for Richard is theater, role playing: he plays himself and thereby re-creates himself. Mere language is insufficient in the world, however, and he, as does Hamlet, fails. Philosophy surrenders to action; bare thought cannot confer being. Shakespeare would have restated the Cartesian axiom: I *act*, therefore I am. The claim carries its own irony: acting is simultaneously genuine and pretense.

Of course Shakespeare did not invent the concept of the theatricality of everyday life. It was a cultural phenomenon that invoked a medieval *Theatrum Mundi*. Yet Shakespeare knew, better than anyone else, how deeply rooted was theatricality in the development of human behavior and relationships: not merely as stages on or through which we strut and fret to enact numberable "ages of man" but as a central construct in forming our selves.

Is the self, then, only a series of masks and poses? Is there no person behind the persona? The question dilates into psychology and philosophy. At a lower stage the history of Shakespeare productions offers a theatrical emblem of the problem. When a critic leaves a contemporary production of *Twelfth Night,* performed in a twenty-first-century subway system to punk rock and strobe lights, muttering something to the effect that "it was interesting, but it wasn't Shakespeare," what does he mean? Can he be measuring the production against an original standard that he or Shakespeare criticism considers authentic? Surely not, since no reader of Shakespeare criticism could hope to find such a standard. The history of Shakespeare productions, like the history of Shakespeare criticism, traces a trajectory of cultural values: particular stagings mirror their historical circumstances. Yet however unique or bizarre a particular production may be, most directors and actors proceed from some idea of an authentic, original Shakespeare. Who is he? What is that?

In his discussion of Derrida's theory of representation, Edward Said recounts a travesty of *Hamlet* described in *Great Expectations* (Said 1983, 196–99). The performance is quintessentially Dickensian. Characters are woefully miscast and comically attired; actors forget their lines or butcher them; members of the audience heckle uproariously (poor Mr. Wopsle plays the Prince). There are in fact several other, extraneous plays vying with *Hamlet* for attention and applause. Yet even as it is being mangled, violated, and travestied, Shakespeare's play not only survives but also controls its distortions. It sounds through the melee; the text asserts itself through its misquotings. Like the Ghost beneath the stage, an idea of original authority underlies all its variant representations. That idea persists in memory: in Dickens's narrated travesty "the royal phantom also carried a ghostly manuscript, to which it had the appearance of occasionally referring" (1964, 273–77). We measure textual or dramatic distortions against an ideal that we cannot recover (and that never existed anyway).

Idealization is the cardinal temptation for anyone conceptualizing Shakespeare. Efforts to surpass predecessors in quotable praise are noteworthy and notorious in the critical tradition from Jonson's day to our own: "To draw no envy (Shakespeare) on thy name, / ... I confess thy writings to be such, / As neither Man, nor Muse, can praise too much." Like Jonson's primary tribute, most idealizations contain a germ or virulent agent of ambivalence. Idealization requires denial, which then resurfaces, like the return of the repressed. (Such a scheme, by the way, helps in understanding the interplay of bardolatry and anti-Stratfordianism in nineteenth- and twentieth-century Shakespeare criticism.) Shakespeare is *the* occasion for idealization in English literature. Given conventional evaluative hierarchies, with their need for a pantheon, some author must represent the head. That Shakespeare is unarguably the appropriate figurehead attests both to his genius and to our need to mythologize authors as cultural heroes. The only times in which Shakespeare's genius went without saying were those periods when he was undervalued as an author. Today, when his genius is assured, it goes with saying repeatedly.

Anti-Stratfordians persist, of course, long after Delia Bacon's demise. One new book supports the claim of the Earl of Oxford, and doubtless champions of other claimants (though no new ones) await in the wings. Like "the Facts" of Shakespeare, the evidence of these debunkers is of minimal interest. What is of interest is the sheer persistence of the myth of debunking. That challenges to Shakespeare's identity should persist so tenaciously in the face of lucid evidence of their contraries indicates a significant critical and historical phenomenon. Manic skepticism about Shakespeare as genuine author represents the lunatic fringe of a real issue in Shakespeare scholarship: the issue of conjecture, or speculation. The identity question is the wildest instance; a milder one is the birthdate. We all know that Shakespeare was born on April 23, 1564, and that he probably was not. The birthdate has an aesthetic, not a historical, veracity. April 23 is Saint George's Day; it is the day on which Shakespeare died in 1616, rounding his little life with an artistically pleasing sleep. It is thus the best conjectural date. Shakespeare's historical life *begins* with conjecture. That conjecture matches the known facts is precisely what is so fascinating about the case. Shakespeare, like King Hamlet's Ghost—a character the author is conjectured to have played—originates in a questionable shape that answers to our identifications.

Another set of emblems is the various portraits. All of them—the Chandos, the Droeshout, the Jannsen, the Flower, the Felton, *et alia*—are attempts to paint a *like*ness. They are still-life versions of performances of Shakespeare's plays: they re-present an original in acts of variant authenticity, where neither original nor authority remains. My favorite is the Chandos. I admire the healthy complexion, the neatly trimmed beard, the penetrating yet playful eyes, the simple yet elegant clothes, and that burnished gold hoop in the left ear. The face is almost a perfect oval, like an egg or a zero. The power and serenity of the gaze enchant me. Among the portraits the Chandos may be the least legitimate, according to experts. It is thereby the most legitimate to me, since it, like the birthdate, emblematizes the place of conjecture in Shakespeare studies. It is the *sign* of Shakespeare and therefore more than a mere portrait. It is also, of course, a mirror. Samuel Schoenbaum relates that "Desmond McCarthy has said somewhere that trying to work out Shakespeare's personality was like looking at a very dark glazed portrait in the National Portrait Gallery: at first you see nothing, then you begin to recognize features, and then you realize that they are your own" (1970, ix).

Signs can be deceptive; they often carry more weight than what they signify, yet they are often all we have. Eighteenth-century reports indicate that the wooden signboard of the Globe Playhouse was a painting of Hercules with the world on his shoulders. This sign signifies more than global theater or the equation of stage with world. It is the sign of deception, of momentary usurpation, of displacement. (Hercules first tricked Atlas into gathering the golden apples of the Hesperides, then tricked him again into resuming his fated burden.) It signifies an essential aspect of the idea of Shakespeare: the author as usurper.

Shakespeare's first public notice describes him as a thief. He is the upstart crow beautified with others' feathers, a player with a tiger's heart (Greene, quoted in Halliday 1958, 45). Another contemporary writes, "Shakespeare, that nimble Mercury thy brain, / Lulls many Argus-eyes asleep" (Freeman, quoted in Halliday 1958, 47). (Mercury put Argus to sleep by telling him the tale of Pan and Syrinx as he played on a pipe; he then decapitated him in order to steal Io, the white cow loved by Zeus.) Dryden called Shakespeare "the very Janus of poets; he wears almost everywhere two faces" (quoted in Halliday 1958, 57). Nietzsche remarked that "dramatists are in general rather wicked men" and that Shakespeare in particular had a "close relationship with the passions" (1909–11, 6:176). Yeats, in his famous thesis about "some one myth" for every man, wrote, "Shakespeare's myth, it may be, describes a wise man who was blind from very wisdom, and an empty man who thrust him from his place, and saw all that could be seen for very emptiness" ([1924] 1961, 107). (Hamlet and Fortinbras, or Richard and Bolingbroke, exemplify the pattern.)

Nineteenth-century phrenologists, following Renaissance science, believed that the organ of robbery and the organ of dramaturgy were the same (Schoenbaum 1970, 298). Shakespeare's career offers evidence for the correlation: almost all of his plots are taken from elsewhere, and much of his language consists of passages from Holinshed or North magically transmuted into perfect iambic pentameter. Trained from boyhood in classical modes of *imitatio,* as a playwright he turned others' workmanlike prose into his own flawless poetry. His goal was not traditional translation but transformation (from history or romance to drama). Shakespeare adapted many but was influenced by few. Instead of simply imitating previous styles, he used them. Whereas Jonson imitated classical dramatic forms, and Spenser imitated medieval allegory, Shakespeare explored, examined, and finally exhausted previous genres. He not only used them, he used them up. His approach to tradition was aggressive and exhaustive: he explored, found the limits of, and then exploded conventional categories of dramatic and poetic expression. This pattern of development persists from *Titus Andronicus* and *The Comedy of Errors* through *King Lear* and *The Tempest.* Shakespeare vigorously manipulated dramatic categories, styles, and devices until they wore out under his handling. He played with the history of literary genres: he was *homo ludens* incarnate. He did not boast of novelty, as Marlowe did, nor did he expect veneration, as Jonson did. Whereas Marlowe translated Ovid with the goal of releasing subversive erotic energies, and Jonson translated Horace with the goal of sustaining Latinate fidelity and grace, Shakespeare used translations to create his own narrative in an individually metamorphosed language. He didn't make translations; rather, he made them over. In this sense he was the truest translator of Ovid because he metamorphosed *Metamorphoses* into drama.

Shakespeare's earliest appreciator, Francis Meres, went so far as to claim reincarnation. "The sweet witty soul of Ovid," wrote Meres in 1598, "lives in mellifluous and honey-tongued Shakespeare." Meres's praise was echoed in ensuing years, when Shakespeare was regularly described as honey-tongued, mellifluous, or flowing sweetly and freely. The upstart crow became the sweet swan of Avon (Greene 1592; Jonson 1623). In Ovid's *Metamorphoses* the tales of Cygnus, who was changed to a swan, and of Corone, who was changed to a crow, are successive stories in book 2. Various myths suit the metamorphic, polytropic Shakespeare—Hercules, Mercury, Proteus. One that fits best, however, is suggested in Coleridge's famous characterization of Richard II: "He scatters himself into a multitude of images" (1960, 2:146). Although Coleridge does not make it explicit, the image or event that enacts this idea is Richard's breaking of the mirror. He scatters his own image into fragments; he shatters his narcissism in a psychic disintegration that he tries futilely to repair in prison.

The myth of Narcissus lies at the heart of Shakespeare's dramatic art, as it lies at the heart of much current psychoanalytic theory. Shakespeare is not Narcissus, but he is the reflecting pool, the surface for projection. By looking at Shakespeare's enactments, we can see ourselves. "Who is it that can tell me who I am?" asks Lear. "Lear's shadow," replies the Fool. Actors reflect our identities as shadows projected on the ground: they give us back images of our selves. We in turn attribute to Shakespeare all that we are. "They told me I was everything" could well be Shakespeare's comment to his readers. To characterize Shakespeare's identity, read his critics.

Shakespeare is a ground for narcissistic projection and for our echoing song: he is the mirror in which we see our idealized selves. For literary critics idealization cooperates with identification. By recreating Shakespeare in our own images, critic by critic and age by age, we reconstitute an icon of linguistic perfection, thereby reanimating an aesthetic ideal while participating in its production. Proclamations of Shakespeare's linguistic omnipotence abound: Hazlitt, for instance, wrote that Shakespeare "has a magic power over words: they come winged at his bidding. . . . His language is hieroglyphical. It translates thoughts into visible images" (Halliday 1958, 91).

My own style of idealization follows Hazlitt's, though it falls short of attributing magical animism. For me Shakespeare simply personifies the English language. His genius represents English at its most flexible and creative. That Shakespeare was born into a culture that enabled and encouraged such linguistic creativity is an accident of history wonderful to contemplate. Elizabethan English was a polyglot, protean tongue, developing during a period that experimented simultaneously with vernacular novelties and classical neologisms. It consisted of ageless proverbs and contemporary inventions; its idioms came from humanist scholars and local shopkeepers. Its literary styles, rooted in medieval allegory, blossomed into an abundance of analogy before being pruned by eighteenth-century rules of decorum and poetic diction. Syntax, punctuation, spelling—the smaller codes of discourse—were amorphous boundaries to be established or trespassed according to creative will or whim. Vocabulary was a flux of significance: words were almost too full of meaning. Not until the eighteenth century would they be codified within the systematic confines of dictionaries, sentenced to terminal definition, buried in a linguistic graveyard where proper usage was carved in the tombstones of convention and precedent.

Elizabethan English was a language of imperial acquisition: foreign terms that strayed too close were quickly appropriated. The contrast with Renaissance Latin, in which useful toil Shakespeare early labored, was sharp. As William Kerrigan puts it: "Humanist Latin boasted a barren immutability—all but completed, intolerant of novelty—while English was forever coming into being" (1980, 288). This historical moment precedes seventeenth- and eighteenth-century applications of the author function as a principle of limitation to restrict "dangerous proliferations of meaning" (Foucault 1977, 123). At the core of Shakespeare's linguistic genius lies polysemous proliferation. Henry James, although he doubted the poet's identity, most admired Shakespeare's medium of "Expression": Shakespeare had access to a storehouse of language that burst "out of all doors and windows"; his use of it was "something that was to make of our poor world a great flat table for receiving the glitter and clink of outpoured treasure" ([1907] 1964, 302). James's metaphor conveys the tangible weight of Shakespeare's style, its connection to a fundamental economy of Midas-like transmutation, and the rich scope of piratical plunder Shakespeare's expansive expression achieved.

What best symbolizes Shakespeare's English—the language of his time and his uses of it—is its analogical base, its love of metaphor. Shakespeare *thought* in metaphor, analogy, terms of likeness: he represented one thing by another. Like Homer's Odysseus, he was polytropic; a man of many ways whose language had many turns. He is *l'homme aux modes,* the Proteus of poetry. Analogy is the broad quality of this style, and the pun is its smaller emblem. The pun is a sign in miniature of Shakespeare's uses of, and attitude toward, language: it is equivocal and multivocal, it dilates significance rather than restricts it. Compared to a plain style of straightforward, controlled discourse, puns represent misdirection and liberation. They create layers of polysemous significance. Shakespeare's puns remind us that his language is never superficial. To the extent that the pun symbolizes Shakespeare's seminal, serpentine linguistic medium—the creative matrix of his thought—Samuel Johnson was uncannily perceptive when he complained, "A quibble was to him the fatal Cleopatra for which he lost the world, and was content to lose it" ([1765] 1960, 68).

Johnson's objection reveals the aridity of his own eighteenth-century idea of language while suggesting the fecundity of Shakespeare's. The erotics of Shakespearean writing marries a masculine ideal of verbal virility to a seductive style of feminine polysemy. Of course, Shakespeare criticism, primarily a male tradition, has erected forms of veneration that imitate masculine ideals. My own idealizations participate in these fantasies of masculine power; they are compelling. Yet I believe that a Shakespearean personification of language offers an alternative to the more limited impersonations of masculine or feminine discourse that pervade current critical theory. If any individual use of language can effectively question the structures and boundaries of genderized convention, it is Shakespeare's.

Beyond this dream of authorial androgyny, my idealization of Shakespeare enthrones him at the intersection of *author,* in the personal sense, and *language,* in the impersonal sense. As the personification of language he signifies an ideal wherein neither writer nor writing need be privileged or subordinated in relation to the other. In this sense Shakespeare's work both divides and bridges medieval and modern notions of textual production. It becomes a watershed of literary history, linking the culmination of anonymous or idealized texts, such as classical mythology and medieval scholasticism, to the incipience of secular self-consciousness and dramatic self-representation. It links textual faith with textual skepticism; it marks the goal of tradition and the origin of modernity.

But by thus idealizing Shakespeare's poetic genius, I can share in his glory while repeatedly granting it to him in a version of aggressive affection—a veneration that also appropriates the god's power. I can recharge my individual and collective faith in the (English) Word, and then replenish its verbal vigor by echoing it. Typically, Shakespeare's critics tend to identify with Shakespeare's language: we quote it, allude to it, and paraphrase it. Whole books consist of one-half Shakespearean poetry and one-half critical prose. Like King Hamlet's Ghost, Shakespeare's language invites identification and appropriation. We listen to its story until it becomes our own, then we inscribe it in our tables to write down elsewhere. The ongoing discourse of Shakespeare criticism re-presents Shakespeare's art in another form; it is an echo as well as a voice. In addition, Shakespeare criticism is a translation into contemporary terms of issues central to current critical discourse—issues of representation, authority, and sexuality.

Commonplace observation shows that the history of characterizations of Shakespeare, like the history of Shakespearean productions, editions, or critical essays, replicates the development of critical theory and taste—from classicism to romanticism to modernism to our current postmodernist reaction. For instance, nineteenth-century notions of Shakespeare's characters as unique individuals with histories, motives, and personalities have now shifted to conceptions of Shakespearean character as displaced, alienated, and refracted into myriad hues and images. Today's Shakespeare is "subjectivized" by distancing and projective identification. He represents the author who projects himself imaginatively on a surface (a stage), where he sees the reintegration of his fragmentary self, or at least a dramatic reorganization of fragments into a temporary, yet illusory, unity. Such a transformation of Shakespeare into a postmodern figure is inevitable. It reveals both Shakespeare and our current circumstance: the Bard is both our contemporary and for all time. As the mirror in which each age sees itself, Shakespeare provides the constancy of mirroring (form) and the variety of mirrored images (content).

Narcissism provides a theoretical key here. Psychoanalytic theories of narcissism are multiple and complex. I will sketch versions by D. W.

Winnicott, Jacques Lacan, and Heinz Lichtenstein. For Winnicott "the precursor of the mirror is the mother's face" (1971, 111). The infant sees itself reflected in the way in which its mother looks at it and responds to it. This primary interrelationship inaugurates the development of a shared imaginative and social space; it is "the beginning of a significant exchange with the world, a two-way process in which self-enrichment alternates with the discovery of meaning in the world of seen things" (1971, 113). For Lacan the space between infant and image is less beneficially mutual and enriching since the mother is replaced by an actual mirror before which the child imagines an alienated integrity, a fiction of the I. In the mirror stage is constructed "the statue in which man projects himself, [and] the phantoms that dominate him"; "the mirror stage is *a drama*" (1977c, 2–3, 4; my italics). Identity for Lacan is always mistaken—the primary instance of *méconnaissance*. Lichtenstein posits the symbiotic matrix of early mother-infant mirroring as the basis for the existential structure of human reality, and stresses the precariousness of that structure. Since it depends on reflection, being is always questionable (like King Hamlet's Ghost): it must be acquired, created, and maintained throughout life. Re-petitions (seeking again) of mirroring in the larger social world are essential to identity maintenance. Identity then serves, in a shift of the image, as a window through which we perceive reality in our own terms. The mirror window is the ego's original "frame of reference" (1977, 217–18).

Psychoanalysis provides theory; Shakespeare provides dramatic and linguistic enactments of the theory, and *Hamlet* remains the central text. "The purpose of playing," Hamlet asserts,

> both at the first and now, was and is, to hold as 'twere the mirror up to nature: to show virtue her feature, scorn her own image, and the very age and body of the time his form and pressure.
>
> (3.2.21–24)

Hamlet's parents haunt his phrases: his seemingly virtuous mother, now scorned, and the aged body of his father, who comes in questionable form to pressure his son. After looking in the dramatic mirror he constructs ("The play's the thing"), he assaults his mother with a metaphoric mirror in which she sees her maculate soul. Ultimately he stares into the mirror face of his last image—Yorick, the jesting death's head that he orders to his lady's chamber.

Both we and Shakespeare are like Hamlet. The plays are the mirror in which we find reflected images of ourselves, and they are the ground on which Shakespeare saw his own multiple identity dramatically represented. Shakespeare inhabited a reality that could be made to order according to the blueprints of imagination. He could stage a scene, act in it, watch it, criticize it, and change it. In him the "participating" and "observing" egos were co-creating partners. By projecting self-representations onto a reflecting stage peopled by shadows, Shakespeare could see his own face.

Recall Cassius's question to Brutus, "Can you see your face?" Brutus answers that he cannot, "for the eye sees not itself / But by reflection, by some other things." Cassius then offers to mirror Brutus to himself: "I, your glass, / Will modestly discover to yourself / That of yourself which you yet know not of" (*Julius Caesar*, 1.2.51–53, 68–70). The moment is well known. I want to analyze a similar one, in which Shakespeare returns to this theme and amplifies it. The scene is the Greek camp outside Troy. Achilles, who has refused to fight, sulks in his tent, as Ulysses walks by, reading:

ACHILLES: What are you reading?
ULYSSES: A strange fellow here
Writes me that man, how dearly ever parted,
How much in having, or without or in,
Cannot make boast to have that which he hath,
Nor feels not what he owes, but by reflection;
As when his virtues, aiming upon others,
Heat them, and they retort that heat again
To the first giver.
ACHILLES: This is not strange, Ulysses.
The beauty that is borne here in the face
The bearer knows not, but commends itself
To others' eyes; nor doth the eye itself,
That most pure spirit of sense, behold itself,
Not going from itself; but eye to eye opposed,
Salutes each other with each other's form;
For speculation turns not to itself,
Till it hath travell'd and is mirror'd there
Where it may see itself. This is not strange at all.
ULYSSES: I do not strain at the position—
It is familiar—but at the author's drift,
Who in his circumstance expressly proves
That no man is the lord of any thing,
Though in and of him there be much consisting,
Till he communicate his parts to others;

> Nor doth he of himself know them for aught,
> Till he behold them formed in th' applause
> Where th' are extended; who like an arch reverb'rate
> The voice again, or like a gate of steel,
> Fronting the sun, receives and renders back
> His figure and his heat. I was much rapt in this.
> (*Troilus and Cressida*, 3.3.95–123)

Typically vivid and various, Shakespeare's language appeals to our senses of sight ("face," "eye"), sound ("applause"), and touch ("heat"). Its metaphors use imagery from Renaissance science—chemistry, optics, and acoustics. It puns playfully and significantly ("eye," "part," "borne," "sun"). Gradually the speech makes manifest what was structurally latent from the start: the analogy to theater and self-exhibition. It makes us think, not only about the philosophical and ethical issue of virtue showing itself in order to know itself through external validation, but also about Ulysses's motives in instructing Achilles in his duty by subtly appealing to his pride. The language makes us follow it, through a syntax that mirrors sense. Achilles's narcissistic reply consists of links of echoed terms, so that the speech proceeds by repetition and reverberation: a rhetorical self-reflection. Achilles, who clearly and simply understands both Renaissance ocular physics and the unnamed author's philosophical point, finds his understanding just slightly shifted by Ulysses—exactly as Achilles's repeated "This is not *strange*" is slightly shifted by Ulysses's reply, "I do not *strain*" (my italics). Ulysses echoes Achilles with a devious difference: the art of mimicry in the service of politics. Whoever the author is, Ulysses reflects his argument, turning its "drift" into the channel of his own intention. He does not identify the author, but he does identify with him. Reading is an eye (I) reflecting on a text. We are all rapt in it.

Underlying Ulysses's speech is a deep analogy central to Shakespeare's art: that of theatricality, or acting on a stage. The phrase "communicate his parts to others" opens a comparison made manifest in the terms *applause* and *arch* (of the sky or heavens, like the arch under which Achilles and Ulysses stand as actors before an audience). Underlying the theatrical analogy is another simile, the mirror:

> or like a gate of steel,
> Fronting the sun, receives and renders back
> His figure and his heat.

Vividly sensual, the simile presents a brilliant sign of the reflected image ("figure") and power ("heat") of the eye of heaven as it gazes into the metal surface. It is a design perfectly suited to both Ulysses and Achilles, for it simultaneously models antagonism and mutuality (two styles of reciprocity). Shakespeare provides a visual and tangible image of what I have been discussing in abstract, idealized terms. He sets up a mirror for all to see, though it takes close reading and visualization of the passage to see it. The text reflects its meaning when energized by the mimetic power of what Henry James called "our interpretive heat, which adds the last beauty" to the "unwinking and inscrutable" face of serene authorial divinity.

The moment demonstrates salient points of psychoanalytic theories of theatrical performance as narcissistic, exhibitionistic, imitative, and relational. An actor—or a modern person acting—is an eye gazing in a mirror, or a man extending his parts before an other, or someone seeking mutual correspondence. Shakespeare's language at several points suggests phallic and coital senses: "man, how dearly ever parted"; "man, . . . his parts"; "formed in th' applause / Where th' are extended"; "gate of steel"; "his figure and his heat." At the level of character Ulysses cleverly appeals to Achilles's virility, as if to say, "Come on, man, show your stuff!" The speech rests on a subliminal equation: acting is a species of exhibitionism (Fenichel 1946; Barish 1981). The dramatic moment is intensely suggestive and verifies Henry James's assertion that Shakespeare possessed "the most potent aptitude for vivid reflection ever lodged in a human frame" ([1907] 1964, 305).

No less suggestive is the teasing question of the identity of that "strange fellow" whose texts Ulysses reads. It is very tempting to identify him as Shakespeare. Perhaps Ulysses is reading *Julius Caesar*—there was evidently no Quarto, but there must have been a script lying around at the Globe. He might be reading the Sonnets, another particularly apt text, or even *Troilus and Cressida,* the most apt (and textually problematic). Actually, he could be reading his own speech.

In this speculative and imaginative identification Shakespeare becomes the unnamed author of the text-within-the-text, the ghostly authority who expressly proves whatever case we construct from him. The author's pen is translated, through actor's voice or reader's representation, into a speculative understanding of original intent. Such mirroring is recursive. Shakespeare presents Ulysses reading a text by

Shakespeare in a scene where an actor recites a script written by Shakespeare while pretending to read a book by an unknown "strange fellow" who is simultaneously Shakespeare—the real author who designed the scene—and not Shakespeare. For the book is probably only a prop, mere blank pages, the perfect medium for projection—unless the actor playing Ulysses is having trouble with his lines, in which case the prop book is a real one, inscribing the actual text of Ulysses's speech.

Speculation lies at the core of both the dramatic and the interpretive scene, for one of the central lines of the quoted passage is textually corrupt. The line, "Till it hath travell'd and is mirror'd" is rendered in both Quarto and Folio (the only authentic texts) actually thus: "Till it hath *trauail'd* and is *married*" (my italics). Modern editorial conjecture has emended reasonably, but changing "travail'd" to "travell'd" dilutes the energy of the line by literally extracting the *work* from it, and translating "married" into "mirror'd" loses in erotic intimacy what it gains in ocular accuracy.

Travailed or traveled? Married or mirrored? Which is the real Shakespeare? How can we ever know? What is a reader or editor to do? Such permutative possibilities in Shakespearean meanings are all too frequent. How can we establish an authoritative text when the words themselves won't stay still? Stability can be established temporarily, through "definitive" editions, but the unruly vitality of Shakespeare's text should (one can only hope) outlast all attempts to tame it.

Misrecognizing Shakespeare

Barbara Freedman

I have been troubled by a change in me. . . . I no longer believe
in the man from Stratford.

Sigmund Freud

I

Ten years ago Geoffrey Hartman presciently critiqued such a project
as the one at hand, aptly observing that "it is no accident that those
who remain within the fold of ego psychology have been busy with
Shakespeare. Could they but establish an operative concept of identity
in a poet who seems to have no identity, then ego psychology might
hold its own despite subversive pressures from the Continent" (1978a,
xi). The odds even then were hardly good, however, and in the past
decade we have seen these subversive forces come to rule on Anglo-
American turf. The result is a Shakespeare "both less in control and
more active," less the grand master than "a principal agent of a productive ideological practice, most of whose conditions remain outside of
his control: the patronage system, the market/audience, the technical
possibilities of the theater, the political constraints and social ideologies in place, even the exigencies of his personal formation" (Kavanagh 1985, 148).

Many of us prefer this more active Shakespeare and therefore encourage the replacement of unrealistic fantasies of unearthing authorial
intentionality by more productive analyses of the means by which meaning is limited or developed, censored or privileged. Following the shift
from modern to postmodern interpretive paradigms, our concern is
neither with uncovering privileged signifieds nor with bracketing them
in favor of privileging "the play of the signifier" but with exploring the
problematic of referentiality itself. This shift in strategy is less a matter
of exploring every reader's response—as proof of the commutability of

the signified—than a matter of rethinking the basic critical assumptions that direct those responses. If anything, such an approach encourages us, for starters, to consider the connotation of such signifieds as "a reading," "Shakespeare," or even "an author."

The topic of Shakespeare's personality is important, then, not because it suggests a new approach to old playwrights but because it demands a reexamination of the fundamental assumptions concerning the conditions under which and by means of which we think the entity "Shakespeare" can be known. In "What Is an Author?" Michel Foucault reminds us that the concept of authorship is itself a culturally constrained and constraining idea—a fact well known to scholars familiar with the Elizabethans' decidedly different notions of plagiarism and communal authorship. But to conceive of authorship as both product and agent of ideology is decidedly less appealing to these same scholars insofar as it implicates our role in the Shakespeare industry as well. As Foucault reminds us, the idea of an author is inextricably tied to "institutional systems that circumscribe, determine, and articulate the realm of discourse" (1977, 130). A similar understanding of Shakespeare as a privileged site of intersecting codes that reflect and effect discourse production and consumption is well at hand. This view has the advantages of being both literally true today and theoretically more fertile than more conventional constructs.

Given this perspective on authorship, the decision to approach Shakespeare by means of his personality is as mystifying as its supposed object of study. This is particularly so given the successful ongoing efforts of critical theory (on such various fronts as feminism, psychoanalysis, deconstruction, cultural materialism, and semiotics) to decenter the subject of Western discourse, level traditional notions of identity and meaning, and rethink the ways in which subject positions are constructed. Given such rallying cries as Lacan's use of Rimbaud's "Je est un autre," Emile Benveniste's " 'Ego' is he who *says* 'ego,' " and Derrida's "Il n'y a pas dehors-texte," the goal of stumbling upon Shakespeare's "true" personality cannot fail to strike us as either naive or reactionary. The goal appears naive in its obliviousness to the distinction between the personality *per se* and the authorial personality, the latter functioning less as cause than as effect of a given work. The goal appears naive in its denial of the commonsense fact that the observer influences, and is influenced by, that which he or she perceives and is thereby caught up in a continual cycle of changed and changing meanings. But the goal of this project appears reactionary in its attempts to resurrect ego psychology insofar as such a move denies the fact that repression, différance, and the uncanny govern not only texts but psyches as texts. Put simply, the project seems oblivious to recent and not so recent theory in seeking to locate something prior to the text—something stable, unchanging, authentic, and autonomous: the author himself.

From this angle, the assignment to write on Shakespeare's personality is far more interesting than any of the responses to it could ever be. It suggests, above all, how easily literary theory can be divorced from notions of utility and validity. Caught up in unmasking the other, criticism refuses to take responsibility for its own production of meaning. The assignment in turn masks a host of questionable assumptions not only about its own endeavors but also about its object of study: (1) that the personality is a static configuration of drives and defenses shaped in early childhood (thus privileging the past rather than the present, the individual rather than the culture, the ego's defensive strategies rather than its instability and repression); (2) that the personality can be objectively measured through an examination of an author's work, so that a tabulation of the incidence of oral or anal imagery can miraculously transcend the terms of the text to reveal something unique and individual; (3) that the personality of a creative genius is itself inherently fascinating, so that what is of value in the work can be accounted for by some trait in the creator's childhood (thereby idealizing the personality, the creative process, and art as a product of the individual); (4) that the obsessive idealization of Shakespeare's personality is a project worth promoting rather than debunking—that one should encourage discussions that ignore his promotion of an ideology committed above all else to order in the state, submission by the individual, and an aristocratic version of "balanced" perspectives.

No less evident is the fact that our mutual quest for the transcendent author reveals a suspect theological enterprise. Regardless of whether the writers seek God the Father or their own fathers, such a venture suggests, at best, a displacement of the idealizing and unifying qualities of the ego. If there is no stable, autonomous, and unified being in the heavens, in history, in the state, in the family, in the literary text, or in the reader of that text, then (in a last-ditch effort temporarily to house a threatened ego's synthesizing functions) why not resurrect the idealized father of the English language, Shakespeare "himself"? In this dream of a return to an earlier, more comforting critical stance, we bear witness to a common fantasy of denying not only the death of the author but also the death of the period in which so many of us were trained. This revival of the authorial personality makes sense, however, in the context of contemporary theories of mourning. D. W. Winnicott has observed that the exaggerated use of the transitional object before a final acknowledgment of its loss serves as "a denial that there is a threat of its becoming meaningless" (1971, 15). The topic of this anthology may well reflect a similar denial of loss: in this case a denial of the obvious fact that an entire body of criticism is becoming, if not meaningless, at least less relevant. We are resurrecting and then mourning not Shakespeare's personality but the humanistic ideal of the personality.

And perhaps that is why this effort can be construed, ultimately, as liberating us to move on to new and more pressing concerns. Chief among them is an inquiry into the relationship between psychoanalysis and theater. Is there a relationship between the birth of a bourgeois theater of the individual and the representation of an unconscious subject? If so, does the tradition of dramatic theater support or subvert the project of ego psychology? Could it be that Shakespeare's impersonality is a function of theater's analysis of the personality? My general working hypothesis is that *theater knows something about the fictions of the ego,* and so the medium itself foregrounds the limitations of ego psychology. This is not to deny the value of analyzing various dramatic characters in terms of their characteristic means of seeking themselves but to suggest that the traditions of comedy and tragedy alike are predicated upon the inevitable failure of that quest. Whether we follow up on the tragic quest for identity ("Who is it who can tell me who I am?") or the comic disclaimer of identity ("I am not who I am"), what the tradition of Western dramatic theater seems to offer is a dissection of the personality in terms of the fictions on which the ego is based. To return to Hartman's challenge, then, I do believe we can establish an operative concept of identity in a poet who seems to have no identity—but not from the standpoint of ego psychology. If anything, we must work from the standpoint of the ego as imposter and supplement, as both product and source of an interminable series of misrecognitions. As we shall see, the history of misrecognitions *of* Shakespeare's personality competes only with the complexity of misrecognitions *in* Shakespeare's texts. And this minor comparison constitutes the crossroads at which we begin our oedipal and oedipalizing quest.

II

In one of the most interesting misreadings in the history of literary criticism, the statement "I am not who I am" has been lifted from Shakespeare's plays and raised to the level of pseudo-autobiographical confession. For centuries it has appeared to Western culture's greatest minds that such statements constituted a secret code. By means of this code someone of superior class and breeding (Sir Francis Bacon? Edward de Vere, the Earl of Oxford?) was assuring those of us of similar class and breeding that he was by no means to be confused with that misbegotten lout from Stratford. This particular misreading is by all accounts both peculiar and tantalizing. What could lead so many gifted scholars—including that unrivalled student of the personality, Sigmund Freud—to suspect a ghostwriter? What could lead these scholars to seek to displace Shakespeare, deny his identity, and put someone else in his place? What was Freud thinking when he wrote, "The name William Shakespeare is very certainly a pseudonym, behind which a great mysterious stranger is hidden" (quoted in Holland 1966, 58)?

Class considerations motivated many of the queries and complaints. It was unthinkable to an educated upper-class scholar that Shakespeare was not "one of us." Yet the issue of Shakespeare's enrollment or nonenrollment at the Stratford Grammar School cannot answer to the irrational zeal with which the "real" Shakespeare has been hunted down. One explanation is that such conjectures constitute a disguised enactment of what Freud termed the "family romance": the fantasy of exposing one's parents as imposters who have displaced nobler, more illustrious kin. Given Freud's fascination, from an early age, with this father of English letters, the desire to unseat an imposter and in the same move to deny one's motive by putting someone else in his place suggests such a fantasy. Further, such critics may well be responding to the peculiar and recurrent invitation by Shakespeare's characters to displace or usurp the self. Works as various as *Two Gentlemen of Verona, Richard II*, and *The Winter's Tale* foreground this invitation, which in the comedies takes the form of a "take my wife" motif; in the tragedies, of a "take my crown" motif; and in the Sonnets, of the free-for-all "take all my loves." A fantasy of being displaced runs throughout Shakespeare's works, and it may well be that such critics are simply taking Shakespeare up on the offer.

More compelling reasons exist, however, for fascination with Shakespeare's personality and for its equation with the statement "I am not who I am." Shakespeare has long been characterized as an elusive or absent author, whose genius, as Coleridge suggested, resides in his ability to identify with, and reflect, a variety of opinions and personality types. Ben Jonson therefore described him as "not for an age, but for all time"—an assessment which is currently under fire by feminist and Marxist scholars alike. Harriet Hawkins aptly describes the implications of this style for the literary critic: "Shakespeare's tendencies to stack the deck, then shuffle it; to deal the cards, then leave the game; to let his witnesses speak for themselves, to confront the strongest cases in favour of someone or something with the strongest cases against them . . . all help account for the richness of his plays. But their very richness is a source of genuine difficulty for those who produce, teach, and interpret them" (1982, 155).

Whereas Hawkins explores the effect of this authorial trait on Shakespearean criticism, much work has been concerned with its cause. Whether the particular cause to be championed is discovered in Elizabethan rhetoric, theater, or cultural history, critics have discovered a wide variety of sources and analogues. Joel Altman (1978), for example, associates Shakespeare's style of writing with the influence on Renaissance drama of the *argumentum in utramque partem*—a technique by which one convincingly argues for opposing sides of the same argument. Norman Rabkin reminds us that Shakespearean drama is a drama of complementarity, from which standpoint Shakespeare's self-displacing strategies might be understood as an inevitable component of good dramaturgy. And Norman Holland traces the roots of this authorial style in an identity theme based on a defensive resolution of oedipal rivalries. Before considering the relationship of cultural and personal styles, of philosophical and psychological stances, we might first clarify the psychological approach. How has psychoanalysis "explained" Shakespeare's personality to date?

Rather than reading "I am not who I am" as a philosophically informed statement, traditional psychoanalytic theory has insisted on interpreting it as a disclosure about the author's personality structure. As Murray Schwartz reminds us, "Absence in its many forms—

forgetting, denying, repressing, or just being silent—is always perceived psychoanalytically as a form of presence. The psychoanalyst
asks, 'In what way is this person announcing himself?' " (1978, 2–3).
Since psychoanalysis negates negation and hears absence of communication, psychoanalytic literary critics have come up with some of the
most enticing schemes for making this very absent author present.

The most attractive of these approaches has been to explain Shakespeare's "absence" as in fact an omnipresence—an effect of his capacity
for shifting emotional identifications. This capacity in turn is analyzed
as a defensive strategy rooted in early childhood conflicts. Norman
Holland attributes Shakespeare's success as an actor and playwright to
"the astonishingly wide range and flexibility of his defenses in the oedipal triangle we all once faced," observing that Shakespeare can "identify as need be with any one of the three protagonists, father, mother, or
child, . . . condense two figures into one or . . . split one into two; project his feelings into any one of the three or introject theirs into himself"
(1966, 135). Holland reminds us that the Dutch psychoanalyst Conrad
van Emde Boas offers an even more precise formulation of this strategy
based on the Sonnets, where a rejected suitor instigates and identifies
with his rival's success. Van Emde Boas explains narcissistic identification with the same-sexed object in terms of frustration by the maternal
object: the subject re-creates the ideal mother-son relationship by identifying with the mother in maternally loving the young man who is, at the
same time, himself. An example of this strategy is the young boy who
compensates for his inability to compete with siblings for maternal
affection by first facilitating the mother's desire to satisfy the rival and
then imagining his rival sibling's satisfaction as his own. The birth of
Shakespeare's younger brother and the ensuing need to cope with the
sibling rivalry it occasioned suggests to some critics the origin of this
defensive strategy. Richard Wheeler's analysis of the Sonnets, which
expands upon these ideas, explores how these poems reveal "the need to
relocate selfhood in another" (1972, 156). Such lines as "Upon thy side
against myself I'll fight" (Sonnet 88), "Thy adverse party is thy advo-
cate" (Sonnet 35), and "The injuries that to myself I do, / Doing thee
vantage, double-vantage me" (Sonnet 88) exemplify "the paradoxical
sense of relief and security that attends the very denial of self-interest"
(1972, 154).

Another way of analyzing Shakespeare is through the insights of
relational psychology, which rightly acknowledges that we can never

study a personality in isolation. As Murray Schwartz and David Willbern remind us, "Literary works carry their psychology within themselves, in the very structure of relations they embody and invite us to form with them as readers" (1982, 205). If we are always in relation to Shakespeare, it is certainly worth inquiring whether, over a period of almost four hundred years, there is not some degree of consistency in reports on the quality and nature of that relationship from his "lovers." Rather than hypothesizing about an inaccessible person, we can explore the transference that occurs in readings and writings on the ever-living author.

The flaw in such an approach is that the literary work does not simply "embody" certain relationships and "invite" us to form others in a social and historical vacuum. Rather, our culture determines how we read literature, what relationships we privilege, and how we can, and cannot, conceive of them. If we fasten on a common style of structuring relationships within and by means of the Shakespearean text, whatever style we discover will tell us less about Shakespeare's character than about ourselves and the place of our desire. And yet such a discovery is well worth exploring. The aspect of the plays that I privilege, and that I think our culture privileges, is their ability to foreground a process of misrecognition in relationship similar to characters' relationships *within* Shakespeare, insofar as both reveal blind spots in our vision as intrinsic to our relationships with ourselves and with others. Object-relations theorists may attribute this characteristic to a failure of empathic mirroring in Shakespeare's personal history. Curiously, however, critics seem to feel adequately mirrored but unable to mirror, seen but unable to reflect, confirmed but unable to reciprocate. Shakespeare can reflect us, the critics seem to say, but we can never reflect him—a fact about which they report feeling variously amazed and distressed, awed and frustrated.

This same inability to be seen, or to be seen rightly, functions as a principle of plot and character construction and is developed at the level of theme throughout the Shakespearean corpus. Not only do the plays present themselves as unable to be mirrored or figured out, as always anticipating and then displacing our view, but the characters continually complain that they cannot be mirrored, as well. The plays work like dramatic anamorphisms in reverse, insofar as they expose the fantasy of a privileged place of vision. In a sense, Shakespeare's plays, like his characters, are only properly viewed when seen to reflect the impossibility of right vision. This is perhaps most evident in the characters and themes of the tragedies, where the heroes seek and fail to find confirmation and recognition by parental figures whose demands on their children are literally self-destructive. Romeo and Juliet are directed by Friar Laurence in their quest for approval; Brutus seeks an honorable reputation and consequently follows a deadly course determined by perceived familial obligations; King Hamlet's ghost double-binds the prince with self-destructive guidelines for being. Coriolanus as a character is built on the necessity and impossibility of acknowledgment, so that he plays out the roles of mother and son as cause and effect. He plays double-binding mother to the people when he suggests that he cannot recognize them as either dependent or independent; he plays son to them when he repeatedly demands that they acknowledge the fact that he needs no acknowledgment.

But Shakespeare was not a Kohutian, and the problem here is not simply the parental other as potential mirror but the nature of human interactions. Drama subverts the settled and stable identity by means of the reflecting gaze of the other; if "the eye sees not itself / But by reflection" (*Julius Caesar*, 1.2.52–53), these reflections change in time and quality from person to person. If "no man is the lord of any thing / . . . Till he communicate his parts to others" (*Troilus and Cressida*, 3.3.115–17), and if that communication is subject to "envious and calumniating Time" (3.3.174), then no man is lord of himself. By *Troilus and Cressida* the split between an idealized, authentic, private self and an untenable, public self is undone. From this vantage point the positions of Hector and Achilles are similarly inauthentic: whether one is a self-deceived and noble fool or a shifty survivor who changes with the times ultimately does not matter.

Whereas the tragedies address a failure of mirroring at the level of character and theme, the comedies work to subvert the level of representation, so that, for example, the characters critique the very notion of character. Consider how impossible it is to separate Kate from her role at the close of *The Taming of the Shrew,* or consider how characters like Petruchio are elusive and enigmatic throughout. As in Epimenides the Cretan's paradox "I am always lying," Shakespeare's comic heroes and heroines often describe themselves as role playing and so render the assessment of character a literal impossibility. In his famous soliloquy in *1 Henry IV* Hal informs us that he has only been pretending to be bad and will only be pretending to reform, so that

"My reformation, glitt'ring o'er my fault, / Shall show more goodly and attract more eyes / Than that which hath no foil to set it off" (1.2.213–15). Yet when Hal promises to be "more myself," we can only wonder what this might mean. In a play where our sense of each character is constantly being revised by means of the distorting lens of another character's vision, this narrative design is itself suspect. It is, moreover, sorely at odds with the imaginative direction of the play, which begins with a father-son conflict, concludes with its resolution, and appears to work through that conflict in the intervening scenes between Hal and his surrogate father, Falstaff. Finally, if we cannot trust any of these characters' views of each other, why trust a given character's view of himself? The result is that some critics choose to disbelieve the play and to believe Hal, while others choose to believe Hal and disbelieve the play. Instead, we might take the debate as intentionally reflective of the problem of representing history. In short, the comedies work to subvert, at the level of representation, the principles of character and plot that the tragedies seek and fail to resolve at the thematic level.

In question is whether we want to code this information in terms of relational strategies or philosophical positions, or whether we need or want to separate the two. Granted, the insistence that one can only be seen as one who cannot be seen connects the crises of identity and interpretation set up both within and by means of the plays. But is this a reason to suppose that we have hit upon Shakespeare's personal strategy or the key to his "identity theme"? Must every Renaissance artist who created and undermined anamorphic projects be analyzed as exhibiting defensive strategies as a result of oedipal crises or inadequate parental mirroring? And which of us can escape a similar charge? Granted, the defensive strategy of shifting and elusive identifications with others as a mode of self-disclosure does appear to function as a means of problematizing both identity and meaning throughout the plays. Yet what we have termed a defensive strategy might simply be labeled by Henry IV as good business procedure, and what we have termed Shakespeare's propensity toward a paradoxical mode of self-disclosure may well describe the work of any successful dramatist. What we are describing may be less an identity style than a means by which obstacles in interpretation elicit interpretation—not unlike the means by which transference operates in the psychoanalytic process.

To understand how the Shakespearean critic's desire is manipulated, we might take a lesson from the manipulation of desire within the plays. The tenable place that Shakespeare's most successful characters seek is a stance that is designed to trap the observer's gaze while preserving the inviolability of the self; a stance that succeeds in holding another's gaze by withholding and disguising its own. Acting is the strategy of choice here, Shakespeare's characters suggest, for insofar as acting calls into question the reality of what is seen, it displaces tension from the observed to the observer. The observed finds a place by usurping the observer's stable position and so plunging the observer into uncertainty. The ambiguity of meaning characteristic of Shakespeare's plays and central to their continuing popularity derives, in part, from their withdrawal of a stable place from which to observe them. The observer's place is recurrently undermined and its interpretations disconfirmed, while that which is perceived holds mastery over it.

The manipulation of the critic's desire here suggests that we seek to be displaced, if not defined, in relation to that part of ourselves where *we* are not "our own." Hal knew that being wanted he might be more wondered at, and Shakespeare knew that he would be both wanted and wondered at if he could prolong our gaze, protect himself from entrapment, and trap us instead. The problems of identity and meaning set up in the Shakespearean text are therefore intricately related. The elusiveness of the author's and the characters' personalities functions, like the ambiguity of the plays' meaning, to successfully ensure them a tenable place in our eyes as permanent objects of desire. Like his characters, then, Shakespeare asks us to see that we can't see him. When we understand the rules of the game, we can play from something of a vantage point at long last.

III

" 'Have I caught thee?' " (*The Merry Wives of Windsor,* 3.3.43), Falstaff asks the merry wives after they successfully trap the buffoon into misinterpreting them. Have we caught Shakespeare? Or has he caught us in another misinterpretation? Can we catch ourselves? In question is whether we have uncovered Shakespeare's personality or the impossibility of fixing a personality; identity, or its fiction. What, after all, have we uncovered but the most predictable of self-fulfilling prophecies? Question: "Given an author who has been dead for almost four hundred years and who, in over thirty-five plays, never revealed much of his character, what can you tell us about his personality?" Answer: "The author reveals the personality of the type of person who does not reveal his personality." If there is any value to such a reading, it is not in the strategic gains of an interpersonal game of "hide the personality" but in the larger connections between psychoanalysis and philosophy, art and theater, personal and cultural styles.

Whereas ego psychologists and object-relations theorists alike fasten on the elusiveness of Shakespeare's personality, that may well be one of his least idiosyncratic traits. Cultural historians offer a host of alternative explanations for this behavior, chief among them the fact of a repressive social atmosphere in Shakespeare's day. Given the presence of an appointed censor with the power to throw writers into prison, this canny playwright's elusive personal style might well reflect nothing more than practical wisdom. Or it might reflect nothing less than an interpersonal style characteristic of Elizabethan society. Lawrence Stone maintains, "Alienation and distrust of one's fellow man are the predominant features of the Elizabethan and early Stuart view of human character and conduct" (1977, 78). He goes on to observe that in the Elizabethan family "at all social levels . . . there was a general psychological atmosphere of distance, manipulation, and deference" (88).

This personal style of impersonality is reflected in the apparently widespread ambivalence toward individualism in Elizabethan England. As the vogue of tragedy suggests, the ideal of the heroic individual both attracted and repulsed the average Elizabethan: genuine hostility was evoked by the attempt to "stand / As if a man were author of himself, / And knew no other kin" (*Coriolanus*, 5.3.35–37). Perhaps this attitude explains why the word *individual*—which had long referred to a state of being complete and indivisible—took on, in Shakespeare's time, the modern sense of one who is special, distinct, and dividable from a larger group. Whether we study why Elizabethans chose to spell their names differently on different days, or why Shakespeare failed to concern himself with published editions of his works, we are continually struck by the idea that the concept of the individual was undergoing change in the Renaissance, and that such change reflected and evoked both anxiety and ambivalence. The result was a growing hunger for narratives in which the resulting admiration, scorn, ridicule, and fear regarding individualism could be expressed. Whether we root the growing attractiveness of individualism in increased social and economic mobility, Puritanism, literacy, colonialism, nationalism, or some combination of all these forces, it is clear that this cultural phenomenon provided grist for the mills of comedy and tragedy alike. Shakespeare's plays, then, offered their Elizabethan audiences a chance to laugh at very real fears: the loss of a secure and stable place within family and community, the horrors of usurpation and of one's own and others' fantasies of displacement, and the inevitable reliance of one's sense of identity and worth on an untrustworthy market.

The fact that the Elizabethans conceived of such terms as *individual, author, self,* and *personality* so differently from us suggests that, in a very real sense, they must have experienced them differently. We would do best, therefore, to learn as much as we can about the Renaissance sense of personality from Shakespeare's plays rather than simply impose an alien personality scheme on them. More familiar to the Elizabethan mindset, as Stephen Greenblatt (1980) points out, was a conception of the personality as an object to be fashioned which in turn was less indicative of faith in an authentic self than of its impossibility. The Elizabethan obsession with the fashioning, presentation, and confirmation of an inherently theatrical self implied a belief that the personality was, above all, a social construct; identity was something that could be borrowed, imitated, fashioned, displayed, updated, and, finally, marketed. From a cultural perspective it is hardly surprising that Shakespearean drama enacts the quest for confirmation of one's authenticity as doomed from the start, or that the quest for recognition is always inscribed within the sphere of illusion. Shakespeare's theater is a drama of the fictions by means of which the ego sustains itself in the eyes of the other (comedy) and is undone through the gaze of the other (tragedy). What is surprising is how long it has taken us to discover the fact that Shakespearean drama repeats this process with its audiences, trapping them in a funhouse of distorting mirrors and recognitions from which we have yet to escape.

The psychoanalytic approach best suited to expose the ideal of autonomous individuality as a comfortable fiction is one that meets early modern skepticism toward the ego with equal skepticism. In contemporary theory this stance has been represented by the work of the French psychoanalyst Jacques Lacan, who believes that psychoanalysis must expose our attachment to the ego as a misrecognition that sustains its power. Not only do Shakespeare and Lacan share a fundamental skepticism toward individualism but they also are committed to undermining the myth of self-presence through the problematic of self-representation. Lacan's seminar on the gaze is only one among many that reveals a fondness for paradoxes more complex than "I am not who I am." Lacanian theory is based on the premise "I am not wherever I am the plaything of my thought; I think of what I am where I do not think to think" ("The Agency of the Letter in the Unconscious," 1977a, 166).

Rather than encourage the strengthening of the ego's defenses, Lacan proposes "we should start instead from the function of *méconnaissance* that characterizes the ego in all its structures" (1977c, 6). By *méconnaissance* Lacan refers to the process of ego construction by means of which the subject misidentifies with a mirror image of its coherence as well as to the further misrecognitions of language, gender, and ideology by means of which the ego is sustained. Had we world enough and time, I would suggest that Shakespeare, too, starts "from the function of *méconnaissance* that characterizes the ego"— and continues to explore its effects from *The Comedy of Errors* through *The Tempest*. Further, I would suggest that the plays trace levels of misrecognition at work in their construction and reception, represent their own conflict with repression, and alert us to the constitutive role of the unconscious in both identity and meaning. When we recall that Shakespearean drama meets postmodern theory in a critique of the idea of the autonomous individual, when we realize the antipathy toward glorified humanism at work in both early modern and postmodern cultures, we see some sense in bringing them into dialogue.

We close, then, with questions rather than answers, questions that suggest another topic, another book. How does the dramatic text interrogate and expose its own production of meaning, its particular staging of mimesis? What does theater tell us about the nature of character, the gaze of the Other, and the role of desire in the construction and representation of subjectivity? Why has drama been the occasion of so much psychoanalytic theory? To what extent is its insistent exhibition of the mask reflective not only of personal strategies but also of the strategies by means of which theater performs the personality? In short, to what extent does drama function to subvert identity itself? Shakespeare's plays raise, rather than answer, these questions, but the study of misrecognition provided there offers directions for further study. If comedy and tragedy continually rehearse the problem of finding or losing a place in relationship to another, the theatrical mask is a sign that the self is always already purloined by the Other's gaze. Rather than rehearse the narrative of the self in relationship to others, we might explore how theatrical misrecognition exposes the illusions of the humanistic self and so foregrounds the fictions by which the ego is constructed and maintained. Shakespeare's characters speak to us of our own imagoes and proclaim the moment, jubilant or joyless, when one's image is revealed as divorced from oneself, when the *je* confronts the *moi*, the speaking subject faces the subject of speech. Shakespeare centers and decenters the subject as it circles in endless fascination with, and fantasied appropriation of, its mirror image. His theater stages the rivalry between ego and persona in the quest for subjectivity, and the humanistic enterprise is enacted as person succumbs to persona, character to mask. Rewriting and refusing the illusions that sustain the heroic self and always opposing the uncritical celebration of autonomy, the Shakespearean project concerning identity is a study of the illusory constructs by means of which the ego stands and falls and by means of which we continually prop it up.

Shakespeare's characters' awareness of their entrapment in representation mirrors the textuality of the psyche, revealing the representational paradoxes in which identity is necessarily always already represented and therefore never on its own. These characters are neither the conquerors nor the helpless subjects of the reign of the signifier; rather, they are trapped in a cycle of repression and representation from which neither they nor we can escape. If the tragedies' assumption of authenticity results in a crisis of representation, the comedies can subvert their own representational levels without harm. The comedies' characters call character into question; they speak to us from a place we know but mistake. They parade their plasticity in an atmosphere of the uncanny, pronounce themselves to us as image, and laugh at their vanquished rivals, who would find in them a different kind of truth. Those seeking to know Shakespeare might well be answered with Olivia's response to Viola: "You are now out of your text; but we will draw the curtain, and show you the picture. Look you, sir, such a one I was this present. Is it not well done?" (*Twelfth Night*, 1.5.232–35). The result, of course, is but another mask. As we continually seek and fail to find the "real" identities of a Kate, Viola, Hal, Hamlet, Coriolanus, or Shakespeare—so temptingly referred to, but withheld from, our view—we miss the fact that, like our own identities, these are phantom images that function as unattainable objects of desire. Always trapping and never fulfilling our gaze, always succeeding in holding us in a stance of servitude and blindness, these characters suggest the triumph of the truth of the mask.

The Shakespearean project of misrecognition was well described by Heidegger when, as Geoffrey Hartman reminds us, he discussed self-identity as

> a *Sich-Verhören,* a word that in German denotes at one and the same time our attempt to know the truth by taking the self into custody and interrogating it, and the failure of that attempt, since a mishearing or mistaking of what has been said is inevitable. Language gives the lie to the ego's capture of a specular identity just as it gives the lie to itself. . . . The most art can do, as a mirror of language, is to burn through, in its cold way, the desire for self-definition . . . to expose the desire to own one's own name.
>
> (1978b, 106–7)

Just as the Lacanian subject misapprehends itself as a coherent unity in the mirror stage and thereby forges the fictional outlines of the ego, so language is misapprehended in the equally delusive mirror of literary criticism, which promises an equally false stability and coherence. Yet literature reveals that aspect of language that traditional literary criticism, as its self-fashioned master, would deny: the fact that language cannot be mastered and is by nature a plenitude of signification that is anything but stable and contained. What, then, is the true mirror of the subject, the ego's double, if not the always elusive mask of the theatrical character?

In sum, the Shakespearean project is an interrogation of the dramatic conditions of the personality. It is based on the theatrical insight that identity is neither unified, autonomous, nor knowable, but the product and process of entrapment in representational and relational paradoxes alike. Based on the idea that the I is an other, Shakespeare's theater directs us back to the shared root of theater and theory in *theatron,* the gaze. Shakespeare's works are valuable, not because they hold the mirror up to nature, but because they focus our attention on the mirror's distorting lens. They stage theater staging itself and characters playing themselves, and thereby expose how the mirror we hold up to ourselves obscures what we see. It is perhaps no surprise that in

what is arguably Shakespeare's greatest tragedy, *King Lear,* the protagonist remains hunched over the corpse of his fantasy, obsessed with
nothing more nor less than the illusions of a looking-glass: "Do you
see this? Look on her! Look her lips, / Look there, look there!"
(5.3.311–12); or that one of his greatest comedies, *A Midsummer
Night's Dream,* stages a play within a play, which begins with the
humble "All for your delight / We are not here" (5.1.114–15).

Bibliography

Abenheimer, K. M. 1946. "Shakespeare's *Tempest:* A Psychological Analysis." *Psychoanalytic Review* 33:399–415.

Adams, John F. 1961. "*All's Well That Ends Well:* The Paradox of Procreation." *Shakespeare Quarterly* 12:261–70.

Adelman, Janet. 1973. *The Common Liar: An Essay on "Antony and Cleopatra"*. New Haven: Yale University Press.

———. 1980. " 'Anger's My Meat': Feeding, Dependency, and Aggression in *Coriolanus.*" In *Representing Shakespeare,* edited by Murray Schwartz and Coppélia Kahn, 129–49. Baltimore: Johns Hopkins University Press.

Altman, Joel. 1978. *The Tudor Play of Mind: Rhetorical Inquiry and the Development of Elizabethan Drama.* Berkeley and Los Angeles: University of California Press.

Aristotle. 1941. *Nicomachean Ethics.* Translated by W. D. Ross. In *The Basic Works of Aristotle,* edited by Richard McKeon, 935–1112. New York: Random House.

Auden, W. H. 1962. *The Dyer's Hand.* New York: Random House.

Barber, C. L. 1959. *Shakespeare's Festive Comedy.* Princeton: Princeton University Press.

———. 1960. "An Essay on the Sonnets." In *The Sonnets,* 7–33. The Laurel Shakespeare. New York: Dell. Reprinted in *Elizabethan Poetry,* edited by Paul Alpers, 299–320. New York: Oxford University Press, 1967.

———. 1980. "The Family in Shakespeare's Development: Tragedy and Sacredness." In *Representing Shakespeare,* edited by Murray Schwartz and Coppélia Kahn, 70–109. Baltimore: Johns Hopkins University Press.

Barber, C. L., and Richard Wheeler. 1986. *The Whole Journey: Shakespeare's Power of Development.* Berkeley and Los Angeles: University of California Press.

Barish, Jonas. 1981. *The Antitheatrical Prejudice.* Berkeley and Los Angeles: University of California Press.

Barthes, Roland. 1977. "The Death of the Author." In *Image/Music/Text,* translated by Stephen Heath, 142–47. New York: Hill & Wang.

Becker, Ernest. 1973. *The Denial of Death.* New York: Free Press.

Belsey, Catherine. 1985. "Disrupting Sexual Difference: Meaning and Gender in the Comedies." In *Alternative Shakespeares,* edited by John Drakakis, 166–90. New York: Methuen.

Benveniste, Emile. 1971. *Problems in General Linguistics.* Translated by Mary Elizabeth Meek. Coral Gables, Fla.: University of Miami Press.

Berger, Harry, Jr. 1970. "Miraculous Harp: A Reading of Shakespeare's *Tempest.*" *Shakespeare Studies* 5:254–83.

Berry, Edward. 1975. *Patterns of Decay: Shakespeare's Early Histories.* Charlottesville: University of Virginia Press.

Berry, Ralph. 1976/77. "Language and Structure in *Measure for Measure.*" *The University of Toronto Quarterly* 46:147–61.

Bloom, Harold. 1973. *The Anxiety of Influence.* New York: Oxford University Press.

Borges, Jorge Luis. 1964. "Everything and Nothing." In *Labyrinths,* edited and translated by Donald Yates and James Irby, 248–49. New York: New Directions.

Bradbrook, M. C. 1980. *Shakespeare: The Poet in His World.* London: Methuen.

Braden, Gordon, and William Kerrigan. Forthcoming. "Milton's Coy Eve: *Paradise Lost* and Renaissance Love Poetry." *Milton Studies.*

Bradley, A. C. [1909] 1963. "Shakespeare the Man." In *Oxford Lectures on Poetry.* London: Macmillan.

Brandes, Georg. 1899. *William Shakespeare: A Critical Study.* New York: Macmillan.

Brenner, Gerry. 1980. "Shakespeare's Politically Ambitious Friar." *Shakespeare Studies* 13:47–58.

Bullen, A. H., ed. 1895. *Speculum Amantis: Love-Poems from Rare Song-Books and Miscellanies of the Seventeenth Century.*

Bullough, Geoffrey, ed. 1958. *Narrative and Dramatic Sources of Shakespeare.* Vol. 2: *The Comedies, 1597–1603.* New York: Columbia University Press; London: Routledge and Kegan Paul.

————. 1960. *Narrative and Dramatic Sources of Shakespeare.* Vol. 3: *Earlier English History Plays: Henry VI, Richard III, Richard II.* New York: Columbia University Press; London: Routledge and Kegan Paul.

Burke, Kenneth. 1953. *Counter-Statement.* 2d ed. Los Altos, Calif.: Hermes Publications.

Campbell, Lily B. 1968. *Shakespeare's Histories: Mirrors of Elizabethan Policy.* San Marino, Calif.: Huntington Library.

Cassirer, E., P. O. Kristeller, and J. H. Randall. 1956. *The Renaissance Philosophy of Man.* Chicago: University of Chicago Press.

Cavell, Stanley. 1969. *Must We Mean What We Say?* New York: Scribner's.

————. 1979. *The Claim of Reason: Wittgenstein, Skepticism, Morality, and Tragedy.* Oxford and New York: Oxford University Press.

————. 1981. *Pursuits of Happiness: The Hollywood Comedies of Remarriage.* Cambridge, Mass.: Harvard University Press.

Chambers, Edmund K. 1930. *William Shakespeare: A Study of Facts and Problems.* Vol. 2. Oxford: Clarendon Press.

Charney, Maurice. n.d. " 'Be That You Are, / That Is, a Woman': The 'Prenzie' Angelo and the 'Enskied' Isabella." Unpublished MS.

Chettle, Henry. [1592] 1974. "To the Gentlemen Readers." In *Kind-Hartes Dreame*, in *The Riverside Shakespeare*, edited by G. Blakemore Evans, 1835. Boston: Houghton Mifflin.

Clemens, Samuel. 1906. *Is Shakespeare Dead?* New York: Harper.

Coleridge, Samuel Taylor. 1960. *Shakespearean Criticism*. Vol. 2. Edited by T. M. Raysor. Everyman's Library. London: J. M. Dent.

Cook, Judith. 1980. *Women in Shakespeare*. London: George G. Harrap.

Cressy, David. 1980. *Literacy and the Social Order: Reading and Writing in Tudor and Stuart England*. Cambridge: Cambridge University Press.

Daniel, Samuel. 1958. *The Civil Wars*. Edited by Laurence Michel. New Haven: Yale University Press.

Dash, Irene. 1981. *Wooing, Wedding, and Power: Women in Shakespeare*. New York: Columbia University Press.

Davies, Stevie. 1986. *The Feminine Reclaimed: The Idea of Woman in Spenser, Shakespeare and Milton*. Lexington: University of Kentucky Press.

Derrida, Jacques. 1978. *Spurs Nietzsche's Styles/Eperons Les Styles de Nietzsche*. Translated by Barbara Harlow. Chicago: University of Chicago Press.

Desai, Rupin W. 1977. "Freudian Undertones in the Isabella-Angelo Relationship of *Measure for Measure*." *Psychoanalytic Review* 64:487–94.

Dickens, Charles. 1964. *Great Expectations*. New York: Bobbs-Merrill.

Dinnerstein, Dorothy. 1976. *The Mermaid and the Minotaur*. New York: Harper and Row.

Dobree, Bonamy. 1952. "*The Tempest*." *New Series of Essays and Studies* 5:13–25.

Dowden, Edward. 1910. "Is Shakespeare Self-revealed?" In *Essays Modern and Elizabethan*, 250–81. London: J. M. Dent.

Drakakis, John, ed. 1985. *Alternative Shakespeares*. London: Methuen.

Dryden, John. 1672. *Essay on the Dramatic Poetry of the Last Age*. London.

Dusinberre, Juliet. 1975. *Shakespeare and the Nature of Women*. London: Macmillan.

Ebel, Henry. 1975. "Caesar's Wounds: A Study of William Shakespeare." *Psychoanalytic Review* 62:107–30.

Eccles, Mark. 1961. *Shakespeare in Warwickshire*. Madison: University of Wisconsin Press.

Edel, Leon. 1972. *Henry James: The Master: 1901–1916*. Philadelphia: Lippincott.

Eliot, T. S. 1950. "Tradition and the Individual Talent." In *Selected Essays*, new edition, 3–11. New York: Harcourt, Brace and World.

Empson, William. 1935. *Some Versions of Pastoral*. London: Chatto and Windus.

Erickson, Peter. 1982. "Sexual Politics in *As You Like It*." *Massachusetts Review* (Spring 1982): 65–83.

———. 1985a. *Patriarchal Structures in Shakespeare's Drama*. Berkeley and Los Angeles: University of California Press.

———. 1985b. "Shakespeare and the Author Function." In *Shakespeare's*

"Rough Magic": Renaissance Essays in Honor of C. L. Barber, edited by Peter Erickson and Coppélia Kahn. Newark: University of Delaware Press.

Essler, Anthony. 1966. *The Aspiring Mind of the Elizabethan Younger Generation.* Durham, N.C.: Duke University Press.

Evans, Malcolm. 1985. "Deconstructing Shakespeare's Comedies." In *Alternative Shakespeares,* edited by John Drakakis, 67–94. London: Methuen.

Farrell, Kirby. 1984. "Self-Effacement and Autonomy in Shakespeare." *Shakespeare Studies* 16:75–99.

Feiring, Candice. 1983. "Behavioral Styles in Infancy and Adulthood: The Work of Karen Horney and Attachment Theorists Collaterally Considered." *Journal of the American Academy of Child Psychiatry* 22:1–7.

Fenichel, Otto. 1946. "On Acting." *Psychoanalytic Quarterly* 15:144–60.

Fiedler, Leslie. 1972. *The Stranger in Shakespeare.* New York: Stein and Day.

Fineman, Joel. 1980. "Fratricide and Cuckoldry: Shakespeare's Doubles." In *Representing Shakespeare,* edited by Murray Schwartz and Coppélia Kahn, 70–109. Baltimore: Johns Hopkins University Press.

Foucault, Michel. 1977. "What Is an Author?" In *Language, Counter-Memory, Practice: Selected Essays and Interviews,* edited by Donald F. Bouchard, 113–138. Ithaca, N.Y.: Cornell University Press.

Freud, Sigmund. 1953. "On the Universal Tendency to Debasement in the Sphere of Love (Contributions to the Psychology of Love II)." In *The Standard Edition of the Complete Psychological Works of Sigmund Freud,* vol. 12, translated by James Strachey et al. London: Hogarth Press.

———. 1955. "The 'Uncanny.' " In *The Standard Edition of the Complete Psychological Works of Sigmund Freud,* vol. 17, translated by James Strachey et al. London: Hogarth Press.

———. 1963a. "A Disturbance of Memory on the Acropolis." Translated by James Strachey. In *Character and Culture,* edited by Philip Rieff, 311–20. The Collected Papers of Sigmund Freud. New York: Collier.

———. 1963b. "A Special Type of Object Choice Made by Men." Translated by Joan Riviere. In *Sexuality and the Psychology of Love,* 49–58. The Collected Papers of Sigmund Freud. New York: Collier.

Fripp, Edgar I. 1929. *Shakespeare's Haunts near Stratford.* London: Oxford University Press.

Frye, Northrop. 1969a. *Anatomy of Criticism.* New York: Atheneum.

Frye, Northrop, ed. 1969b. Introduction to *The Tempest.* In William Shakespeare, *The Complete Works,* edited by Alfred Harbage, 1369–72. Baltimore: Penguin Books.

Garber, Marjorie. 1981. *Coming of Age in Shakespeare.* New York: Methuen.

Garner, Shirley Nelson. 1976. "Shakespeare's Desdemona." *Shakespeare Studies* 9:233–52.

———. 1981. "*A Midsummer Night's Dream:* 'Jack Shall Have Jill, / Nought Shall Go Ill.' " *Women's Studies: An Interdisciplinary Journal* 9:47–63. Special Issue on Feminist Criticism of Shakespeare, vol. 1, edited by Gayle Greene and Carolyn Ruth Swift.

Gibbons, Brian, ed. 1980. *Romeo and Juliet,* by William Shakespeare. London and New York: Methuen.

Gohlke (Sprengnether), Madelon. 1980a. " 'And When I Love Thee Not': Women and the Psychic Integrity of the Tragic Hero." *Hebrew University Studies in Literature* 8:44–65.

———. 1980b. " 'I Wooed Thee with My Sword': Shakespeare's Tragic Paradigms." In *The Woman's Part: Feminist Criticism of Shakespeare,* edited by Carolyn Ruth Swift Lenz, Gayle Greene, and Carol Neely, 150–70. Urbana: University of Illinois Press. Reprinted in *Representing Shakespeare,* edited by Murray Schwartz and Coppélia Kahn, 170–87.

———. 1982. " 'All That Is Spoke Is Marred': Language and Consciousness in *Othello.*" *Women's Studies: An Interdisciplinary Journal,* 9:157–76. Special Issue on Feminist Criticism of Shakespeare, vol. 2, edited by Gayle Greene and Carolyn Ruth Swift.

Greenblatt, Stephen. 1980. *Renaissance Self-Fashioning: From More to Shakespeare.* Chicago: University of Chicago Press.

———. 1986. "Psychoanalysis and Renaissance Culture." In *Literary Theory / Renaissance Texts,* edited by Patricia Parker and David Quint, 210–24. Baltimore: Johns Hopkins University Press.

Greene, Robert. [1592] 1974. *Groats-worth of Wit.* In *The Riverside Shakespeare,* edited by G. Blakemore Evans. Boston: Houghton Mifflin.

Halliday, F. E. 1958. *Shakespeare and His Critics.* New York: Schocken Books.

Harbage, Alfred. 1941. *Shakespeare's Audience.* New York: Columbia University Press.

———. 1966. *Conceptions of Shakespeare.* Cambridge, Mass.: Harvard University Press.

———. 1970. *William Shakespeare: A Reader's Guide.* New York: Farrar.

Hartman, Geoffrey. 1978a. "Preface." In *Psychoanalysis and the Question of the Text,* edited by Geoffrey Hartman, vii–xix. Baltimore: Johns Hopkins University Press.

———. 1978b. "Psychoanalysis: The French Connection." In *Psychoanalysis and the Question of the Text,*" edited by Geoffrey Hartman, 86–113. Baltimore: Johns Hopkins University Press.

Harvey, Gabriel. 1974. "Manuscript Note on *Hamlet* and *Venus and Adonis* and *Lucrece.*" In *The Riverside Shakespeare,* edited by G. Blakemore Evans. Boston: Houghton Mifflin.

Hawkins, Harriet. 1982. "The Year's Contribution to Shakespearean Study." In *Shakespeare Survey 35,* edited by Stanley Wells, 153–92. Cambridge: Cambridge University Press.

Hawkins, Sherman. 1975. "Virtue and Kingship in Shakespeare's *Henry IV.*" *English Literary Renaissance* 5:313–43.

Hawthorne, Nathaniel. 1962. *The English Notebooks.* Edited by Randall Stewart. New York: Russell & Russell.

Hayles, Nancy K. 1980. "Sexual Disguise in *Cymbeline.*" *Modern Language Quarterly* 41:231–47.

Hays, Janice. 1980. "Those 'Soft and Delicate Desires': *Much Ado* and Distrust of Women." In *The Woman's Part: Feminist Criticism of Shakespeare*, edited by Carolyn Ruth Swift Lenz, Gayle Greene, and Carol Neely, 79–100. Urbana: University of Illinois Press.

Hazlitt, William. 1818. *Lectures on the English Poets*. London.

Holland, Norman. 1964. *The Shakespearean Imagination*. New York: Macmillan.

————. 1966. *Psychoanalysis and Shakespeare*. New York: McGraw-Hill.

————. 1985. *The I*. New Haven: Yale University Press.

Holloway, John. 1961. *The Story of the Night*. London: Routledge and Kegan Paul.

Horney, Karen. 1950. *Neurosis and Human Growth*. New York: Norton.

Hyman, Lawrence W. 1975. "The Unity of *Measure for Measure*." *Modern Language Quarterly* 36:3–20.

Irving, Washington. 1983. *The Sketchbook of Geoffrey Crayon, Gent*. In *Washington Irving: History, Tales & Sketches*, edited by J. W. Tuttleton, 983–1001. New York: Library of America.

James, Henry. 1903. "The Birthplace." In *The Better Sort*, 245–311. Freeport, N.Y.: Books for Libraries Press.

————. [1907] 1964. "Introduction to *The Tempest*." In *Selected Literary Criticism*, edited by M. Shapira, 297–310. New York: McGraw-Hill.

Jardine, Lisa. 1983. *Still Harping on Daughters: Women and Drama in the Age of Shakespeare*. Totowa, N.J.: Barnes and Noble Books; Sussex: Harvester Press.

Johnson, Samuel. [1765] 1960. "Preface." In *Dr. Johnson on Shakespeare*, edited by William Wimsatt. New York: Hill & Wang.

Jones, Ernest. 1949. *Hamlet and Oedipus*. New York: Norton.

Jonson, Ben. [1623] 1974. "To the Reader." From *Timber; or, Discoveries*. In *The Riverside Shakespeare*, edited by G. Blakemore Evans, 58, 1846–47. Boston: Houghton Mifflin.

Joyce, James. 1934. *Ulysses*. New York: Modern Library.

Kahn, Coppélia. 1981. *Man's Estate: Masculine Identity in Shakespeare*. Berkeley and Los Angeles: University of California Press.

Kavanagh, James H. 1985. "Shakespeare in Ideology." In *Alternative Shakespeares*, edited by John Drakakis, 144–65. London: Methuen.

Kelly, Joan. 1984. *Women, History, and Theory: The Essays of Joan Kelly*. Chicago: University of Chicago Press.

Kermode, Frank. 1971. "Shakespeare's Learning." In *Shakespeare, Spenser, Donne: Renaissance Essays*, 181–99. New York: Viking.

Kerrigan, William. 1980. "The Articulation of the Ego in the English Renaissance." In *The Literary Freud: Mechanisms of Defense and the Poetic Will*, edited by Joseph Smith, 261–308. Psychiatry and the Humanities, vol. 4. New Haven: Yale University Press.

————. 1984. "Life's Iamb: The Scansion of Late Creativity in the Culture of the Renaissance." In *Working Papers*. Madison, Wis.: Center for Twentieth-Century Studies.

King, Henry. 1914. *The English Poems of Henry King*. Edited by Lawrence Mason. New Haven: Yale University Press.

Kirsch, Arthur. 1981. *Shakespeare and the Experience of Love*. Cambridge: Cambridge University Press.

Knight, E. Nicholas. 1973. *Shakespeare's Hidden Life: Shakespeare at the Law*. New York: Mason and Lipscomb.

Kohut, Heinz. 1971. *The Analysis of the Self*. New York: International Universities.

Kott, Jan. 1966. *Shakespeare Our Contemporary*. Translated by Boleslaw Taborski. New York: Doubleday.

Kristeva, Julia. 1986. "Stabat Mater." In *The Kristeva Reader,* edited by Toril Moi, 160–86. New York: Columbia University Press.

Kuhn, Maura Slattery. 1977. "Much Virtue in If." *Shakespeare Quarterly* 28:40–50.

Lacan, Jacques. 1976. *The Four Fundamental Concepts of Psycho-Analysis*. Edited by Jacques-Alain Miller. Translated by Alan Sheridan. New York: Norton.

———. 1977a. "The Agency of the Letter in the Unconscious, or Reason Since Freud." In *Ecrits: A Selection*, translated by Alan Sheridan, 146–75. New York: Norton.

———. 1977b. "Aggressivity in Psychoanalysis." in *Ecrits: A Selection*, translated by Alan Sheridan, 8–29. New York: Norton.

———. 1977c. "The Mirror Stage as Formative of the Function of the I." In *Ecrits: A Selection*, translated by Alan Sheridan, 1–7. New York: Norton.

Laslett, Peter. 1971. *The World We Have Lost*. 2d ed. New York: Scribner's.

———. 1984. *The World We Have Lost Further Explored*. 3d ed. New York: Scribner's.

Leech, Christopher. 1958. "The Structure of the Last Plays." *Shakespeare Survey* 11:19–30.

Leeman, Fred. 1979. *Hidden Images: Games of Perception, Anamorphic Art, Illusion*. Translated by Ellyn Childs Allison and Margaret L. Kaplan. New York: Harry N. Abrams.

Lenz, Carolyn Ruth Swift, Gayle Greene, and Carol Neely, eds. 1980. *The Woman's Part: Feminist Criticism of Shakespeare*. Urbana: University of Illinois Press.

Levin, Richard A. 1982. "Duke Vincentio and Angelo: Would 'A Feather Turn the Scale'?" *Studies in English Literature* 22:257–70.

Lewis, Wyndham. 1927. *The Lion and the Fox*. London: G. Richards.

Lichtenstein, Heinz. 1977. "Narcissism and Primary Identity." In *The Dilemma of Human Identity*, 207–22. New York: Aronson.

Lovejoy, Arthur O. 1936. *The Great Chain of Being: A Study of the History of an Idea*. Cambridge, Mass.: Harvard University Press.

McCurdy, Harold Grier. 1953. *The Personality of Shakespeare*. New Haven: Yale University Press.

Maclean, Hugh, ed. 1982. *Edmund Spenser's Poetry.* 2d ed. New York: Norton.

McNaron, Toni A. H. "Female Bonding in Shakespeare's Plays: Its Absence and Its Presence." Unpublished paper.

Mair, Lucy. 1977. *Marriage.* London: Scholar Press.

Marcus, Leah. 1986. "Shakespeare's Comic Heroines: Elizabeth I and the Political Uses of Androgyny." In *Women in the Middle Ages and the Renaissance: Literary and Historical Perspectives,* edited by Mary Beth Rose, 135–53. Syracuse, N.Y.: Syracuse University Press.

Marlowe, Christopher. 1969. *Tamburlaine the Great. Parts I and II.* In *The Complete Plays,* edited by J. B. Steane. Harmondsworth: Penguin.

Meres, Francis. 1598. *Palladis Tamia: Wits Treasury.* London.

Montaigne, Michel de. 1928. *The Essayes of Michael Lord of Montaigne.* Translated by John Florio. New York: Dutton; London: J. M. Dent.

Montrose, Louis. 1981. " 'The Place of a Brother' in *As You Like It:* Social Process and Comic Form." *Shakespeare Quarterly* 32:28–54.

Nagarajan, S. 1963. "*Measure for Measure* and Elizabethan Betrothals." *Shakespeare Quarterly* 14:115–19.

Neely, Carol Thomas. 1981. "Feminist Modes of Shakespearean Criticism: Compensatory, Justificatory, Transformational." In *Women's Studies: An Interdisciplinary Journal* 9:3–15. Special Issue on Feminist Criticism of Shakespeare, vol. 1, edited by Gayle Greene and Carolyn Ruth Swift.

———. 1985. *Broken Nuptials in Shakespeare's Plays.* New Haven: Yale University Press.

Nietzsche, Friedrich. 1909–11. *Complete Works.* Edited by Oscar Levy. Vol. 6. New York: Russell & Russell.

Novy, Marianne. 1984. *Love's Argument: Gender Relations in Shakespeare.* Chapel Hill, N.C.: University of North Carolina Press.

Nuttall, A. D. 1975. "*Measure for Measure:* The Bed Trick." *Shakespeare Survey* 28:51–56.

Oliver, H. J., ed. 1978. "Introduction." *The Merry Wives of Windsor,* by William Shakespeare. Arden Edition. London: Methuen.

Orgel, Stephen. 1975. *The Illusion of Power: Political Theater in the English Renaissance.* Berkeley and Los Angeles: University of California Press.

Ovid. 1960. *Metamorphoses.* Baltimore: Penguin.

Padel, J. H. 1975. " 'That the Thought of Hearts Can Mend': An Introduction to Shakespeare's Sonnets for Psychotherapists and Others." *Times Literary Supplement,* December 19, 1975, 1519–21.

Palmer, John. 1948. *Political Characters of Shakespeare.* London: Macmillan.

Paris, Bernard J. 1977. "Hamlet and His Problems: A Horneyan Analysis." *Centennial Review* 21:36–66.

———. 1980. "Bargains with Fate: A Psychological Approach to Shakespeare's Major Tragedies." *Aligarh Journal of English Studies* 5:144–61.

———. 1981. "The Inner Conflicts of *Measure for Measure.*" *Centennial Review* 25:266–76.

———. 1982. "Bargains with Fate: The Case of Macbeth." *American Journal of Psychoanalysis* 42:7–20.

———. 1984a. " 'His Scorn I Approve': The Self-effacing Desdemona." *American Journal of Psychoanalysis* 44:413–24.

———. 1984b. "Iago's Motives: A Horneyan Analysis." *Revue Belge de Philologie et d'Histoire* 62:504–20.

Pearson, Lu Emily. 1957. *Elizabethans at Home.* Stanford, Calif.: Stanford University Press.

Plato. 1937. *Euthydemis.* In *The Dialogues of Plato,* translated by Benjamin Jowett. Vol. 1, 133–70. New York: Random House.

Plautus. 1960. *The Twin Menaechmi.* Translated by Richard W. Hyde and Edward Weist. In *Anthology of Roman Drama,* edited by Philip Whaley Harsh. New York: Holt, Rinehart and Winston.

Priestley, J. B. 1963. "The Character of Shakespeare." *Show* 3:82.

Prynne, William. 1633. *Histrio-Mastix.* London: E. A. and W. I. for Michael Sparke.

Quaife, G. R. 1979. *Wanton Wenches and Wayward Wives: Peasants and Illicit Sex in Early Seventeenth-Century England.* New Brunswick, N.J.: Rutgers University Press.

Quint, David. 1986. "Introduction." In *Literary Theory / Renaissance Texts,* edited by Patricia Parker and David Quint, 1–19. Baltimore: Johns Hopkins University Press.

Rabkin, Norman. 1967. *Shakespeare and the Common Understanding.* New York: Free Press.

———. 1980. *Shakespeare and the Problem of Meaning.* Chicago: University of Chicago Press.

Rainoldes, John. 1599. *Th' Overthrow of Stage-Playes.* Middleburg: R. Schilders.

Ranald, Margaret Loftus. 1979. " 'As Marriage Binds and Blood Breaks': English Marriage and Shakespeare." *Shakespeare Quarterly* 30:68–81.

Reid, Stephen A. 1970. "A Psychoanalytic Reading of *Troilus and Cressida* and *Measure for Measure.*" *Psychoanalytic Review* 57:263–82.

Riefer, Marcia. 1984. " 'Instruments of Some More Mightier Member': The Constriction of Female Power in *Measure for Measure.*" *Shakespeare Quarterly* 35:157–69.

Riggs, David. 1971. *Shakespeare's Heroical Histories: "Henry VI" and Its Literary Tradition.* Cambridge, Mass.: Harvard University Press.

Rosenberg, Marvin. 1972. "Shakespeare's Fantastic Trick: *Measure for Measure.*" *Sewanee Review* 80:51–72.

Said, Edward. 1983. *The World, the Text, and the Critic.* Cambridge, Mass.: Harvard University Press.

Salingar, Leo. 1974. *Shakespeare and the Traditions of Comedy.* Cambridge: Cambridge University Press.

Schoenbaum, Samuel. 1970. *Shakespeare's Lives.* Oxford: Oxford University Press.

————. 1975. *William Shakespeare: A Documentary Life.* Oxford: Clarendon Press.

————. 1977. *William Shakespeare: A Compact Documentary Life.* New York: Oxford University Press.

Schwartz, Murray M. 1978. "Critic, Define Thyself." In *Psychoanalysis and the Question of the Text,* edited by Geoffrey Hartman, 1–17. Baltimore: Johns Hopkins University Press.

Schwartz, Murray M., and David Willbern. 1982. "Literature and Psychology." In *Interrelations of Literature,* edited by Jean-Pierre Barricelli and Joseph Gibaldi, 205–24. New York: Modern Language Association.

Schwartz, Murray M., and Coppélia Kahn, eds. 1980. *Representing Shakespeare: New Psychoanalytic Essays.* Baltimore: Johns Hopkins University Press.

Shakespeare, William. 1623. *Mr. William Shakespeare's Comedies, Histories, and Tragedies.* Edited by John Heminge and Henry Condell. London.

————. 1974. *The Riverside Shakespeare.* Edited by G. Blakemore Evans. Boston: Houghton Mifflin. (This is the text cited by all essays in the collection.)

Sidney, Philip. 1904. *An Apologie for Poetrie.* In *Elizabethan Critical Essays,* edited by Gregory Smith. Vol. 1, 148–207. Oxford: Oxford University Press.

Skura, Meredith Anne. 1980. "Interpreting Posthumus' Dream from Above and Below: Families, Psychoanalysts, and Literary Critics." In *Representing Shakespeare,* edited by Murray Schwartz and Coppélia Kahn, 203–16. Baltimore: Johns Hopkins University Press.

————. 1981. *The Literary Use of the Psychoanalytic Process.* New Haven: Yale University Press.

Spencer, Theodore. 1942. *Shakespeare and the Nature of Man.* Lowell Lectures, 1942. New York: Macmillan.

Sprengnether (Gohlke), Madelon. 1986. "Annihilating Intimacy in *Coriolanus.*" In *Women in the Middle Ages and the Renaissance: Literary and Historical Perspectives,* edited by Mary Beth Rose, 89–111. Syracuse, N.Y.: Syracuse University Press.

Stone, Lawrence. 1975. "The Rise of the Nuclear Family in Early Modern England: The Patriarchal Stage." In *The Family in History,* edited by C. E. Rosenberg, 13–57. Philadelphia: University of Pennsylvania Press.

————. 1977. *The Family, Sex and Marriage in England 1500–1800.* New York: Harper and Row.

Stopes, Charlotte C. 1901. *Shakespeare's Family.* London: Elliot Stock.

Storr, Anthony. 1968. *Human Aggression.* New York: Atheneum.

Stubbes, Phillip. 1583. *The Anatomie of Abuses.* London: Richard Jones.

Sundelson, David. 1980. "So Rare a Wonder'd Father: Prospero's *Tempest.*" In *Representing Shakespeare,* edited by Murray Schwartz and Coppélia Kahn, 33–53. Baltimore: Johns Hopkins University Press.

————. 1983. *Shakespeare's Restorations of the Father.* New Brunswick, N.J.: Rutgers University Press.

Thirsk, Joan. 1969. "Younger Sons in the Seventeenth Century." *History* (London) 54:358–77.

Thompson, Roger. 1974. *Women in Stuart England and America: A Comparative Study.* London: Routledge and Kegan Paul.

Tillyard, E. M. W. 1943. *The Elizabethan World-Picture.* London: Macmillan.

———. 1964. *Shakespeare's History Plays.* New York: Barnes and Noble Books.

van Emde Boas, Conrad. 1951. *Shakespeare's Sonnetten en hun Verband met de Travesti-Double Spelen.* Amsterdam: Wereld Bibliotheek.

Warner, Marina. 1983. *Alone of All Her Sex: The Myth and the Cult of the Virgin Mary.* New York: Random House.

Wheeler, Richard P. 1972. "Poetry and Fantasy in Shakespeare's Sonnets 88–96." *Literature and Psychology* 22:151–62.

———. 1981. *Shakespeare's Development and the Problem Comedies: Turn and Counter-Turn.* Berkeley and Los Angeles: University of California Press.

Williamson, Marilyn. 1982. "Doubling, Women's Anger, and Genre." *Women's Studies* 9:107–19.

Wilson, John Dover. 1932. *The Essential Shakespeare.* Cambridge: Cambridge University Press.

Winnicott, D. W. 1971. *Playing and Reality.* London: Tavistock.

Wrightson, Keith. 1982. *English Society 1580–1680.* New Brunswick, N.J.: Rutgers University Press.

Yates, Frances A. 1975. *Astrea: The Imperial Theme in the Sixteenth Century.* London: Routledge and Kegan Paul.

Yeats, William B. [1924] 1961. "At Stratford-on-Avon." In *Essays and Introductions,* 106–7. New York: Macmillan.

Notes on Contributors

Janet Adelman is Professor of English at the University of California, Berkeley. She is the author of *The Common Liar: An Essay on "Antony and Cleopatra"* and of essays on other Shakespearean plays and on Chaucer and Milton.

C. L. Barber was an exceptionally gifted teacher of Shakespeare whose *Shakespeare's Festive Comedy* remains a widely consulted classic. A Junior Fellow at Harvard, Barber taught at Amherst College, the State University of New York at Buffalo, and the University of California at Santa Cruz. He died in 1983.

Kirby Farrell teaches at the University of Massachusetts and is the author of *Shakespeare's Creation* and *Play, Death, and Heroism in Shakespeare,* and of a novel, *Cony-Catching.*

Barbara Freedman is Associate Professor of English and Chair of the Humanities Division at St. John's University. More recently, she has been teaching and writing on Shakespeare and psychoanalysis at Harvard University. Along with numerous essays published in scholarly journals, she is the author of the forthcoming book *Self and Other in Shakespearean Comedy* and is editor of the Garland Shakespeare Bibliography on *The Comedy of Errors.*

Shirley Nelson Garner is Associate Professor of English at the University of Minnesota. She is a co-editor of *The (M)other Tongue: Essays in Feminist Psychoanalytic Criticism* and is a founder of *Hurricane Alice,* a feminist review.

Sherman Hawkins is Professor of English at Wesleyan University. He has published essays on Chaucer, Spenser, Shakespeare, and Milton, and is currently working on a book on Shakespeare's history plays.

Norman N. Holland is Marston-Milbauer Eminent Scholar in the Department of English at the University of Florida. He is well known for his psychoanalytic approach to literary criticism. The most recent of his many books is *The Brain of Robert Frost.*

William Kerrigan is Professor of English at the University of Massachusetts. Along with articles on Renaissance poetry and philosophical subjects, he is the author of *The Prophetic Milton* and *The Sacred Complex: On the Psy-*

chogenesis of Paradise Lost, winner of the James Holly Hanford Prize of the Milton Society of America. His latest book (with Gordon Braden) is *The Idea of the Renaissance.*

Carol Thomas Neely is Professor of English and Women's Studies at the University of Illinois. She is co-editor of *The Woman's Part: Feminist Criticism of Shakespeare* and author of *Broken Nuptials in Shakespeare's Plays.*

Marianne Novy teaches in the English Department and the Women's Studies Program at the University of Pittsburgh. She is the author of *Love's Argument: Gender Relations in Shakespeare.* Her anthology of essays on women's responses to Shakespeare is forthcoming from the University of Illinois Press.

Bernard J. Paris is Professor of English and Director of the Institute for Psychological Study of the Arts at the University of Florida. He is the author of many books, including the forthcoming *Bargains with Fate: A Psychological Approach to Shakespeare.*

Madelon Sprengnether is Professor of English at the University of Minnesota. She has published articles on Spenser, Lyly, Nashe, and Shakespeare and has co-edited a collection of feminist psychoanalytic essays entitled *The (M)other Tongue.*

Richard P. Wheeler is Professor of English at the University of Illinois, where he teaches in the Unit for Criticism and Interpretive Theory. His publications include essays on Shakespeare, Renaissance drama, Yeats, and D. H. Lawrence. The University of California Press recently published *The Whole Journey: Shakespeare's Power of Development,* an unfinished manuscript by C. L. Barber that was completed by Wheeler after Barber's death.

David Willbern is Associate Professor of English and Associate Dean of Arts and Letters at SUNY/Buffalo. He has published essays on Shakespeare, Renaissance drama, Freud, D. H. Lawrence, and Robert Duncan, and has a work in progress entitled *Poetic Will: Shakespeare and the Play of Language.*

Index

Abenheimer, K. M., 214
Acting: as displacing tension, 254; as exhibitionism, 242
Actor-director role, 11–12
Adams, John F., 157
Adelman, Janet, 11, 196
Admiration, epics and, 57
Adultery, 108, 184
The Aeneid (Virgil), 189
Aggression, 7–8; and antagonism, 242; dual nature of, 58–64; father and, 12, 85; history plays and, 45; into irony, 38; justified, 13; legitimate, 8, 59; magic and, 13; master-servant relationship and, 88; oral forms of, 70; positive use of, 36–37; raised to heroism, 48; in service of community, 61–62; turned inward, 89–90; violent, 206; Western culture and, 209; will to power and, 61
Alcoholism, 28–31
All's Well That Ends Well: bed tricks and, 153–62; betrayal in, 11; father-daughter relationship in, 82; marriage contracts in, 122; separation from family in, 155, 156; sexual paradoxes in, 154; sexual substitution in, 75; source for, 153; and unborn child, 162; women in, 119, 125, 130–31
Alter ego, rebellion against, 94
Altman, Joel, 249
Ambition, 47; character development and, 175–76; cultural prohibitions against, 59; redemption of, 55; sovereignty and, 176
Androgyny, 204
Anger, men and, 112. *See also* Aggression
Annihilation, fear of, 99–100
Anthropology, marriage and, 179
Antichrist, 90
Antony and Cleopatra: art and nature in, 200; betrayal in, 148; boy actor and, 191–205; cross-dressing in, 195; death test and, 187–88; female sexuality

and, 185–87; femininity in, 191–205; misogynous rage and, 189; sex disgust and, 12, 187
Anxiety, infant's loss of mother and, 107
Arden, Agnes, 122–23
Arden, Mary. *See* Shakespeare, Mary Arden
Arden, Robert, 122
Aristocracy, admiration for, 37
Aristotle, 60
Arrogant-vindictive trends, 207, 209, 223
Asp, symbol of, 188–89
As You Like It: brotherly love in, 103–4; cuckoldry jokes in, 108; erotic ethic in, 60; father-son relationship in, 69; fratricidal struggle in, 49; images of brotherhood in, 104–5; inheritance in, 124; leaving-home motif in, 70–71; masculinized women in, 79; masterless women in, 130; relevance of primogeniture to, 106
Auden, W. H., 214
Author(s): community and, 245; as dead father, 229; death of, 1; deconstruction of, 4; idealization of, 246; institutional systems and, 245; invention of, 229–30; resurrection of, 247; as text, 2–3; transcendent, 227, 229, 246; as usurper, 233
Author-function, 2–3, 7, 230, 236
Authority, impulse to subvert, 205
Autonomy/isolation pattern, 209

Bacon, Francis, 51
Barber, C. L., 7–8, 10, 39, 46, 76, 85, 107, 110, 114
Bardolatry, 176, 227
Barish, Jonas, 195
Barthes, Roland, 229
The Battle of Agincourt (Drayton), 63
Bawds, 125
Becker, Ernest, 87
Bed tricks, 151–74
Belott, Stephen, 121